WORM

THE HISTORY OF
A HIGH PEAK VILLAGE

Christopher Drewry

Christopher Drewry

ASHRIDGE PRESS/COUNTRY BOOKS

Published by Country Books/Ashridge Press
Courtyard Cottage, Little Longstone, Bakewell, Derbyshire DE45 1NN

Tel/Fax: 01629 640670
e-mail: dickrichardson@country-books.co.uk

ISBN 978 1 901214 82 6

Printed and bound by: HSW Print

CONTENTS

INTRODUCTION

There were a number of motives for me to compile a history of the village of Wormhill in the High Peak of Derbyshire. The most compelling was a direct personal interest in the subject because I was born and bred here and have always kept my home in the village, even though my professional career took me away for long periods to other parts of the United Kingdom and abroad. In that sense too I can claim a degree of local credibility not shared by all – it is said that you can come to the High Peak as a babe in arms and die here aged 90 but there will still be someone at your funeral who will say "Aye, 'e were a great chap but 'e wunner born 'ere, tha' knows"!

Having collected together many snippets of information over the years, the leisure of retirement left me no excuse not to attempt a synthesis of everything I had learned, after a further period of sustained research in local libraries and other institutions.

My efforts in this regard began as a purely personal venture – to record as much as I could about my own property at the north end of the village at Hargate Wall and about the history of the Drewry family. Many people, I think, feel the urge to tackle such issues for the benefit of posterity but not all have the good fortune to access a wealth of relevant material or the time to harness it into a coherent story. In my own case I quickly found that a history of Hargate Wall could not be separated from the wider history of the whole parish of Wormhill or from the even more extensive history of this fascinating region right in the middle of England. As other local historians have discovered, the history of any particular place needs to be placed in context and only makes sense if treated as a microcosm of the history of the nation.

After adopting therefore a necessarily wider focus than I had at first intended, it was only a matter of time before friends and neighbours became aware that what I was doing had a potentially wider interest. I began to receive requests to give illustrated talks on the subject to various audiences in the local area. Speaking to one group of people tended to spawn further requests to talk to other groups elsewhere. I was either unable or unwilling to satisfy every request for a verbal presentation and this prompted the thought that there could be a market for a more durable account in the form of a written publication. Hence the genesis of this little book.

The sources for the information it contains are many and various. Amongst the early histories of the county of Derbyshire it is well known that most are either incomplete or of questionable value. James Pilkington's *View of the Present State of Derbyshire with an account of its most remarkable Antiquities* of 1789 in two volumes tells us more about 18th century Derbyshire than its early history but is valuable for that reason all the same. Stephen Glover's *History of Derbyshire* of 1829 in two volumes does much the same for the following century. John Tilley's wonderfully illustrated five volumes on *The Old Halls, Manors and Families of Derbyshire* published in 1892 would appear to be, on the surface, an absolute mine of useful information but sadly much of the detail is either impenetrably complex genealogical data or it is mutually contradictory and notoriously unreliable. Another historian called John Pym Yeatman attempted a five volume *Feudal History of the County of Derby* between 1886 and 1907 but went bankrupt before completing the work. The formal *Victoria County History* series covering each of the counties of England started on Derbyshire but never finished it. Many other writers of local histories and guidebooks have completed some commendable works of great interest and they are acknowledged in my text where I have drawn or quoted from them. Likewise I owe a debt of gratitude to those who have allowed me to photograph items of historical interest and to those, particularly Angela Taylor and Tony Hill, who have allowed me to draw from their photographic collections.

I have also referred to other Gazetteers and Directories of Derbyshire, starting with Bagshaw's in 1846 and Francis White in 1857 and followed by many versions of Kelly's which are useful and patently accurate accounts of the county at the time of their publication. More recently a spate of local guide books, folklore and romantic tales by the likes of Chrichton Porteous have made good reading but are geared more to the tourist trade than historical interest. But even amongst these there are exceptions which prove the rule, of which Mike Langham's *Buxton – a People's History* of 2001 is a distinguished example.

The Histories of Derbyshire would be thin indeed, were it not for the masterpiece of 1800 pages in four volumes by Gladwyn Turbutt in 1999. This extraordinarily well researched tome took Gladwyn 20 years to complete and is, without doubt, the definitive history of the county. Much of my knowledge of the history of this part of the county has been culled from or confirmed by this monumental work, without which this volume would be much less well informed.

I have consulted hundreds of lesser written sources which contain references to the village, many of which are to be found in the excellent Local Studies section of the Buxton Library and the County Library in Matlock. Amongst these are many gems written by local enthusiasts – Nancy Hunter of Elm Tree House for example had a go at the history of Wormhill in the 1960s (*Wormhill Wakes*) and at least two vicars of Tideswell[1] have produced their own histories of the area.

---

[1] *A guide to Tideswell and its Church* by Rev JMJ Fletcher 1902 and *The Parish Church of St John The Baptist Tideswell 1350-1950* by Rev Leslie L Lowther

Specialist books on old carriageways, industries, crimes and mysteries throw additional light on local events. Hart's *North Derbyshire Archaeological Survey* of 1981 and many volumes of the Derbyshire Archaeological Journal are very valuable sources of scientific and historical research. Anyone who has time to visit the County Record Office at Matlock will be rewarded by the find of many original documents (for example the 1822 Enclosure Award for Wormhill) and exhaustive microfiches of parish records, surveys and censuses.

More productive still has been the ever-expanding mountain of information contained in thousands of web-sites on the Internet. Type in 'Hargate Wall', 'Herdewycke Waella', 'Wormhill' or 'Wormehul' or any of the other spellings recorded in Cameron's *Place Names of Derbyshire* on any good modern search engine and watch the results with amazement. Here is the record of a legal trans-action for land at Hargate Wall in the 13th century and there is another for a field which had the same name in 1402 as the one it has today. Numerous family pedigrees on the Internet corroborate ownership of the manor back to the Norman Conquest and beyond. One of many American web-sites traces an émigré family back to a young farm girl born in Number 4 Hargate Cottages in the 1730s. Her parents' initials are still on the date stone above the front door and on a lintel above a walled-up doorway in the Lambing Sheds. Similarly a short spell of sustained detective work on the Internet cracks the previously unsolved mystery of the date stone on a nearby farmhouse which reads 'HTAT REFD 1623'.

Despite this fund of data I must sound some notes of caution. At the outset of my research Gladwyn Turbutt gave me a stern warning that local histories are notoriously dangerous and unreliable. The first thing that usually makes them so is the shortage of authoritative reference material. Frequently they are breaking new ground and, in the absence of concrete proof, the temptation to speculate or guess is strong. In the second place they are often dependent on old wives' tales handed down in village folklore as gospel truth when in fact the folklore is none other than the speculation and guesswork of previous generations. And in the third place they tend to be distorted by the fanciful or false claims of either the author or other people seeking to exaggerate the achievements and longevity of their fore-bears in the local area.

I have certainly found examples of all of these phenomena and I have no doubt that my own version is far from faultless in these respects. I would claim only that I have tried to be conscious of the pitfalls; to expose or exclude previous speculation and guesswork where I know the authenticity is doubtful; and to puncture dubious claims by producing additional evidence pointing to their falsity. Indeed I have had and still have occasion to revise my own assumptions and assertions when new and contradictory evidence has come to my attention or as further reflection has caused me to revisit 'facts' which I had wrongly taken for granted. I have no doubt at all that more such errors remain in this edition and deserve to be similarly reviewed in due course. I can only apologise in advance for any that the reader finds.

My final observation by way of introduction is that I have deliberately drawn a line under the more recent events from the mid 20th century onwards and have excluded reference to people who are still alive. To have done otherwise would have risked bringing 'history' too close for comfort and, in the worst case, could have raised accusations of invidiousness or misrepresentation – self-evident pit-falls which I have obviously been at pains to avoid!

Thus I hope this volume will prove of interest not just to those directly associated with Wormhill and the surrounding district but also to a wider public keen to learn about the evolution of a small village community – typical no doubt of many others in the land – from the earliest times to the modern day. Unusually perhaps we can trace our predecessors right back to the first settlers and farmers of around 5000 years ago and their bones still lie in the original burial sites around the village. Over five millennia we have good evidence of other tribes and peoples who have farmed the limestone plateau and exploited its mineral wealth and still do so today. Each period of this 5000 year village history has been influenced and buffeted sometimes literally by the force of climate change and more often by the events of our wider national history – invasion, occupation, invention or importation of new technologies, new industries, new infrastructure, war, civil war, royal patronage, new patterns of ownership, authority, administration and tax-ation. In many ways the history of this village is the history of England under the microscope but all the more fascinating because we can see the impact on real people throughout the ages. Pulling this history together has been a matter of considerable personal satisfaction to me and I hope it will be of equal value and interest to succeeding generations.

PREHISTORY

One of the first things to surprise people about the High Peak or Peak District of Derbyshire with its dales and rolling hills rising up to 2000 feet above sea level at the southern end of the Pennine Chain is that, in prehistoric times around 280 million years ago, it was actually a shallow maritime lake lying below sea level. Over millions of years the fossils of a species of starfish called Entrochi were deposited on the floor of the saltwater lake, eventually forming a continuous bed 20 miles long, 20 miles wide and up to 1500 feet deep. This created the limestone bedrock which was subsequently raised up by huge upheavals driven by movement of the Earth's tectonic plates. The so-called 'limestone dome' of the High Peak was forced clear of the surrounding geological formations of gritstone and shales, making it for ever afterwards the dominant characteristic of the local landscape. It also made it the principal factor determining the uses to which that landscape would be put by the human beings who would later come to live here. This unique landscape has given the area the name of 'the White Peak' to distinguish the land which lies on limestone from that which overlies gritstone and is known as 'the Dark Peak'.

However, the various Ice Ages of the Pleistocene Period preserved a glacial climate which prevented any form of animal or human life until the melting glaciers broke away, scouring out the lines of the dales and the river valleys. At this southern end of the Pennines the melt waters at Buxton carried non-indigenous rocks all the way down the Wye valley as far as Matlock.

As the climate warmed and vegetation grew, herds of migrating animals moved into and through the area attracting in their wake a range of predators, some of which are now extinct and others of which are not now to be found outside equatorial regions. In 1911 workmen at the Victory Quarry Dove Holes broke into a cave on the quarry face which was 90 feet long, 4 feet wide and 15 feet high. In the sand on the floor of the cave were the bones and teeth of these exotic animals, later identified by the famous local antiquarian Sir William Boyd Dawkins as those of mastodon, sabre-toothed tiger, rhinoceros and elephant. Some of the bones had clear marks of hyenas' teeth on them, prompting speculation that the cave had been a hyena's den. In a further find some distance away at Windy Knoll below Mam Tor in the Hope Valley Boyd Dawkins and a Mr Rooke found 6800 bones, tusks and teeth from the same period. They concluded that the site had been an ancient watering hole for herds of bison, deer, some tropical animals, reindeer, wolves and bears. Just as great herds migrate today in some parts of the world in search of fresh pastures, these herds may well have migrated from the plains of Central and Northern France (there was no sea gap separating us from the Continent at the time) via the inland valleys like the Trent to the coastal plains of the Dee and Mersey and back again in time with the seasons.

With so much fresh meat on the hoof, it was only a matter of time before Early Man arrived to hunt it during the Palaeolithic Era or First Stone Age around 10,000 BC and perhaps earlier still in the intervals between the twenty or so Ice Ages. Not far away at Creswell Crags near Bolsover in North-East Derbyshire are signs of some of the earliest human cave dwellings in the British Isles. There is evidence of the caves in the fertile gorge being used for temporary shelter and protection by Neanderthal and pre-Modern Man. Cave drawings there include deer, wild horse and hunting scenes. Finds in the caves have included decorated implements and weapons made from the bones of prehistoric animals like woolly rhino. At this time the country was not yet an island and remained part of the European Continent, from which these first humans are assumed to have come in pursuit of the migrating herds.

The Early Stone Age gave way to the Mesolithic Era or Middle Stone Age around 8,500 BC and this period is thought to have lasted for about 4,500 years. Human progress in other words was incredibly slow by later standards. It was during this period however that the first humans are known to have arrived in the Peak District. They too were cave-dwellers and nomadic hunter-gatherers who followed the migrating herds and exploited the natural crops of acorns, bracken roots, herbaceous leaves and plants, hazel nuts, fungi and blackberries in season. After the flooding of the North Sea Basin and the separation of the British Isles from the Continent, caused by the melting ice caps and the rising oceans, Mesolithic Man moved west onto the higher ground but did not settle. There are recognised Mesolithic camps at Fox Hill Cave in Earl Sterndale and at Lismore Fields in Buxton along with their rough non-geometric flint implements and arrow heads. Pit debris at these sites has been radiocarbon dated at 5220 +/- 80 BC.

Stone Age to Bronze Age

The period from 3750 BC through to 400 BC is difficult to divide up into separate 'Ages' and there do not appear to have been major incursions of foreign peoples into the newly formed British Isles. There were however a number of evolutionary developments in the tools and materials employed by the indigenous population and it is these developments which historians frequently use to differentiate between one part of the period and another. The Neolithic Era or Late Stone Age spans the years 3750-1750 BC and is distinguished by the use of novel stone implements and weapons, especially flints. Around 2000 BC is the start of the so-called Beaker Period when beaker-shaped pottery appeared for the first time in burial chambers and around 1750 BC the discovery of bronze led to the manufacture of the first metal tools and weapons, giving rise to the so-called Bronze Age. The 1400 year span of the Bronze Age is sometimes differentiated by the terms Early, Middle and Late but these subtle sub-divisions, however significant to the academic and archaeologist, make little impact on our village story.

At the start of the period beginning around 3750 BC Late Stone Age or Neolithic Man arrived in the Peak District from two directions – from the south via the Trent valley and from the south-west and Southern Ireland via the Cheshire Plain. The main thing to distinguish these new arrivals from their nomadic predecessors was that they were no longer just hunter-gatherers subsisting on the natural harvest wherever and whenever they could find it; they decided to settle and to generate new types of food supply by farming. These then were the first people who can be described as inhabitants of Wormhill.

Quite when and why they chose to settle here cannot be proven. Some time between 4000 and 3000 BC pioneers of a Neolithic tribe must have made their way up the Wye valley and the dales or over the moors from Cheshire, looking for a suitable place to establish a settlement. Key considerations for them would presumably have included things like a reliable water supply, an adequate supply of game to hunt and availability of fertile soil which they could clear and cultivate. One such place they did find was Middle Hill at Wormhill.

The following diagram shows the extent of this settlement between the Sitch road and Withered Low. The evidence comes from the presence of large quantities of flint chippings which are regularly exposed on the surface when the fields are ploughed. Significantly the densest scatters of flint straddle the stream which runs above ground from the perched aquifer on the hillside down towards Dale Head before disappearing below ground through porous limestone rock. Flint is not and

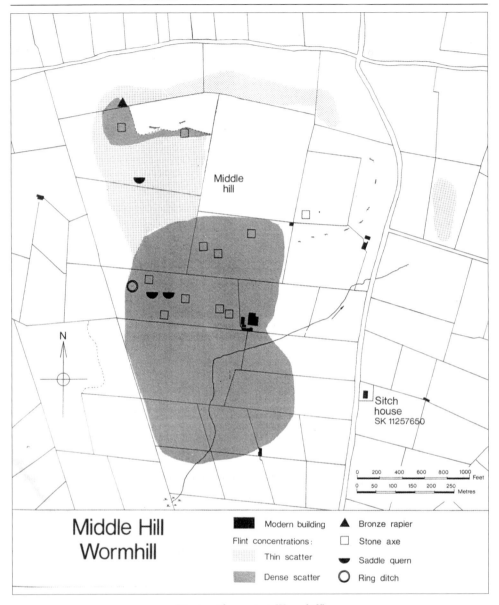

First settlement at Wormhill[2]

never has been an indigenous stone in this part of the country. It must have been imported from a considerable distance away, almost certainly from the Yorkshire and Lincolnshire Wolds and possibly also from the chalk lands of Sussex, Wiltshire and Hampshire or the flint mine at Grimes Graves near Thetford in Norfolk. Large lumps of raw flint would have been chipped away or 'knapped' by

---

[2] From *The North Derbyshire Archaeological Survey* 1981.

our Neolithic settlers to shape useful implements like primitive knives and arrow heads and indeed some of the heaviest concentrations of flint flakes found in the 1960s and 1970s on this site were in piles alongside the stream bed where the settlers would have sat chipping away outside the doorways of their basic huts of wooden frames covered by hides.

Neolithic Flints from Middle Hill

Amongst the thousands of chippings found have been some fine flint arrow heads, eleven polished stone axes used for chopping down timber and clearing the ground for cultivation (possibly 'Langdale' axes made in the Lake District), three saddle querns (shallow stone bowls used for grinding corn) and some 'Peterborough' pottery. A ring ditch shown on the diagram caused some excitement when first discovered because this type of feature can often signify a burial site but excavation of this one revealed nothing of interest. Nor did students from Sheffield University have any success from scanning the fields with a proton magnetometer in an attempt to locate the post-holes of the primitive dwellings. The bronze rapier shown as a triangle at the top of the diagram comes from a period up to 2000 years later and is covered subsequently in this chapter.

Our pioneer settlers would certainly have been proficient hunters, tracking down game anywhere within carrying distance of Middle Hill or going on longer expeditions if conditions were favourable. There have been finds of isolated pieces of worked flint like the fragment of curved hunting knife found on Hayward Farm in 2005 which tend to corroborate such activity. One can imagine a Neolithic hunter cursing as his knife broke while gutting a deer and leaving the fragments where they lay to be discovered 5000 years later! But they were also the pioneers of farming which allowed them to create a larger and denser population because it was inherently a more efficient means of food production than hunting and gathering. Having cleared the ground in the lee of Middle Hill, the land now farmed by Messrs Mosley, Hadfield and Beresford would have been planted in small patches with a primitive form of wheat. Around 2000 BC the local climate was 2-3 degrees C warmer than today which could have made the site highly conducive to cereal production. Our first farmers would also have started to domesticate wild animals over a period of several centuries by, for example, a process of 'loose herding' (following the wild horse and reindeer migrations before feeding and catching up a few of the more docile animals) and then 'close herding' (penning up the sheep and pigs). They eventually kept long-horned ox, pigs, sheep and goats.

The advent of fixed settlements like this meant that the Neolithic people started to pay attention to the burial of their dead and the veneration of their ancestors. No records of burial sites exist from before this time but there is a profusion of evidence beginning at this period. Various grave types have been discovered in the local area. There is a so-called 'passage grave' at Five Wells near Taddington which is a chamber constructed of massive stones, approached by a paved and stone-lined passage and covered by a circular mound of limestone rubble. Then there are 'round barrows' of which the largest local example is at Tideslow north of Tideswell. This has a diameter of 132 feet and a series of stone cists or burial chambers but no paved entrance passages. A third type is the 'earthen long barrow', examples of which have been found in a field opposite the Crescent in Buxton and at Perryfoot near Peak Forest. Many of the Neolithic burial sites in the Peak District are close to the prehistoric trackway from the Hope Valley to Buxton which was used by traders moving between the Lake District, Wales and Ireland – what might be described as the M6 Motorway of its day, though it would have been no more than a rough unpaved track flattened by the regular passage of human feet. The same major trade route was used and developed by successor peoples including the Romans.

These early burial sites appear to have been reserved for the families of local and tribal chiefs, many of them containing multiple skeletons. The Neolithic custom was to 'de-flesh' or excarnate the corpses by leaving them exposed on elevated wooden platforms in the open air until only the bones remained and then to arrange the bones carefully inside the elaborate burial chambers. Some of the burial chambers are said to have been re-visited on a regular basis and the bones re-arranged as a form of ancestor worship. It is thought that these processes allowed the tribes to show respect for the dead and veneration for ancestral leaders of the community but that they were also a way of marking ownership of the surrounding land – 'we own this land because, look, our ancestors are still buried here'. The skeletons show that Neolithic people had a thin physique and long skulls. The average height of men was 5ft 6 in and of women 5ft 2¹/₂in. Life expectancy did not exceed 40 years.

Many of the original Neolithic burial sites were added to over the centuries and some contain multiple burials, sometimes within the same burial chambers, of people who died up to 3000 years apart, making dating of the remains problematic. Some contain evidence of Neolithic, Beaker, Bronze and Iron Age remains. In other cases the burial sites were looted by grave-robbers in the 18th and early 19th centuries and valuable grave goods which would have dated the burials with greater certainty were removed.

At Wormhill there are five 'round barrow' tumuli at three separate sites – at Wind Low[3] near Hargate Wall, at Bole Hill and at Withered Low. All of these are now registered national monuments. (*See colour plate 1.*)

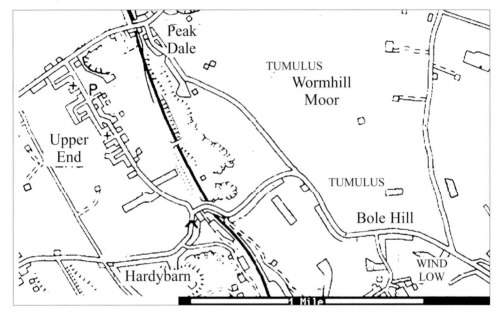

The Wormhill Tumuli

The barrows of Derbyshire, Staffordshire and South Yorkshire were hastily and unscientifically excavated by William Bateman (1787-1835) and his son Thomas Bateman (1821-1861) using large teams of workmen and often leaving big pits and spoil-heaps in the fields. Thomas Bateman gives a detailed account in his *Vestiges of the Antiquities of Derbyshire* published in 1848 of his findings at the barrows of Wind Low, Bole Hill and Withered Low. He was more than a touch irritated to discover that, in some cases, he was not the first to have dug into the graves and that, in other cases, they had been stripped of moveable stone by landowners using it for the new enclosures 20-30 years before his excavations.

---

[3] From the Old English word *hlaw* meaning burial mound

His account of opening the barrow at Wind Low is as follows:

On 12th August 1846 was opened a low flat barrow at Windle (Wind Lowe) Nook near Hargate Wall Derbyshire. It was about 20 yards in diameter, 2 feet high and encircled by a ring of large flat limestones placed in a sloping manner on one side about 3 yards from the margin of the tumulus, apparently for the purpose of preserving its symmetry. The top of this barrow is surmounted by a large square sandstone which has originally formed the base of one of the wayside crosses of which numerous examples remain in the north of Derbyshire[4]. About the centre of the barrow was a cist measuring near 6 feet by 4 feet in horizontal area and 3 feet in depth. It was of unusual construction, the sides being built of large stones set on end, some of which appeared above the turf. An examination of the contents of this cist led to the conclusion that it had been applied to sepulchral purposes at various distinct periods and that the last interment had been partially disturbed at a comparatively recent date. The contents were as follows : small pieces of urn, calcined[5] bones and flints, skeletons of two persons of full stature and of two infants, one of them very young, and various animal bones amongst which those of the rat, weasel and horse were most conspicuous. All of these articles were so much out of their ordinary arrangement as to leave no doubt of their disinterment at the time of a burial of another skeleton which lay in a contracted position a few inches above the floor of the vault. This skeleton, which from the ornaments discovered with it and the slender proportions of the bones must be attributed to a female, had not entirely escaped spoliation at a recent period. The following circumstances seem to put this question beyond doubt, namely the discovery of sundry pieces of tobacco pipe and nails from rustics' shoes, and from the fact of finding part of a very large ivory pin and a fragment of an armilla or bracelet of Kimmeridge Coal[6] both of which would have been perfect at the time they were deposited. Whoever these former excavators were, they were not very close observers, as they overlooked a necklace of beads of the aforesaid Kimmeridge Coal, terminated by two perforated conical studs of the same, and enriched by six pieces of ivory ornamented with the

---

[4] The base of the Saxon cross is still there and can be seen clearly in the photograph (colour plate 1). As Bateman asserts, this would indeed have been planted on top of the tumulus in about the 12th century as a marker on the road between Buxton and Tideswell. The original road ran from Green Fairfield, across Great Rocks Dale, through Tunstead and Hargate Wall. The Wind Low cross would have been visible soon after the traveller left Green Fairfield. Many similar boundary and route markers exist else where in the High Peak, including the base of a cross and another better preserved mediaeval cross at Wheston on the so-called Crossgate road from Tideswell; one at Fairfield; the base of a cross 1/2 mile north-east of Wormhill church on the public footpath and a more intact cross on the slopes of Kinder Scout. Sometimes ancient crosses were modified for other purposes and presented to churches – one such example is the cross in Wormhill churchyard with a large stone base, two sets of square steps and about 3 feet of shaft supporting a sundial which was a gift from Robert Meverell in 1670.

[5] Cremated.

[6] A form of jet. Kimmeridge coal or shale comes from the Isle of Purbeck in Dorset, where veins of it are exposed by coastal erosion.

everlasting chevron or zigzag pattern so universally prevalent on Celtic[7] remains. The beads, exclusive of the studs and ornaments, are 76 in number and are identical with two that are figured in Plate 3 Vol 1 of Sir Richard Hoare's excellent work. The ivory ornaments are quite novel, no other example having been published.

Wind Low Necklace, now in the Weston Park Museum Sheffield

In other words what Thomas Bateman found at Wind Low was the burial site of a Neolithic, Beaker or Bronze Age chieftain and family (two adults and two children) plus the cremated remains of lesser mortals, perhaps slaves who were sacrificed and buried with their master. The bones of animals with mystic connotations went in with them. Later, during the Iron Age, a senior female member of a Celtic tribe had been buried on top of them.

Some time before Bateman's arrival on the scene, a pipe-smoking grave-robber wearing hob-nailed boots had stolen most of the ivory pins from the Celtic shroud and most of the Celtic jet bracelet – before Bateman himself completed the looting by removing the Celtic necklace!

Three days later, on 15th August 1846, he moved on to open the first of two barrows at Bole Hill on the other side of the road. This was also surrounded by a circle of very large stones. In the centre was a pile of very big flat stones with regularly walled-in courses and, at its base, a rock 4 feet by 5 feet by 1 foot deep weighing nearly a ton. Quite how the tribes would have moved and positioned a rock of this weight defies belief. They had no lifting gear and no wheels or carts; so they would have

Thomas Bateman

---

[7] Ie Iron Age (400 BC – 43 AD). Corroboration for this finding by Bateman comes from the fact that the female skeleton in the top grave had been buried in a contracted or trussed position which was certainly a Bronze and Iron Age custom. The large ivory pin would have held together the burial shroud.

levered it and rolled it on wooden logs for as far as it had to be transported, just as they did for the massive stones in the henges. Bateman's fertile imagination led him to speculate that this huge rock was a 'cromlech' or altar for human sacrifice used by the Iron Age Druids. But this appears unlikely because underneath it lay a classic Bronze Age warrior, a skeleton of large proportions lying on its left side in contracted posture. Behind the head was an Early Bronze Age flat riveted dagger, $6^{1}/_{2}$ inches in length and in the highest state of preservation. He said that it was in such good condition that it appeared to have been silvered. The dagger had been enclosed in a wooden sheath, the remains of which were clearly perceptible. There were also two flint instruments beside the body. This was an Early Bronze Age and not an Iron Age burial. It is unlikely to have been disturbed by grave-robbers before Bateman's arrival on the scene because of the weight of the covering rock.

Four days after that he opened another barrow close to this one and also on Bole Hill. This had been damaged by the removal of stones for making the new field boundaries demanded by the Enclosure Act of 1822. Bateman did however discover that two bronze 'celts' or axe-heads had been discovered at this site when the locals started taking the stone in 1826 and had subsequently been removed by the finders. Could they still be in use as door-stops in some farmhouse in the village? Bateman's excavation of the remaining intact part of the barrow revealed two skeletons, one male and one female.

By 1st September he had travelled along the ridge to the high ground at the top of Withered Low where he opened another two barrows which had been substantially damaged by the removal of stone for walling. Here he found another two bodies, one of which was female.

Some of the 19th century barrow-diggers, Bateman included, used to leave a metal tablet in the mound when they filled it in, showing who had dug it and when. In Bateman's case nine such lead tablets have since been recovered, all of them curiously with the same spelling mistake T Batemen. Whether there are similar tablets in the Wormhill tumuli is not known because they have very properly lain undisturbed since Bateman filled them in after his excavations in 1846.

Thomas Bateman Lead Tablet

The conclusion is that the Neolithic, Beaker and Bronze Age people buried their clan chiefs and occasionally also the members of their families at these prestigious hill-top locations. The presence of male and female skeletons in three of the barrows and of children in one of them raises the question of whether the tribes indulged in the practice of sacrificing wives and children when a clan chief died or whether wives and children were interred subsequently in the clan chiefs' graves. What is however clear is that alongside them went the cremated remains of lower castes of the tribe, perhaps slaves who were sacrificed at the time of their masters' death, and the bones of various animals with mystical and pagan connotations. If the clan chief was of sufficient stature, he was buried with his most treasured possessions such as a bronze dagger. Some 1500 years later the Celts arrived during the Iron Age and chose to bury the most important members of their tribes in the same hill-top graves. And this time they buried them with their jewellery. Thus the Hargate barrow at Wind Low spans a period of 4200 years – a Neolithic family of around 3000 BC, an Iron Age noblewoman of around 400 BC, an Anglo-Saxon cross made about 800 AD and planted on top of the tumulus as a marker around 1200 AD. It lay undisturbed until some time in the late 18th century and then finally revealed its secrets in 1846.

Also associated with the Neolithic and Beaker periods are the Stone Circles and Henges, of which Stonehenge in Wiltshire and Avebury in Gloucestershire are the best known national examples. There are however two lesser known henges in the local area.

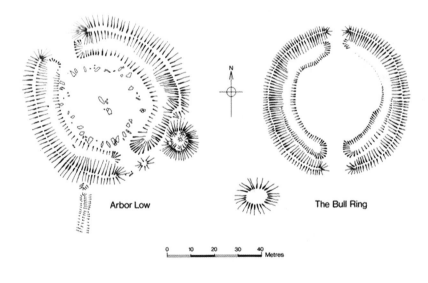

Local Henges

The closest henge, now almost unrecognisable as such, is the Bull Ring at Dove Holes. The name 'Bull Ring' remains a mystery but it is conceivable that it refers to the 18th and early 19th century practice of bull-baiting[8] in which a bull was tethered to a ring embedded in a heavy stone and attacked by dogs on which bets would be placed. The first dog to pin the bull by the nose was judged the winner. If so, the amphitheatre formed by the henge may have provided the seating for the spectators. A similar bull-ring stone is in the field in front of Well-head Farm at Wormhill. The original Dove Holes henge, allegedly built towards the latter end of the Neolithic period between 3000 and 2000 BC, was a circular enclosure with a surrounding ditch and outer bank with a diameter of 257 feet. It had two entrances. The ditch was dug 4-7 feet into the limestone and the spoil was thrown onto the outer bank which was 6 feet high. Fragments of Beaker pottery have been found there but no standing stones. The eighteenth century historian James Pilkington records seeing one solitary stone standing in the centre of the enclosure but it is assumed that all the stones were removed at some stage for local buildings and roads. The Dove Holes henge would have been the gathering place for the Neolithic and Beaker populations north of the river Wye including those from the settlement at Middle Hill less than 2 miles away.

The Bull Ring at Dove Holes

There is much speculation as to why henges were constructed, other than as a gathering place for the tribes. Circles are thought to have had a magical connotation, capable of either confining or excluding the ancestral spirits which primitive societies feared could inflict misfortune on the living. In this interpreta-

---

[8] Bear-baiting and bull-baiting were outlawed in England in 1835.

tion some theorists suggest that henges had a function in burial ceremonies and were treated as a half way house or place of limbo through which corpses were taken on the way to their burial chambers.

Another purpose is alleged to have been for the observation of the sun and moon and their alignment with the stones. This could have enabled the tribes to compile a primitive calendar in order to fix the dates of important feasts, religious ceremonies and farming activities. The Beaker calendar was a year of 16 months, with each month containing between 22 and 24 days.

More elaborate theories revolve around the idea that the alignment of stones and henge entrances, extended outwards cross country in so-called 'ley lines', provided a primitive form of mapping and direction-finding.

The popular supposition that the henges were used by the Druids for religious ceremonies is possible but doubtful as the Druids did not arrive in England before 400 BC, some 1400 years after the henges were abandoned by their original builders.

A more intact henge, used by the tribes south of the river Wye, is at Arbor Low (*colour plate 2*). It is the best preserved henge in the north of England. Again this has a circular arena, ditch and outer bank with a slightly smaller diameter of 250 feet. Many of the original 50 stones within the circle are still there, though now lying flat rather than upright. They were originally arranged in pairs in a rough ellipse and it is known that they were vertical, as at Stonehenge, because several stone stumps in an upright position are still visible. In the centre is a group of four stones forming a 'cove' or sanctuary. Excavations in the early 20th century found burial sites in the outer ditch of Neolithic and Beaker people and a typical tanged and barbed arrow head from the Beaker period.

By the start of the Bronze Age in 1750 BC the use of henges appears to have lapsed, to be replaced by a larger number of small stone circles used solely for the purpose of burial sites. Most of the later Bronze Age burials were cremations and the ashes were placed in urns before interment in the 15-100 foot diameter circles with stones standing only 2-3 feet high.

The Bronze Age pioneered the crafts of leatherwork and carpentry and produced more advanced forms of pottery but the most significant milestone in human progress came from the discovery and use of metals. Quite how they discovered that mixing the molten ore of 90% copper and 10% tin created a strong, durable and resilient alloy which we now know as bronze remains a mystery. It probably came about by trial and error or accident. Copper was found and mined throughout the country, though there are certain well-known copper-mining centres which were extensively worked from 1900 to 900 BC such as the Great Orme mine at Llandudno in North Wales. This would have been on the line of the ancient trade route from Ireland via Wales and the Peak District to the Lake District and could therefore have been an important source of bronze for our local population. Tin, the other and minor ingredient of bronze, was to be found principally in the West Country and arrived here presumably by the same west coast route. Some smelting of bronze may have taken place throughout the British Isles but it is likely that there would have been key centres for the manufacture of the more prestige bronze items like swords which were then widely traded in exchange for agricultural produce and other goods.

The two burial sites at Bole Hill contained bronze – a dagger in one grave and two axe-heads in the other – whereas those at Wind Low and Withered Low did not. There must however be some possibility that bronze artefacts had been removed from the latter by grave-robbers before Bateman got to them. A bronze spearhead from the Middle Bronze Age was found by a quarryman at Tunstead in 1930 and is now in the Buxton Museum.

It is the trade route which most probably accounts for the bronze sword ploughed up by Mr Fred Mosley at the top of Middle Hill in 1954. His attention was drawn to it by the sound of the ploughshare breaking the blade in two. One can only speculate about why something as valuable as a sword should have been left on the hillside. It is not something which it would have been easy simply to lose. It might have been thrown away because it was broken or had come to the end of its useful life. Or it might have been left for the gods as part of some ancient ceremony overlooking the former Neolithic settlement. Or just conceivably it might have marked the site of a skirmish between Bronze Age tribes competing for the dwindling amount of fertile land and have been abandoned along with the other debris of a battlefield. Just as plausibly, because the site of the find overlooks the ancient trade route running from Buxton to Smalldale to Peak Forest to the Hope Valley, the sword could have marked the location of a highway raid on the traders and their rich pickings.

What we do know is that, early on in the Bronze Age around 1400-1300 BC there was a sharp deterioration in the climate and average temperatures fell to 2 degrees C below those of today. This could have shortened the growing season by up to 5 weeks per year. Wet, stormy weather replaced the warm and relatively dry climate which had enabled the original Neolithic settlers to grow wheat on Middle Hill. Crops failed to reach maturity and the fertility of the shallow soils worked without crop rotation by the Neolithic, Beaker and Bronze Age tribes had been exhausted. It became a time of famine on the limestone plateau which was consequently deserted but not before traditional social patterns had changed from relatively harmonious and peaceful co-existence to a situation of inter-communal rivalry and violence. Driven off the higher ground, the inhabitants moved down to the wooded slopes of the river valleys. Defensive sites were established for the first time to protect family and clan.

So by the end of the Bronze Age in around 400 BC life and livelihood in the Peak District had become distinctly tricky. And then, as if that wasn't bad enough, an impetuous and warlike crowd of foreigners arrived from across the North Sea and the English Channel.

THE IRON AGE AND CELTIC BRITAIN

The Celts and their Druid priests were an enterprising race who had spread along the coasts of Western Europe from the Iberian Peninsula to Normandy and Brittany and thence by sea to Cornwall, Wales, Ireland, Scotland and eventually to mainland England. The Celtic connection in language and culture remains distinct even today in those outer parts of their colonies which were not quickly overrun by subsequent invaders. Their arrival in the inland territories of England took longer than their occupation of the coastal lands but the Bronze Age inhabitants of Wormhill would have met them by about 400 BC.

They were renowned as a fearless and boastful warrior race and good horsemen and they were the first to use two-wheeled chariots in battle. Their weakness was a lack of discipline and a chaotic failure to coordinate their battle tactics – characteristics which caused them to lose out to the later Roman invaders.

They did however bring with them a new and important technology – iron. The use of iron had begun in Asia and spread to Western Europe before the Celts imported it here. It had a number of qualities which made it superior to bronze. Iron ore was more readily available than copper and tin and it was relatively easy to smelt. Molten ore would have been poured into stone moulds, typically to create blades of different sizes. The end result would have been wrought iron of varying hardness. By forging together a series of harder and softer blades, the Celts would have created a tough metal which held a sharper edge than bronze.

The Iron Age lasted a mere 350 years but that was sufficient for the Celts to establish tribal colonies throughout Britain. The Peak District may have been largely uninhabited at the time of their arrival here except in the river valleys but an Iron Age tribe called the Coritani[9], whose capital was at Leicester occupied a region which extended from the Trent valley and North Midlands to the foothills of the Pennines. To the west of the Coritani in the Cheshire Plain and reaching up into south Lancashire lived the Cornovii and to the north of them both in the Pennines lived a wild and warlike tribe called the Brigantes. These tribal names were the ones attributed to them later by the Romans. The Brigantes took their name from the Celtic goddess Brigantia[10] and their capital was at Almondbury near Huddersfield. Where the boundary lay between the Coritani and the Brigantes or

---

[9] Modern historians increasingly refer to them by the alternative name of *Corieltauvi*.
[10] Meaning 'The High One'.

whether there was even any formal border at all between their areas of interest is a matter of speculation but it is possible that the line of the later Roman Ryknield Street[11] represented roughly the limits of their respective regions. 'Wye'[12] and 'Sitch'[13] are place names with a Celtic derivation.

An Iron Age noblewoman of either the Coritani or, more probably, the Brigantes tribe is buried in the Wind Low barrow at Hargate but there is no firm evidence of Iron Age settlements nearer than Tideswell and the Wye valley. On the other hand the Iron Age noblewoman at Wind Low is unlikely to have been buried far from the settlement from which she came and there must therefore be at least a probability of an Iron Age settlement close to the burial site. Where that might have been is unknown and I am in danger of falling into the trap I mentioned at the outset of promoting speculation and guesswork. But a possible clue lies in the Wormhill field name noted by Cameron as 'Castle Lidget'. The term 'Castle' usually implies some form of ancient fortified enclosure and 'Lidget/Lydgate/ Ludgate' is a regularly used place name meaning a swing gate leading to the Commons. As shown in the 1822 Enclosure Award for Wormhill, Castle Lidget was the former name of the Commons area now encompassing the Sitch Wood and Sitch Barn, ie the ridge above the stream bed running down to Dale Head. It is conceivable that this area might have been a small Iron Age enclosure and that any

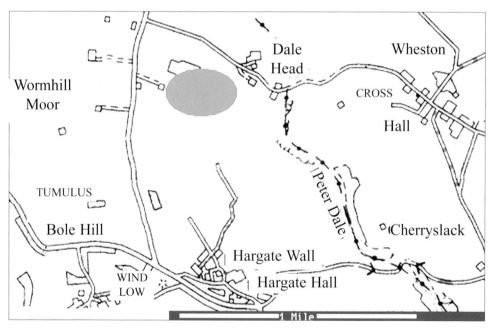

Castle Lidget

---

[11] The modern day A38 dual carriageway from Lichfield to Derby and Chesterfield.
[12] Meaning 'Water'.
[13] Meaning 'Stream'.

remaining stone fortifications may have been removed to make the new walls demanded by the Enclosure Act of 1822. A round quern stone lid was ploughed up in the nearby field called the 'Little 8'[14] in the autumn of 2003.

If there had been a Celtic enclosure on the Sitch, it was clearly not of the same size, significance or complexity as the major Iron Age hill forts which are dotted about the Peak District. On one of the southern Pennine outposts above Castle Naze rocks at Combs Edge is a Celtic stronghold perfectly situated for defence on the ancient trackway from Cheshire. It is triangular in shape, $2^1/_2$ acres in area and 1400 feet above sea level (ASL). Another typical hill fort and the best preserved can be seen at Mam Tor near Castleton. This covers 16 acres and is at 1696 feet ASL. It is surrounded by a deep ditch and a double rampart facing south. This would have been surmounted by a wooden palisade from where the defenders would have hurled their javelins and rocks at attackers. Part of the outer rampart has been worn away by erosion of the shale on the famous 'Shivering Mountain' but the entire outline of the fort is clearly visible from the air.

Mam Tor Hill Fort

The tribes lived inside the forts for protection against raiding neighbours and would have kept their stock inside the ramparts at night for security against thieves and predators, of which lynx, wolves and bears were the main threat. Another function of the hill forts was to store locally produced goods with which to barter

---

[14] Ordnance Survey Number 502.

for the rarer raw materials like salt and iron brought in from outside the area. Hill top locations provided a commanding view of the surrounding countryside, guarded against being surprised by approaching enemies and offered a dominating defensive position. How the tribes survived arctic winters at such high altitude with only basic shelters made of wood and hides is another question. Impressive though they were and formidably defended by the use of sling shot from the ramparts, these hill forts would have proved ineffective against the tactics of the Roman legions, who advanced in a phalanx under a roof of hand-held shields before engaging in deadly close combat with their wide-bladed swords.

It is thought that the North Derbyshire forts were predominantly outposts of the Brigantes tribe, though the five other hill forts in the local area are believed to have been used primarily as stock enclosures rather than defensive positions. These are: Fin Cop in Monsal Dale north of Ashford (12 acres and 1025 feet ASL); Burr Tor near Great Hucklow (12 acres and 1300 feet ASL); Ball Cross north-east of Bakewell (1½ acres and subsequently destroyed by the Romans); Castle Ring on the north edge of Harthill Moor (½ acre); Gardom's Edge near Baslow (12 acres).

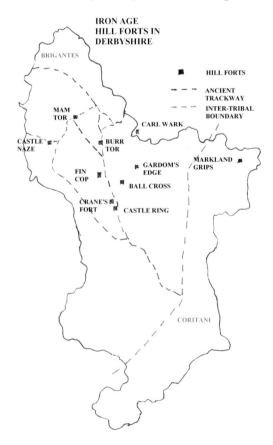

Iron Age Derbyshire

And so towards the end of the Iron Age the inhabitants of this part of North Derbyshire would have been a mixture of different tribes and races. The remnants of the Bronze Age people would have been clinging onto a rather meagre existence in the valleys of the Wye and the Derwent where they had been forced to go by the abrupt climate change of 1300 years previously. The first settlement at Wormhill in the lee of Middle Hill would have been for ever abandoned from that time. They would have been joined by the Celtic colonists some 400 years previously who had quickly dominated local tribal society but probably intermingled and interbred with the indigenous people they had found here. The Celtic tribes had established power bases and areas of influence which they chose to defend from hill forts and other outposts, of which there just might have been a minor example in the Sitch fields. Their allegiance was to a tribal queen living to the north in the Pennines. But otherwise what we now call Wormhill and the surrounding area would have been vacant territory.

At this point of time, shortly before the birth of Christ and the consequent change in our modern date line from BC to AD, human beings had already been present in the Peak District for 10,000 years – or over 80% of the 12,000 years that humans are known to have been here. Yet over that huge period of time human civilization had hardly advanced at all. Cave dwellers wearing animal hides, hunting the migratory wild herds and living off the land had developed into settlers and primitive farmers who wore wool, kept domesticated animals and had started to use more effective implements made of bronze, iron and pottery. Beyond that not much had changed. But huge, rapid and revolutionary change was about to arrive with the Romans.

THE ROMAN OCCUPATION

By the time that the Romans started their occupation of Britain in 47 AD, their civilisation was already far more advanced than anything that the resident Britons had experienced. In every respect – culture, systems of trade, industry, finance, social organisation, military competence and equipment, understanding of the principles of construction and infrastructure – they were centuries ahead of the peoples that they subjugated. In Britain their arrival must have been comparable to a 21st century first world nation taking over a third world nation living in the 18th.

The Emperor Claudius invaded England through the island of Thanet in north Kent in 43 AD. To the Romans, whose empire had been extended throughout Europe to the Rhine, Danube and Euphrates, Britain was the furthest extent of the known world and was erroneously reputed to contain huge mineral wealth. Julius Caesar had launched two expeditions to Britain in 55 and 54 BC but had withdrawn to the Continent on both occasions without leaving an occupation force behind. Claudius quickly subdued and occupied southern and eastern England, pushing the boundaries of Roman Britain out to the river Exe in the south-west, along the south coast of the Bristol Channel and up to a line bounded by the rivers Severn and Trent.

The Romans suppressed the Celtic and Druid cultures of the indigenous Britons and there were rebellions by some of the tribes in the occupied territories, most notably by Queen Boudicca[15] of the Iceni in Norfolk. Boudicca raised the whole of south east England in revolt and, while the main Roman legions were campaigning in Wales and destroying the Druid base on Anglesey, she burnt London, Colchester and St Albans. Finally brought to battle somewhere between London and Chester in 62 AD, possibly near Mancetter in Warwickshire, the Celtic tribes were annihilated and Boudicca poisoned herself. The Roman historian Tacitus put the Britons' casualties at 80,000 – perhaps a far-fetched figure but, taking into account the inevitable massacre of camp followers, perhaps not.

Another British chieftain, Caractacus, learned quickly from his defeats in pitched battles and the siege of his hill forts. He fought a long guerrilla campaign against the Romans, withdrawing eventually to North Wales and then to the Pennines where he was betrayed by the Brigantes in 51 AD and handed over to the Romans who took him back to Rome in chains and paraded him through the streets. The Brigantes, our local tribe, appear to have adopted a more pragmatic

---

[15] Boadicea.

approach to the insuperable invaders and their queen Cartimandua reached an uneasy accommodation with them in exchange for retaining the independence of her Kingdom. Handing over one of the most notorious Celtic 'terrorists' would have ingratiated her even more in the eyes of the Romans.

By about 78 AD the Romans under Governor Agricola had pushed further north to the foothills of the Pennines in order to defend against the marauding northern tribes of Britain. By this time the deal struck by the Brigantes, a fickle and untrustworthy lot, was obviously wearing a bit thin. Buxton was occupied, possibly made into a small fort and first developed as a spa, the Romans having recognised the significance of the hot water spring which they had obviously seen before at places like Bath and elsewhere in Europe.

The Roman name for Buxton was Aquae Arnemetiae, meaning 'waters of the goddess of the sacred grove'. Arnemetia appears to be a Romanised version of a Celtic word or phrase. Anu or Arnu was the Celtic goddess Mother Earth, from which the more recent name of St Ann's Well is derived, and Nemeton is another Celtic term meaning a sacred grove where religious ceremonies took place. Some Celtic historians deduce from this that Buxton was the site of a Celtic temple complex associated with the spa waters and may have been comparable to the known Celtic complex at Bath (named Sulis Minerva by the Romans). In Celtic cultures the female deity or Earth Mother was frequently associated with springs and water. The spring was the place where the Underworld communicated with our world and it therefore made sense to make contact with the deity there. Many springs and wells in Ireland and the west of Britain are presided over today by Christian female saints, as in the case of St Ann at Buxton.

The Roman baths were on the same site as the present spa in the Crescent where various Roman constructions were found as early as 1695 and where a horde of 232 Roman coins, three bronze bracelets and a wire clasp were discovered in 1975. All of these coins and jewellery were votive offerings thrown into St Ann's Well to honour the goddess Anu.

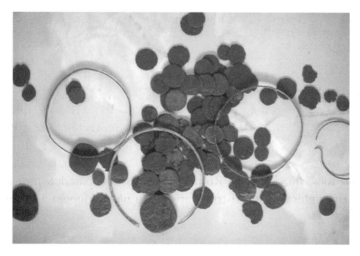

The coin horde contained at least one coin from each of the Emperors' reigns during the Roman occupation of Britain, possibly indicating continuous settlement at Buxton. Excavation of Poole's Cavern in the 1980s revealed a collection of Roman brooches, metal working equipment and jewellery made of bronze, lead and iron, adding to an earlier discovery of jewellery, coins, Samian pottery and human and animal remains in the cavern. Dating of the evidence showed that the Romans or Britons working for them had occupied the cavern from 100-150 AD. The use of money was perhaps one of the greatest changes brought about by the Roman occupation. No longer was the local population dependent on barter for trade; they became merchants and dealt for the first time in cash.

Buxton became a key junction on three routes in the Roman road network – one coming from Ashbourne to the south[16], one heading north-west to Mantia[17] and one leading north-east to Navio[18]. All of these routes appear to have been in use for centuries before the Roman occupation as trade routes and ancient trackways. The Romans merely developed and improved them with permanent pavement and drainage. Part of a Roman mile-stone found at Silverlands in Buxton showed the distance to Navio as 11 Roman miles[19]. This road is called variously Bath-way, Bathingate or in modern parlance Batham Gate[20]. It follows the ancient trade route from Buxton via Smalldale, to the north of Middle Hill, past Dam Dale Farm, crossing the A623 at Mount Pleasant Farm, and via Tideswell Moor to Bradwell. In dry summers it can be clearly seen by the discolouration of the grass over the Roman paveway beneath, cutting across the fields in a straight line by the turning to Smalldale on the Wormhill to Peak Forest road.

The fort called Navio at Brough[21], another at Ardotalia or Melandra[22] near Glossop, a third at Chesterfield[23] and a fourth at Templeborough near Rotherham were part of a chain of Roman installations stretching from Manchester across to South Yorkshire. Each of them was approximately 20 miles from the next – a reasonable day's march for the legions. Both Ardotalia and Navio were constructed on the south side of rivers, suggesting a defensive posture facing North, and were probably the northernmost outposts of the Roman occupation at the time on the frontier with the Brigantes. If so, the Hope Valley and the Woodlands Valley

---

[16] Subsequently known as 'The Street' from the Old English *straet* meaning a Roman paved road.

[17] Manchester.

[18] The Roman fort at Brough near Bradwell.

[19] About 10 modern miles.

[20] From the Old English *baeth* meaning bath or bathing place and *gaet* meaning track or road.

[21] The modern place name of Brough-on-Noe comes from the Old English *burh* meaning fortification and the Roman *Navio* which in turn came from the Celtic *Nava* meaning running water.

[22] The name *Melandra* for the fort at Glossop does not appear to have been used before the 18th century and its origins are disputed. One interpretation is that it was coined by a local official as an 'in' joke, being an anagram of *Alderman*. *Melandra* was the name given to the fort in 1772 by Rev John Watson in a report to the Society of Antiquaries.

[23] On the site of the present St Mary's Church with the crooked spire.

near Glossop would have represented the dividing line between the Roman Empire and the Brigantes hill tribe. The line of forts would also have served to guard the key east-west route across the base of the Pennines. As can be seen elsewhere, eg at Hadrian's Wall on the Scottish border, the Romans had a habit of securing the border with forts, from which they could not only protect the frontier but also extract customs dues and taxes from traders crossing the boundary. The Mam Tor and Castle Naze hill forts may thus have been some of the Brigantes' southernmost outposts. Relations between the Romans and the Brigantes were always strained and occasionally broke down into open hostility. Some of the rebellions by the hill tribes in the first century AD took up to 4 years to bring under control.

Rev Samuel Pegge

Navio was badly vandalised by collectors in the 18th century. In 1761 the Rev Samuel Pegge recalled seeing a bust of Apollo and of another deity in stone which had been found in the fields. A Roman building 31 feet long by 27 feet wide was found, consisting of hewn gritstone, bricks and tiles. This was some distance from the fort itself and may have been the mansio or hotel for visitors. A tile was found with the word Cahors[24] engraved upon it but without a number and there were further 18th century discoveries of urns full of ashes and a half length figure of a woman with her arms folded. All of these relics were removed by the finders, as was expected in those days, and no trace of them remains.

A datestone was found subsequently which showed that the garrison in 158 AD was manned by the 1st Cohort of Aquitanians from the Garonne region of France. A Roman gritstone altar to the God of War, probably 'collected' from Navio by the Vernon family who came from up the road at Hazlebadge Hall, has found its way to Haddon Hall and its inscription gives us the name of one of this cohort's Prefects – Sittius the Fifth (Quintus) from Sicily (Caecilianus) :

To the God Mars Braciaca, Quintus Sittius Caecilianus, Prefect of the First Cohort of Aquitanians, performs his vow.

Excavation of an underground chamber at Navio has revealed the name of another Prefect on the inscription of an oblong stone slab which translates as:

In honour of the Emperor Titus Oelius Hadrianus Antoninus Augustus Pius[25],

---

[24] Cohort.
[25] Augustus Pius was emperor from 131 to 161 AD.

Father of his country, [erected by] the 1ˢᵗ Cohort of Aquitanians under Julius Verus Governor of Britain, and under the direct orders of Capitonius Fuscus, Prefect of the Cohort.

During the same period the garrison at Ardotalia came from the 1ˢᵗ Cohort of Frisiavonians who were recruited from the Rhineland between Aachen and Cologne. Ardotalia was occupied from 78 to 140 AD, guarded the approaches to Longdendale and secured the important road known as the Doctor's Gate over the Snake Pass from Brough. This road was so named after Dr John Talbot, vicar of Glossop from 1494 to 1550 and an illegitimate son of the Earl of Shrewsbury. The doctor used the road when he visited his father at his castle at Sheffield.

When these forts were built in the first century AD, the Romans had their principal bases at Chester (the 20ᵗʰ Legion) and York (the 9th Legion). A legion consisted of 5000 men and was divided into 10 cohorts. The first cohort of each legion contained 800 men and the remaining cohorts were around 480 strong. Each cohort consisted of six centuries (each about 80-100 men strong) commanded by centurions.

Over and above the Regular Roman Legions there were Auxiliary Cohorts of 'foreigners' recruited from throughout the conquered areas of the Roman Empire, of which the garrisons at Navio and Ardotalia were examples. In common with other mercenary forces down the ages the Romans appear to have appointed their own native Roman commanders to the auxiliary formations in order to guarantee their loyalty and discipline. A successful career as an auxiliary earned Roman citizenship after 25 years' service, the gift of 30-40 acres of land and the privilege to hold slaves and freedmen.

A diagram of the fort at Brough (*colour plate 3*) following excavations in the 1960s is shown on the following page. One finding was that the fort was occupied from about 78 AD to 350 AD. It was originally constructed with timber inside ditches, trenches and ramparts and remained like that until the garrison was sent north under Emperor Hadrian to pacify the Scots. It was re-occupied in 154-158 under the governorship of Julius Verus during a renewed rebellion by the Brigantes and was then more extensively built in stone. It was redesigned for a second time during the governorship of Severus (193-211) and further modified in 300 AD for a garrison which included cavalry. Artillery catapults or 'ballistae' were also incorporated then, as evidenced by the discovery of $1\frac{1}{2}$ - 6 inch gritstone cannonballs. Two of these are to be found today built into the fireplace of one of the nearby houses. Unlike the forts at Ardotalia and Chesterfield, which were abandoned by the mid 2nd century, Navio continued to be garrisoned well into the 4th century, probably to control the lead mining industry in the area. It is known that some of the Roman stonework at Navio was removed in the 12th century to build Peveril Castle at the head of the valley.

In the following diagram the excavated walls, watchtowers and barrack blocks

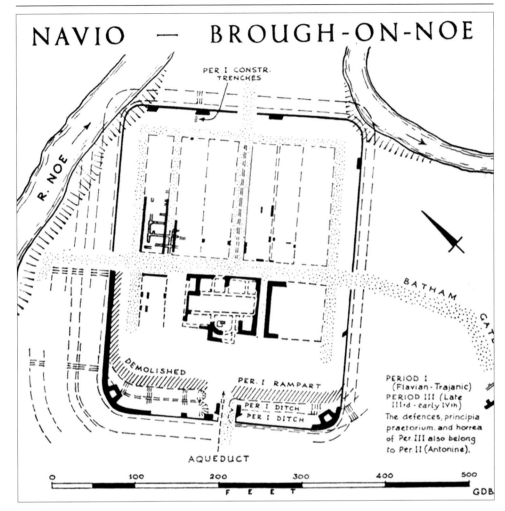

NAVIO — BROUGH-ON-NOE

PER. I CONSTR.
TRENCHES

R. NOE

BATHAM GAT

DEMOLISHED

PER. I RAMPART

PER. I DITCH

PER. I DITCH

AQUEDUCT

PERIOD I
(Flavian - Trajanic)
PERIOD III (Late
IIIrd - early IVth)
The defences, principia
praetorium, and horrea
of Per. III also belong
to Per. II (Antonine).

0   100   200   300   400   500

F E E T

GDB

are shown in thick black lines. Outside the fort on the south and south-east sides was a settlement or vicus of local inhabitants who gathered there to trade and provide services for the 500 strong garrison. The locals would have had no access to the fort itself except to negotiate business.

The Romans are known to have mined lead in the local area and to have exported pottery and corn. The earliest Derbyshire lead ingot comes from the reign of Emperor Hadrian (117-138). Another was discovered in 1777 on Cromford Moor with the inscription 'IMP.CAES.HADRIANI.AUG.MEI.LVT' – Inscribed by the 6th Legion in memory of Emperor Hadrian in 130 AD. The overall administrative centre for the lead mining industry was at Lutudarum[26] and the associated symbol LVT appears on 20 of the 28 surviving ingots known to have originated in Derbyshire. The Romans transported High Peak lead by road along

---

[26] Thought to be either a place near Wirksworth or the name of the Roman contractors handling the lead.

the Old Portway from Bradwell to Wardlow Mires to Ashford where it was loaded onto barges and floated down the Wye, Derwent, Trent and Humber to the coast. From there it was shipped either to the south of England or to the Continent. The labour force in the lead mines consisted of slaves, prisoners and convicted criminals. Some of the modern inhabitants of Bradwell are said to descend from Roman convicts sent to work there – the so-called 'damnati in metalla' (those condemned to work in metal mines) – but there is another saying that it is probably wise not to mention this in Bradwell!

Romans also mined Blue John spar at Castleton, the only place on earth where this distinct type of fluorspar is found. It is probable that they discovered it while mining for lead. Other fluorspars bearing a resemblance to it but easily distinguishable to the geologist are to be found in Iran on the border with Afghanistan, in China and in the USA. The Romans are known to have also mined fluorspar in Iran and Northern Italy and these are more likely to be the sources of the ornaments found at Pompeii. Pliny mentions that Petronius gave 300 talents[27] for a big vase of fluorspar. When he was condemned to death by Nero, he broke it, supposing that the emperor coveted the vase. For another fluorspar vase Nero is said to have paid the equivalent of nearly £50,000. The ashes of Governor Severus however were placed in what is definitely a Blue John urn at York in the year 211.

Coal was first mined in the High Peak in the early 2nd century and was used in the Roman forts as a heating fuel and for smelting lead. Stone and marble quarries were also developed to a limited extent.

The local population, witnessing all these sudden explosions of technological, industrial and social advance, must have been in awe of their Roman masters. Most of them, it appears, could not be trusted for employment in the Roman army or in the key industries but they seem to have been used to provide basic services such as food production, transport and labour. The extent of the local population at the time of the Roman invasion is a matter of some dispute among historians. Some maintain that the Peak District had been largely vacant until the Romans persuaded friendly tribes to colonise it towards the end of the first century. Others claim that the Peak District had been continuously inhabited and that the local tribes merely acquiesced in the Roman occupation and got on with their lives with minimum interference from the invaders. Clearly there were settlements in the district at the time of the Roman invasion, though on what scale and of what type is more difficult to assess. It is known that the Romans were responsible for introducing pottery kilns into the Peak District from the Trent valley and the so-called Derbyshire Pottery found in the settlements dates from the second century and not earlier. So it is conceivable that the Romans introduced not only new instruments and techniques but also indulged in some plantation of more reliable tribes from the south.

---

[27] About £30,000 equivalent in modern money.

What is certain is that, during the second century, there were many small Romano-British settlements throughout the district – some 120-140 have been identified in the county. These settlements, many containing four to five houses at most, were concentrated in the river valleys at approximately 1 mile intervals and are most numerous in the Wye, Derwent and Dove valleys. There was a string of settlements beside the river Wye including the sites at Staden outside Buxton, Cow Low and Chee Tor. The Chee Tor settlement on the south side of Chee Dale and reaching up to Blackwell was one of the larger sites and is still clearly visible from the Millers Dale to Wormhill road.

Chee Tor Lynchet Banks

From their typical thatched roundhouses surrounded by an outer wall, the foundations of which can be seen at Blackwell Farm, the Romano-British cultivated strips of land right down to the side of Chee Dale and Blackwell Dale. The roundhouses usually had an entrance facing south-east towards the sunrise and the simple interior was divided into sections for living and sleeping. The houses were occasionally accompanied by small walled yards. The Chee Tor site contains a typical tight-knit group of 4-5 houses which would have been occupied by members of the same family group.

The so-called lynchet banks running down to the dale sides are among the best preserved examples of Romano-British agriculture and were formed by the regular ploughing by oxen of the terraces of land. Steady soil erosion caused the earth to slip downhill and bank up against the walls and hedges of the field boundaries, leading to high berms on the edges of the fields. Some of these are still 2-4 metres high. Between the Chee Tor lynchets and the settlement itself there is a flattened area known as the Mediaeval Open Field. This would also have been cultivated as lynchets by the Romano-British but was more extensively ploughed by later settlers in the Middle Ages, eliminating the former field boundaries and banks of earth.

The North Derbyshire Archaeological Survey[28] also lists Hargate Wall as a Romano-British settlement, noting that the remains are barely visible after later ploughing. The evidence offered for this conclusion is that there are fields at Hargate Wall associated with Romano-British occupation. The only conceivable sign of lynchet banks of which I am aware are in the fields to the south of Rocky Low[29] where there are two distinct straight ridges running east-west along roughly level ground on the slope, one of them coinciding with a former field boundary removed in the 1970s and another supporting the boundary wall between OS[30] 618 and 621. A further potential lynchet bank can be seen under the top wall on the south side of the Lambing Croft[31]. However it seems equally possible that these ridges could be natural geological features formed by the underlying rock or by natural erosion of the topsoil down to the boundary walls.

A survey of early settlements and fields in the Southern Pennines by L H Butcher notes three stony banks about one foot high and three feet wide in Rocky Low[32] itself and further earth and stone enclosure banks around the site of the former barn called Cherryslack on the north side of Peter Dale. All of these observations are very questionable in my opinion.

The first settlers at Hargate Wall, whether in Romano-British or Anglo-Saxon times, would have focussed their cultivations close to the spring at Dakins Farm and to the stream which would have flowed down the back lane to Peter Dale before it was piped in 1900. It is no coincidence that the oldest field names in this part of Hargate are concentrated on either side of that stream bed. This lends some credence to the possibility of a Romano-British settlement at Hargate Wall but, without further hard evidence, this must be highly speculative in my view.

Other developments during the Roman era include the advent of Christianity which was marginally tolerated by the invaders. Place names containing Eccles[33] suggest early Christian religious congregations and gathering-places but not churches themselves, the first of which were not built until many centuries later. Examples are Eccles Pike at Chapel-en-le-Frith and Eccles House at Hope[34].

---

[28] C R Hart 1981 page 96.
[29] Ordnance Survey No 619 formerly known as Sitch Pingle and OS No 618 formerly known as Lower Lunch.
[30] Field with Ordnance Survey number [ ].
[31] OS 625.
[32] OS 849.
[33] From the Latin *ecclesia* meaning church.
[34] But not Eccles Hall at Tideswell which is named after the lawyer called Samuel Eccles who built the house in 1724.

The Roman Empire in Britain expanded up to Hadrian's Wall on the Scottish borders and, for a while, into the lowlands of Scotland. In the first, second and third centuries AD the Roman garrison of Britain contained 50,000 men. It survived for three centuries but, with growing manpower shortages caused by Roman campaigns on the Danube, the province's garrison was reduced to around 20,000 and then eventually collapsed around 410 AD, at which point the Romans conducted a complete withdrawal from Britain. So the Roman era lasted less than 400 years and was a comparative 'blip' in terms of our history's time span but its influence on our civilisation was enormous.

When it all came to an abrupt end, there was a Romano-British settlement at Chee Tor and possibly another at Hargate but still no 'village' and no place that anyone was yet calling 'Wormhill'. That was to come as a result of the next invasion from across the North Sea but, this time, by a mixture of Jutes, Angles and Saxons from Denmark and North Germany.

ANGLO-SAXON BRITAIN

Romano-British and Celtic communities remained after the Roman withdrawal but Anglo-Saxon immigrations into Britain began with the arrival of Hengist in Kent in 428. Angles landed in East Anglia and Lincolnshire and Saxons in the Thames Estuary and on the South Coast. Their control of England was not complete before 584. Strong and prolonged resistance was mounted by the Ancient Britons which kept the Anglo-Saxons contained within their bridgeheads on the coasts. In the fifth century the resistance was led by Kings Vortigern and Vortimer, and then by Ambrosius Aurelianus who is thought by some historians to be synonymous with King Arthur, though there is no proof for this. The history of this period is speculative and confined to often conflicting reports in chronicles and annals. It is further complicated by the mediaeval romances written 600 years later about the Arthurian Legend which relied more on poetic licence and fiction than fact. It is likely however than Arthur and others succeeded in defeating the invaders over a sustained period between 490 and Arthur's death at the battle of Camlann in 517 against his former viceroy Medraut who had joined forces with the Angles. The Anglo-Saxons did not manage to break out into western and northern Britain before 571 but their conquest was complete by 584. Thereafter they consolidated their power in England for the next five centuries and it was their language and legal system which came to predominate over the Roman and Celtic practices.

The Anglo-Saxon occupation and influence in South Derbyshire probably started towards the end of the sixth century. The Kingdom of Mercia was founded by Crida in about 585. The Midlands were primarily an Anglian territory with the invaders claiming descent from Angeln in Schleswig, North Germany. The grandfather of Crida, Icel, was probably the first to lead a band of Anglian migrants to the east coast of Britain early in the 6th century. Place-names containing 'ing' (eg Hartington, Taddington) are of typical Anglo-Saxon origin. 'Ton' is the Anglo-Saxon word for a settlement or village and 'ing' denotes the owner; hence 'settlement belonging to Hart' and 'settlement belonging to Tadd or Tada'.

The map[35] which follows shows Anglo-Saxon cemeteries and burial sites by the end of the 7th century and hence the extent of Anglo-Saxon colonisation by about 700. There is a distinct concentration in North Derbyshire which is circled.

---

[35] After S Chadwick Hawkes.

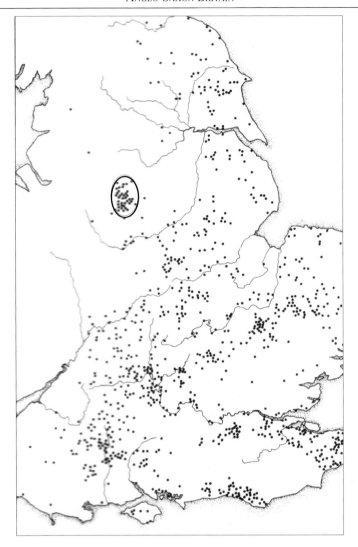

Anglo-Saxon Colonisation by 700

The earliest known name of the village of Wormhill is 'WRUENELE' which is how it appeared in the Domesday Survey of 1086. Although the very reputable expert, Cameron, prefers to attribute the name to 'Wyrma's Hill', the Anglo-Saxon derivation of this name is said to come from 'wruen' meaning worm/reptile/ dragon and 'ele' meaning hill. The more imaginative of the theorists of early dragon mythology quote Wormhill as one of the sites associated with dragons and refer to the hill at Knotlow[36] near Millers Dale where a dragon was reputed to have lived, with the terraces around the hill being the marks left by the dragon's coil.

---

[36] Derived from the Middle English *knot* meaning hill and *hlaw* meaning burial site.

Knotlow is in fact a good example of a volcanic outcrop of darker coloured rock called Toadstone which can be seen in the small quarry on the Wormhill side of the hill. Thus it is thought by geologists to be the lava 'plug' of an ancient volcano, sealing the centre of a crater from many millions of years ago. It is tempting but too fanciful to suggest that ancient tales of fire, smoke and molten rock roaring and spewing from this local volcano came to be associated with the myth of a dragon (*colour plate 4*).

Nor does it escape the dragon enthusiasts' attention that in St Margaret's Church there is a carving of St Margaret and the Dragon, as if there could seriously be any connection between the two! Some eighteenth century historians speculated that the name of the village had originally been 'Wolfhill'[37] but this was pure fantasy and bears no relation to reality.

Nowadays only those with a vivid imagination or a very unwise sense of humour would dare to suggest that there are any dragons left in Wormhill.

Hargate Wall also derives its name from the Anglo-Saxon *Herdwyk-waella* meaning 'Herd-farm by the Spring'[38]. The Mercian word 'waella' became Middle English 'walle' and is difficult to distinguish from 'wall'. The origin of the name Hargate Wall therefore goes back to Anglo-Saxon times before the Norman Conquest and, if we discount the dubious claim of a Romano-British settlement here around AD 200, can be dated back to the establishment of the first settlement in AD 700-950. Some local history books speculate that the first settlement at Hargate Wall began around 1100, ie 34 years after the Norman Conquest, which is clearly wrong. The name suggests that Hargate Wall has always been a farm where cattle have been reared for up to thirteen centuries (but up to eighteen centuries if the first settlers were Romano-British), taking advantage of the natural springs of water which rise there. The main spring rises at the eastern end of the troughs at Dakins, where the sterks from Dakins Farm used to be watered every morning until a water supply was piped to the farm buildings in the 1960s.

From the start of the 8th century there was a large scale movement away from the Romano-British pattern of dispersed individual farmsteads like that at Chee Tor to settlement of multiple families in villages and hamlets. This was motivated by the new system of communal open field agriculture with common rights for meadowland and pasture, which was to endure until the Enclosure Acts 1000 years later. Wormhill and Hargate Wall were almost certainly established around this time. Within the villages cattle were bred principally for ploughing in the standard 4 or 8 ox team rather than for milk which was more usually provided by sheep. Goats were also kept for milk and meat. Pigs, smaller and darker than today's breeds, roamed in large herds in outlying woodland areas tended by swineherds.

Anglo-Saxon settlements, of which Wormhill is a good example, were built in

---

[37] And this theory was repeated by Chrichton Porteous in the 1960s.
[38] Cameron – *Place Names of Derbyshire.*

linear fashion either along the narrow floor of a dry valley (like Tideswell) or on a plateau above the valley (like Wormhill). The Angles may have taken over some of the Romano-British settlements but they appear to have been the first inhabitants since the Bronze Age to have built on the limestone plateau rather than confining themselves to the river valleys. Long narrow fields of $\frac{1}{2}$ - 1 acre in size and separated by either stone walls or movable hurdles were constructed at right angles to the street, forming the typical early cultivation strips closest to the village (*colour plate 5*). In Wormhill there are two well defined boundary banks either side of and parallel to the village street forming a typical 'town ring' which marked the limits of the fields nearest to the street. The gable walls of the older houses are built on these banks with their doorways facing south.

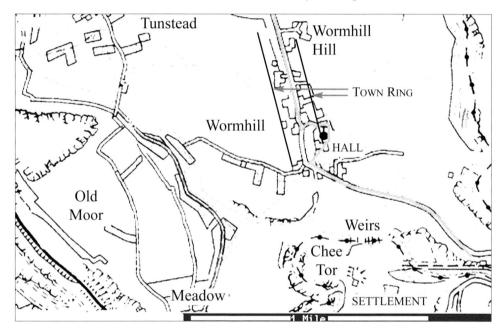

Wormhill Town Ring

Wells and natural springs, which were not universally to be found on the porous limestone plateau, were key to the location of a settlement and these had to be away from the deepest river valleys, from where carriage of water to the fields would have been too inconvenient. Both Wormhill and Hargate Wall meet this description and criteria for an Anglo-Saxon settlement in all respects.

Anglo-Saxon houses were typically rectangular structures, built of timber and roofed in either thatch or shingle. They were around 28 feet long and 17 feet wide with high ridges and low eaves. Archaeologists refer to this type of construction as a Grubenhaus which the Angles brought with them from their homeland in North Germany. The earliest houses in the village may have been of this kind.

41

Anglian Grubenhaus

The capital of the whole Mercian Kingdom was originally at Repton but the Kingdom then divided into North Mercia (north of the Trent) with its capital at Lichfield and South Mercia (south of the Trent) with its capital at Tamworth. It was several generations before the Mercians penetrated into the Peak District which was still occupied according to the 'Tribal Hidage' by a Romano-British tribe called the Pecsaetan (including presumably the inhabitants of our settlement at Chee Tor). The Peak District contained 1200 'hides'[39] or 1200 areas containing 120 acres of arable land and it was on the basis of the 'hidage' that the Mercians organised their taxation laws. A hide was divided into four 'virgates' (about 30 acres each) and each virgate was divided into two 'bovates' (about 15 acres each)[40]. Earthworks and ditches, still visible in places in the Hope Valley, marked the boundary between Mercia and Northumbria.

Legend[41] has it that a major battle took place in the Hope Valley in the early 600s between a joint force from Wessex and Mercia on one side and Northumbria on the other. Cuicholm, King of Wessex, and Edwin, King of Northumbria, had

---

[39] The meaning of the term 'hide' is in some dispute. Historians of the Anglo-Saxon era explain it variously as a unit of taxation, a term relating to the productivity of land or as a measurement of acreage.

[40] The acreage of hides, virgates and bovates varied from county to county.

[41] The legend is questioned by serious historians like Gladwyn Turbutt but that does not stop the Peak Park Authority from advertising it as historical fact in tourist handouts!

become embroiled in a dispute over land boundaries. Cuicholm had sent an envoy to the court of Edwin with orders to murder the King. The plot was foiled by the intervention of Lilla, one of Edwin's chief thegns, who died as a result of his wounds and is commemorated by Lilla Cross high on the North York Moors. To avenge the assassination attempt, Edwin marched south to the Hope Valley, where Cuicholm had amassed a large army, reinforced by the troops of Penda, King of Mercia and another sworn enemy of Edwin. The two armies clashed the following day in the Edale Valley somewhere near the present Townhead Bridge and the river Noe is said to have run red with the blood of the warriors. Edwin, King of Northumbria and a Christian convert, supposedly emerged victorious. The outcome of the battle is alleged to have bequeathed the names of the hills from which the opposing forces were launched – Win Hill for Edwin and Lose Hill for Cuicholm and Penda. This is however disputed by experts on place-names who point out that Win Hill derives from 'withies' or mountain ash trees which still grow there and Lose Hill (pronounced *Loose*) means the hill with the pig-sties (from the Old English *hlose*). In 634 AD Penda[42], grandson of Crida, eventually defeated and killed Edwin in battle in South Yorkshire.

King Oswiu, son of Oswald, took possession of the Kingdom of Mercia in 659 AD and converted the inhabitants to Christianity. A church was built at Lichfield and made a cathedral before it was rebuilt as a much larger edifice in 700. The Venerable Bede (673-735), the English theologian and historian, noted that in his time the inhabitants of Derbyshire and Nottinghamshire amounted to just 7000 families.

Derbyshire became one of the 16 counties of the Kingdom or heptarchy[43] after the eventual success of the Anglo-Saxon conquest. Its inhabitants were known as the Mercii Aquiloranes, which distinguished those who lived on the north side of the river Trent. Derbyshire was divided into six Hundreds and was said to contain about 440 hamlets. The boundaries of Mercia expanded and contracted according to the outcome of enduring conflicts with Northumbria and Wessex but, at its most extensive, Mercia stretched from the Humber in the North to the Thames in the South and the Welsh borders in the West. It was controlled by the Anglo-Saxon earls and dukes who did their best to keep at bay the next invasions which came from Scandinavia.

The first Viking invasion lasted from 793 to 876. The Vikings went on the rampage in the 9th and early 10th century, sacking Derby and all the towns and monasteries down the east side of the country as far as Ely. The Abbey at Repton was destroyed by the Danes in 874. England was divided at the time into separate and rival Kingdoms – Northumbria, Mercia and Wessex – and the Vikings were expert at exploiting these rivalries to their own advantage. Their superior mobility

[42] The *Penny* coin is alleged to have been named after him.
[43] Seven autonomous regions.

on sea and land and the flexibility of their military organisation made them invincible until the Anglo-Saxon Kings had formed alliances and reorganised their forces at the start of the 900s. The 9th century map of England (*colour plate 6*) above shows Wormhill right on the boundary of the Duchy of Mercia under Anglo-Saxon rule and the Danish controlled territories under the rule of the Danelaw.

Alfred was perhaps the most successful of the Anglo-Saxon Kings and it was his achievement of defeating the Viking attempt to conquer the Kingdom of Wessex that prevented England from becoming a Scandinavian colony in the 9th century. But for Alfred, it is sometimes said, we might all be speaking Danish today. Alfred reached an agreement with the Viking Guthrum in c.880 to divide up the country into areas of Anglo-Saxon and Scandinavian influence with the boundary running from Tamworth to Northampton to London. North and east of that line the Norwegian and Danish invaders were dominant. To the south and west the Kingdoms of Mercia and Wessex retained control.

Alfred's son, Edward the Elder, succeeded in rolling back the Scandinavian Conquest in the Midlands and restoring Mercian control, though the achievements of the Mercian King Aethelred I and his wife and successor Queen Aethelfraed should not be lightly overlooked. The Anglo-Saxon Chronicle over-egged the successes of the Wessex Kings to a greater extent then the Mercian Register did for their own monarchs and Edward may have benefited from more 'spin' than he deserved. He bought certain manors back from the Danelaw and no doubt coerced or forced other Vikings into withdrawal. We know from a charter from the early 900s that a Saxon called Uhtred was buying lands from the 'pagans' in Hope and Ashford on the orders of Edward. After the death of Queen Aethelfraed in 918 Edward became the ruler of both Wessex and Mercia until his death in 924. In 920 Edward ordered the building of a military post at what is known as Castle Hill in Bakewell to mark the extent of Mercian re-occupation and to defend against any further Viking raids. This construction and garrisoning of a so-called burh on the northern frontier of Mercia was enough to persuade the Viking ruler of York Ragnall Guthfrithson to formally submit to Edward and thus avoid any further encroachment on his territory. Edward's gains were consolidated by his son and successor, Athelstan, who was the first Anglo-Saxon King to rule over a united England and the first to successfully introduce a universal system of law.

How far the Vikings penetrated into the Peak District before they were driven back into Northumbria is not known but there is only scant evidence of Viking occupation west of Bakewell[44]. The extent of Scandinavian penetration into

---

[44] Some claim that Flagg is a Viking place-name and others that the mediaeval earth-work called Camp Green near Hathersage was once a 'Danes' camp'. Less plausible is the claim of a battle fought against Viking plunderers at Chapel-en-le-Frith – there was nothing at Chapel to plunder until the foresters bought the land and built the first Forest Chapel there in the 13th century.

England can be gauged by the prevalence of place-names ending in 'by'[45] and 'thorp'[46]. These are most common in Yorkshire, Lincolnshire, South Derbyshire, Nottinghamshire, Leicestershire, Northamptonshire, East Anglia and along all the coastlines and outlying islands of the British Isles. They do not generally extend into the uplands of the Pennines.

The main purpose of the Viking invasions was to extract loot and ransom money. They stripped churches and monasteries of their valuables; seized local dignitaries and demanded ransom money for their release; and accepted large payments[47] in return for sparing towns from looting. In many cases this protection money merely encouraged the Vikings to return repeatedly to demand more. The raids, involving from 30 to 200 ships, each manned by 40 warriors, were usually temporary in nature and the invaders returned regularly to Scandinavia once they had secured sufficient loot but some settled for longer periods and established positions of local authority and control.

A further Scandinavian invasion took place from 1016 to 1042 when the Danish King Cnut assumed the throne of England, ruling by once again dividing the country into regions controlled by Anglo-Saxon Earls. During this period there is evidence that the Viking obsession with precious metals led them to pursue mining as well as looting. Both the Anglo-Saxons and the Danes mined lead in the area, the Odin mine at Castleton being named after a Danish God.

By the end of the Anglo-Saxon era, in the reign of Edward The Confessor, England had been united into a single Kingdom and divided up into administrative areas called scirs or shires with Sheriffs[48] representing the King's authority. Shires had been divided up into either Wapentakes[49] or otherwise Hundreds[50]. The High Peak had become one of six Hundreds in Derbyshire – an administrative term which persisted into the 19th century. Codified systems for taxation and justice had been created, based on the new administrative divisions. Feudal society had been formed with a personal bond between the local lord and his dependants.

We know from the Domesday Survey that the last Anglo-Saxon owner[51] of the Wormhill manor was a man called Siward Barn. He owned 9 other manors in the county including one close to Wormhill called *Muchedswelle* which has since disappeared without trace. This was one of several 'lost' manors which were either abandoned or laid waste by the Norman conquerors. All we know about Muchedswelle is that, in the Domesday Survey, it was one of the berewicks[52] in the

---

[45] Old Danish for farmstead or village, eg Derby, Ashby.
[46] Denoting a secondary settlement or hamlet.
[47] Often thousands of pounds in weight of silver.
[48] Shire Reeves.
[49] Wherever there was a history of Danish occupation in the Midland or Northern counties.
[50] Each consisting of 100 settlements or 100 hides.
[51] Or *Thegn* as lords of the manor were then known.
[52] Outlying settlements.

manor of Hope, as was Tideswell. Modern commentators variously ascribe its name to 'Muched's Spring' or even the 'Mucky Well'! So where and what was Muchedswelle? On the other hand, if it was the Mucky Well, do we really want to know?

Siward joined the rebellion of Hereward The Wake in 1070 against the early Norman occupiers and his fate is unknown. Hereward was a small Lincolnshire landowner, whose stronghold in the Isle of Ely was captured by King William in 1071. Legend has it that Hereward and some of his companions escaped through the marshes but nothing was heard of him again. He was one of the last leaders of the Anglo-Saxon resistance. He was not alone because it is alleged that somewhere between 50% and 75% of the Anglo-Saxon aristocracy perished in the first 4 years of Norman rule and their widows fled to the nunneries. It was not a good time to be a dissident Anglian thegn and Siward may have succumbed in the purge, the scale and thoroughness of which would have made Stalin envious. Siward's complicity in the rebellion would explain why his manors were confiscated and handed over to Henry de Ferrers when the Normans came to power.

Finally we owe the Anglo-Saxons credit for some of the most advanced and exquisite jewellery seen up to that time. An Anglian noblewoman was buried at Cow Low just outside the parish to the west of Great Rocks Dale in amongst a series or earlier Romano-British and Bronze Age graves. With her were two gold pins set with garnets and linked by a gold chain as a pair of hair-pins to hold either a headdress or a veil. Next to her was a wooden box with brass hinges and a hasp, fastened by an iron padlock. Inside the box was an ivory comb, a silver pendant necklace, a blue glass bead and other personal possessions. The pins and gold chain are in the Sheffield City Museum.

More significantly still, from the burial mound at Benty Grange, now a derelict farmstead just north-east of the Parsley Hay junction on the Ashbourne to Buxton road, came one of only two examples yet discovered of Anglo-Saxon armour. When it was opened in 1848, the mound revealed traces of chain mail and a warrior's helmet, now also in the Sheffield Museum. The helmet has an iron framework covered in horn plates. It is crowned by a bronze boar with gold tusks and the nosepiece is surmounted by a silver cross. This treasure is second in importance only to the famous helmet at the ship burial at Sutton Hoo in East Anglia but that is now thought to have belonged to the Swedish King Raedwald rather than a genuine Anglo-Saxon. Dating of the Benty Grange helmet is problematic but it might have preceded AD 700 because the folk epic poem called Beowulf written in about that year refers to Mercian warriors amongst whom 'the shapes of boars, adorned with gold, glinted above their helmets'. Boar helmet crests were thought to confer protection in battle. So here we have a Mercian warrior of significant status and Christian faith who may have fought and died with the Mercian army against the Northumbrians in the Hope Valley or later against the Viking invasions. Whether Benty Grange was his home or the site of the battlefield where he died, we are unlikely ever to know and whether he was a 'prince' as some histories claim, is beyond proof.

So the 500 years of Anglo-Saxon control, despite the turmoil and friction of multiple competing Kingdoms and persistent incursions from Viking invaders, had established the geography and local government of England and Derbyshire much as we know it today. It is a period often referred to, undeservedly in my view, as the 'Dark Ages'. Certainly the first 200 years were marked by a degree of instability, chaos and brutality which contrasted sharply with the relative stability and civilisation of the Roman Occupation but such barbarity as did take place did not compare unfavourably with that of their Norman successors. In true Germanic fashion the achievement of the Anglo-Saxons was to bring an unprecedented level of order and organisation within a unified and well administered Kingdom, much of which has lasted through to the present day. If they had had trains, you could be sure that they would have run on time. In this respect their contribution had a more enduring value than their Roman predecessors, whose customs and culture were never transferred to their English colony and disappeared with their abrupt departure. The only exception to this was the continuing use of Latin in church services and records but it was never adopted by the native British in everyday speech. The Normans were lucky to inherit the Anglo-Saxon systems and infra-structure and did little to change them.

The English language has its main roots in this period of Anglo-Saxon rule and it is noteworthy that the rest of the world, when they speak pejoratively about Britain and the English-Speaking peoples, still refers to us as 'Anglo-Saxons'. Likewise it was the Anglo-Saxons who introduced the penny coinage which remained legal tender in Britain for over 1000 years until it was replaced by decimalisation in 1974.

On the local scene, our village and many others in the Peak District were created at this time by families whose recent forebears had started life in North Germany. These Schleswig-Holsteiners had probably absorbed and intermarried with the remnants of the Romano-British tribes and, who knows, there might have been some Viking blood in their veins as well. They had created a new concept for this part of the world – they had formed a community of multiple families as opposed to a settlement confined primarily to one family group. They had created the concept of the 'village' which has lasted, with some exceptions like the change from communal to private ownership of land, for the intervening 1300 years.

NORMANS AND PLANTAGENETS

THE NORMAN CONQUEST

Godfrey Foljambe, whose family was to become the owners of the Wormhill manor for over three centuries, fought at the Battle of Hastings in 1066 with William the Conqueror. He is said to have been a descendant of King Lodbrok of Denmark and of his 30th son King Eric of Sweden and to have been knighted for his feats in battle. On arrival in England he married a Saxon heiress called Uchtred at Elton near Matlock. Their son, Sir Ralph Foljambe (born in about 1101), was the first member of the family to own the manor from the 1100s. He gained ownership by his marriage to Gundred de Ferrers, the daughter of Henry de Ferrers, and the manor could conceivably have been part of her dowry. Their son, the third generation after the Conquest, was Sir Geoffrey Foljambe (1125-1184) who married Matilda Musard[54].

In the Domesday Survey, drawn up in 1086 twenty years after the Battle of Hastings, the manor of 'WRUENELE' belonged to Henry de Ferrers[55], whose descendants became the Earls of Derby[56]. The amount of cultivated land was sufficient for 4 ploughs. The manor contained 20 acres of meadow and underwood one league[57] in length and four furlongs[58] in breadth. The significance of 'under-wood' was that this was, at the time, the only source of fuel and building materials. It therefore determined the population and hence taxation capacity of the manor. It was primarily the taxation capacity that the Domesday Survey sought to establish. In size and character Wruenele was fairly typical of the hundreds of rural manors where the population of England mostly lived. For the purposes of the

---

[54] Their first born child, Henry (born 1152), was a page in the train of King Richard I. Matilda came from the family of Hascoit Musard, a Breton noble and son of the Viscount of Nantes. Hascoit was the eldest of four brothers who fought at Hastings and was granted the barony of Staveley in South Derbyshire

[55] Henry was a Norman knight who had fought at Hastings. His home was originally at Ferriers-St Hilaire in the Eure region of France. He was the Lord of Longueville Normandy and was a Domesday Commissioner. Wruenele was one of 114 manors in Derbyshire which had been granted to him by William the Conqueror after he had been proclaimed King

[56] At the Battle of the Standard in 1138

[57] In the Norman period = 1½ miles.

[58] One furlong = one furrow long = the distance that a team of oxen could pull a plough before they had to be rested – 220 yards. They were then turned round and ploughed another furlong in the opposite direction. Obviously this was an inexact measurement because a beefy ox team would plough a longer distance than a weedy team before they were knackered.

Survey a place only qualified as a 'town' if it had more than 2000 inhabitants and there were only 18 such towns in England at the time.

The Normans quickly introduced their own feudal hierarchy with the King as the Absolute Ruler; Barons and Tenants-in-Chief who were allocated large tracts of land and owed allegiance to the King; Knights occupying one or more manors; and the Peasantry at the bottom of the social pyramid. Most of the villagers owed allegiance to the lord of the manor and 10% were officially described as 'slaves'. Beneath the knights, gentlemen and esquires who made up 5% of the population and managed all the land, the lowest rung of military vassals went by the Anglo-Saxon name of *sokemen* (freehold tenants farming manor smallholdings in exchange for fixed rents and non-military services). Beneath them came the *villeins* (farmers with their own smallholdings), *bordars* (farm labourers) and *cottagers* (lower peasants with no land). This latter category of inhabitants was by far the most numerous and accounted for 75% of the total.

The Domesday Survey showed a total population of about 12,000 and 17 distinct landowners in Derbyshire where the Anglo-Saxon manors were expropriated and handed over to the Norman knights. King William was ruthless in suppressing the vestiges of Anglo-Saxon resistance and, during his campaigns against the Mercian warlords in the Midlands in the early years after the Conquest, he laid waste to many manors in the south of the county. This accounts for the many 'lost' manors in the Domesday Survey which are described as 'waste'. The scorched earth policy was relatively modest in the Midlands compared to the so-called 'Harrying of the North' where the Norman Army committed an early example of genocide in whole regions of Yorkshire, Northumberland and Durham. So complete was this deliberate devastation that some areas were said not to have been populated or cultivated again for 9 years. So much for the Entente Cordiale!

The Ferrers family became one of the leading baronies of the land, taking part in a series of revolts against King John in 1215 and later against King Henry III because of his subservience to the Pope and his generosity to foreign favourites. The third generation of the family after the Conquest took part in the rebellion of 1264, led by Simon de Montfort, which defeated King Henry at Lewes and took him prisoner. However the royalists put down the rebellion, winning victories in 1265 at Evesham and against Robert Ferrers at Chesterfield in 1266. After the defeat Robert is said to have been caught hiding amongst bags of wool in Chesterfield Church. His hiding place was given away by a girl whose lover had been killed in the battle, after being compelled to join the rebels – Hell hath no fury like a woman scorned. Robert Ferrers was thereafter obliged to go into exile.

Quite how long the manor remained in the hands of the Ferrers before Robert went into exile is not known but Wormhill probably passed into the ownership of the Foljambes by Sir Ralph Foljambe's marriage to Gundred de Ferrers around the beginning of the 1100s.

William Peveril, another Norman knight and an illegitimate son of William the

49

Conqueror was granted other manors in the neighbourhood and his son (also called William) built Peveril Castle (colour plate 7) at Castleton and Bolsover Castle[59] near Chesterfield, fled the country after poisoning Ranulf, the Earl of Chester in 1152 and forfeited his estates in 1155 to the Duchy of Lancaster and hence the Crown.

The Normans were the first builders of castles, the ancient Britons having confined themselves to building hill-forts made of timber and surrounded by massive earthworks. These huge stone castles were masterpieces of ingenious fortification, largely unassailable before the invention of gunpowder and so expensive to construct that they threatened to bankrupt their royal builders[60]. Some of the walls of Peveril Castle remain along with the ruins of a gateway and the shell of the keep. The walls were 8 feet thick and nearly 60 feet high, enclosing an area of some 400 square feet. The cost of construction of the Tower (Keep) in 1176 was £135. In the previous year the cost of one of the chambers within the castle walls had been £4-17-0 and a further £49-0-0 was spent in 1177 on unspecified building work. King Henry II (the first of the Plantagenet Kings) had special apartments made on the hill below so that he could come and supervise the building works. He visited several times, in 1157 receiving there the submission of Malcolm the Maiden, King of Scotland and a gay icon of his age. On this occasion it is known that he was accompanied by his wife Eleanor of Aquitaine[61] despite the fact that she had only recently given birth to a son who would in due course become King Richard I. Their daughter Matilda was living at the Castle in 1167. Records of the cost of board and lodging at the Castle show that Henry II's expenses in 1157 were £10-4-0; Malcolm of Scotland's were £37-12-3 (presumably for a larger entourage) and their wine bill came to £3-12-0. The following year Henry II's bill came to £36-5-0 and in 1164 to £8-8-3.

Why the Normans chose to site a substantial castle at the head of the Hope Valley is not recorded. In many parts of the country the Normans built castles to symbolise and maintain their supremacy over the Anglo-Saxons and other rebellious tribes after suppressing them in the years following the Conquest. Peveril Castle could have marked a prestige project for the local warlord, William Peveril, and it was clearly designed as a strongpoint from which to administer the Royal Hunting Forest. But it was also the case that the Normans tended to build

---

[59] The 12th century Bolsover Castle was held by the king after 1155 and was besieged in 1215 during one of the Barons' Revolts against King John. The Barons had invited King Louis VIII (1187-1226) of France to invade and usurp the throne of England. The invasion however was unsuccessful and Louis returned to France. Gerald de Furnival held Bolsover for the king and William de Ferrers mounted the siege on behalf of the barons. One of the towers and part of the curtain wall were breached but it appears to have held out. The mediaeval castle was later allowed to deteriorate and became a ruin before it was rebuilt by Charles Cavendish in 1608.

[60] Harlech Castle in Wales was said to have consumed a third of the royal income during the time of its construction

[61] See *Eleanor of Aquitaine, by the Wrath of God, Queen of England* by Alison Weir.

their castles at key nodal control points on the national road network. Peveril Castle controlled the important Winnats Pass on the east-west route across the base of the Pennines and, in this respect, the castle may have served the same purpose as the Roman fort had done at nearby Brough.

The dale which runs from Peter Dale down to Millers Dale and just to the north of Wormhill village is called Monks Dale. It was William Peveril who caused it to acquire the name. William Peveril (the Second) founded the Abbey of Lenton near Nottingham to pay for his sins or, as he put it, 'for the health of his own soul and of Adelina his wife'. In about 1108 he handed the Abbey a number of manors, 'two thirds of the tithes of all the pastures pertaining to his Lordship in the Peak, the whole tithe of colts and fillies wherever he had a stable in the Peak and the whole tithes of lead and hunting'. As part of this generous gift he granted the 'township' of Blackwell and land at Monks Dale to the monastery which later rewarded him by sheltering him when he went on the run after poisoning the Earl of Chester. A Grange[62] and a chapel were established in Monks Dale, which is referred to as the 'oratory' in some accounts and of which only the barest traces remain on the site of the present Monks Dale Farm overlooking Millers Dale. The monks were said to have made considerable income for the Abbey from the tithes and by operating the flour mill at Millers Dale.

Millers Dale

The Grange probably continued in use by the monks until the dissolution of the monasteries by King Henry VIII in 1520-1540. It is known that the Lenton Priory's ownership of property in nearby Blackwell came to an end in 1538. A fragment of a 14th century traceried stone screen found in Monks Dale in the 1860s was kept in the garden of Tideswell vicarage until 1905 and is now said to be in the parvise over the south porch of Tideswell church. Since the gallery leading to the parvise

---

[62] A Farm worked by monks.

from inside the church was removed in the 19th century and the only other access is via a minute spiral staircase in the porch leading from a locked door to which nobody now seems to have the key, I have no means of verifying whether the stone fragment is still there.

There is also a credible theory, first suggested by W Allan Milton in his *Historic Places around Buxton* of 1926, that the mediaeval cross at Wheston with its elaborate depiction of the Crucifixion and the Virgin Mary is another relic from the Monks Dale Grange. It seems entirely possible that the fiercely Catholic Alleyn family at Wheston could have sought to preserve this cross at the Dissolution by moving it to the spinney alongside Wheston Hall but it is also undoubtedly the case that the Alleyns had enough money and religious zeal to

Wheston Cross
From Monks Dale Grange?

commission and erect a cross of this quality of their own accord. This cross used to be on the Green in front of Wheston Hall but was moved to its present location when the house was rebuilt. It has also lost its top section, though it is not known whether this occurred through natural wear and tear and ageing or through deliberate desecration of Catholic symbols in the 16th century.

The monks of several Orders became wealthy and powerful land-owners at the time throughout the area. They were a rum lot. They were exempt from the laws of the land and had no hesitation in exploiting their immunity. Many of them preferred hunting and poaching to learning and preaching. They brewed and drank heavily, one monastery delivering no less than 460 gallons of ale per annum to a local priest for his personal consumption (equivalent to 10 pints a day every day of the year)! Two abbots in Derbyshire were sacked for keeping concubines.

The monastic order which occupied Monks Dale were Cluniacs – the so-called 'Black Monks' who wore a black robe and black hood and cape. The Cluniacs were an offshoot of the Benedictine Order, founded at Cluny in 910 and favoured by the Norman and Plantagenet Kings because they brought French customs to the English Church and replaced worship of the 'pagan' saints worshipped by the Anglo-Saxons. They liked to wear fine linen underneath and were connoisseurs of wine. At least, unlike the Cistercians or 'White Monks', they did take the trouble to wear underclothes. Walter Map, a twelfth century author and not a fan of the Cistercian Order, wrote that the White Monks wore no underpants 'to preserve coolness in that part of the body, lest sudden heats provoke unchastity'. There was another Cluniac grange at Priestcliffe near Taddington. St Bernard tells of one Cluniac Abbot who had 60 horses in his stables and a greater assortment of wines than anyone could taste at a sitting.

Whether the occupants of the Monks Dale grange were a corrupt and dissolute bunch we will never know and their daily routine can only be guessed at but, if they followed the ritual Benedictine programme of the time, their days would have been filled with prayers and services, interspersed with work on the farm. The normal day started at midnight with the services of Mattins and Lauds. After this the monks retired to bed until dawn (probably about 5am in summer and 7am in winter) when they rose again to sing Prime. They then washed, had a modest breakfast and returned to the chapel for the Chapter-Mass. A chapter meeting followed, dealing with spiritual advice and disciplinary matters, and the next 2 hours were taken up with work. Then came the High Mass at 10am, followed by recitations and lunch at midday taken in silence while one of the monks read a homily from the stone lectern in the dining room. During the summer months the monks were usually allowed a siesta after lunch but otherwise the afternoon was taken up with work on the farm or study until Vespers which was followed by supper. The last service of the day was Compline after which the monks retired to their dormitory (about 7pm in winter and 10pm in summer). What a life!

It is possible that, in common with other granges and abbeys of the time, the Cluniacs in Monks Dale used so-called lay brothers to do the menial work on the farm, leaving the monks themselves more time for their monastic duties. Lay brothers were not inducted as monks and did not wear monastic clothing but lived and ate with them. Sheep-farming was a major and profitable activity for the granges and much of the income of the monasteries came from the sale and export of wool. Lay brothers often took the major share of tending the flocks.

For 100 years the Cluniacs held the tithe rights undisputed until challenged by the Dean and Chapter of Lichfield, who went to court in 1241 with the claim that the rights of the Monks Dale grange belonged to the church of Hope in their diocese and that William Peveril had given away tithes and privileges which didn't belong to him in the first place. However neither side could produce a Royal Charter as evidence of ownership. Five appeals went to the Papal Court at Rome without a finding being reached.

In 1250/51 the Dean of Lichfield, frustrated by this unresolved dispute, sent men to collect the tithe sheep and lambs from the Monks Dale grange and gathered them inside Tideswell church where they thought they would be safe from the retribution of the monks. However the monks were determined to have their rights and broke into the church. 'Some sheep and lambs were killed under the feet of horses in the church; others were dragged out and carried off by force of arms; the Ministers of the church were beaten and savagely wounded; and the church itself violated by the Ministers and monks of the priory, and polluted with blood, and the churchyard likewise.' Such drama for a quiet place like Tideswell! The dispute was eventually settled by the Lenton Monastery agreeing to pay the Diocese of Lichfield 100 marks compensation on top of the £60 already paid for damage. It was agreed that all tithes belonged to Lichfield except two thirds of the tithes on lead, all the tithes on the mill at Millers Dale, and all tithes on stud farming and hunting. The monks were still well in pocket.

William Peveril's estates were confiscated when he went on the run but the monks hung onto the grange and the mill. Many of the lands of the other great landowner in the area, Robert Ferrers, passed to the Crown in 1266 after his defeat at the battle of Chesterfield. These two estates were added to the already major Crown holding, the Royal Forest of High Peak, which ranged from Castleton in the North to the rivers Goyt and Wye in the South.

Despite the association between Monks Dale and William Peveril, the mediaeval history of Wormhill is linked in a much closer and more enduring way with another family called Foljambe, whose modern day descendants pronounce their name 'Fuljam' and sometimes also spell it as 'Fulgam'.

THE FOLJAMBE DYNASTY

We have seen how the manor passed to the Foljambe family through marriage with Gundred de Ferrers in about 1100. Their ownership of the manor lasted remarkably for eleven generations and nearly three centuries through to 1392 before the Wormhill branch of the family died out for want of a male heir.

The Foljambes were amongst the Crusaders who went to the Holy Land, led by King Richard I, Coeur de Lion. Richard I spent most of his 10 years reign of England living in Normandy, visiting England only twice, for 3 months on the first occasion and 2 months on the second. As one of our greatest English heroes, it is remarkable that he spoke no English at all. Nevertheless the Crusades bequeathed him a massive reputation as one of England's most famous warrior Kings. The Foljambe shield is a band between 6 escallops or sea-shells, the escallop being generally recognised as the symbol of a crusader. The Crusader member of the family was Sir Henry Foljambe (the third generation at Wormhill following Sir Ralph – first generation – and Sir Geoffrey – second). As a young boy Henry was a page in the train of King Richard at his coronation. Pages were inducted into the royal court around the age of 7 and were trained as mounted knights during their teenage years. He probably took part in the third Crusade which lasted three years from 1189 to 1192. We can imagine him setting out from the village with a small retinue of servants and horses, making his way over several days to London and thence in a perilous sea journey over the Channel before a long transit of France.

The Third Crusade formed up at Tours in Northern France where the massive armies of King Richard of England and King Philip of France gathered. The mediaeval historian Ambrose wrote "Had ye but seen the host when forth it came!

The Earth trembled with its coming". This must have been an awesome experience for the young Henry but as nothing compared to the months which followed. The crusaders embarked at Marseille and set sail for Sicily where they spent three months. On 10th April 1191 two hundred ships set off from Sicily and many were dispersed in storms before they found landfall in Cyprus. Here there was a further delay while King Richard got married to his bride Berengaria in Limassol on 12th May. On 5th June they landed at Acre and set siege to it, achieving its surrender on 12th July, after which a staggering 3000 Saracens were massacred on the spot. Jaffa (now Tel Aviv) was taken on 9th September but that was the last successful achievement of the campaign. Malaria and dysentery set in; the French and other allies lost heart and went home and the remaining crusaders spent a miserable winter camped outside Jerusalem. They failed to capture Jerusalem the following year and in July 1192 Richard withdrew to Acre. After concluding a 3 year truce with Saladin on 29th September, they set off for home on a sea journey which was every bit as perilous as their outward trip 2 years previously. Some of the crusaders eventually made a safe landing at Marseille but others including King Richard were swept off course and were ship-wrecked in the Adriatic. The King ended up being held captive in Austria and Germany for 2 years while a massive ransom was raised in England for his release.

One of the Derbyshire casualties of the Third Crusade was William de Ferrers who died at the Siege of Acre. Sir Henry Foljambe however married Eleanor (Fitzherbert), had a son and heir called John (1179-1249) and lived until 1208 – so he must have been one of the lucky ones who made it home again to his wife and family.

Sir John Foljambe, the fourth generation at Wormhill and married to Margaret Lutterell, died in 1249. He left 6 sons, the eldest of whom, Thomas (1206-1283), inherited the manor.

Thomas's younger brother, Roger, is recorded in the Forest Pleas in 1251 as incurring the heaviest fine (20 marks) for 'vert' or 'greenhue' offences (damage to or illegal removal of timber from the Forest). His pledge for good behaviour in the future was seconded by John Foljambe (another brother) and Walter Coterell.

Sir Thomas Foljambe (the first) (fifth generation at Wormhill), married to Margaret de Gernon of Bakewell, was Bailiff of the Forest in 1256. He kept the Forest on horseback, attended by a boy. His tenure coincided with the Civil War led by the Barons from 1264 to 1267 and with the royalist victory at Chesterfield in 1266. As a knight of the shire he may well have taken part in the battle on the royalist side. In any event he must have pledged his loyalty to the King, despite his ancestor's marriage to the Ferrers family, because the family would not otherwise have retained ownership of the manor after the King's return to power. Thomas had 4 sons (Thomas, William of Wormhill, Nicholas of Campana and Henry) and a daughter (Cecilie).

In 1275 William Foljambe of Wormhill, brother of Sir Thomas, was leasing glebe land in Wormhill from the Dean and Chapter of Lichfield. Five years later he was convicted and fined heavily for poaching.

Sir Thomas Foljambe was appointed Constable of Peak Castle in 1281. This was a lucrative appointment because he is said to have taken receipts of £260 for his own pocket in the first year. These windfalls however did not last long. He died on 17th January 1283 and was succeeded by his eldest son Thomas (the second) (1258-1297) who married Catherine le Eyr.

Keeping track of the Foljambe family tree is a complex and difficult business. It is not made any easier by the common practice around this time of eldest sons being given the same Christian name as their father. Hence there were four lords of the manor called Thomas who inherited Wormhill one after the other before the favourite name changed to Godfrey and then three Godfreys succeeded each other!

Sir Thomas Foljambe (the second) – the sixth generation at Wormhill – died in 1297, leaving one son Thomas (the third) (died 1314) to inherit.

Sir Thomas (the third) – seventh generation – married Alice de Furnival, by whom he had one son, Thomas (the fourth) (1282-1324). This latter Thomas was summoned in 1301 to the muster of knights at Berwick-on-Tweed to do military service against the Scots. He would have been 19 at the time. He survived and in 1319 he is recorded as holding 15 acres of land in Wormhill in return for the service of finding a footman with bow and arrows to patrol the Royal Forest.

Sir Thomas (the fourth) – eighth generation – married first Aveline and second Alice Darley. By his first wife, Thomas (the fourth) had three sons:

John – became Lord of the manor of Tideswell and owned land in Wormhill[63]. His line of the family died out in 1447.

Thomas – became Lord of the manor of Elton[64] and had land in Tideswell and Litton. His line of the family died out in 1378.

Hugh – lived at Elton and had land in Bakewell. He had a daughter who became a nun but no male children; so his line of the family also died out in the second generation.

By his second wife Thomas (the fourth) had one son, Godfrey

Godfrey became Lord of the manor of Wormhill when his father died in 1324 and went on to have 5 sons. Without Godfrey, the Foljambe dynasty would have disappeared completely in the 15th century. The Wormhill branch led by his eldest

---

[63] He died on 4 Aug 1358 and was buried at Tideswell. The original brass plate on his tomb in Tideswell Church was stolen and was replaced with the present one by one of his descendants two centuries later. The new plate credits him as the founder and main benefactor of the new church which was rebuilt between 1330 and 1380. Some historians think this claim a touch exaggerated. His great-grandson Edward was knighted at Agincourt.

[64] The first Foljambe to arrive in England with William The Conqueror in 1066 (Godfrey) married a Saxon heiress called Uchtred at Elton and the family had presumably held the Elton estate for 3 centuries at this point in time.

son had died out by 1388 but, from his other 4 sons, the Foljambes have survived down to the present day, gaining the earldom of Liverpool on the way.

From the reign of Edward I onwards Derbyshire was represented in Parliament by two knights every year. Parliaments took place in various parts of the country including Cambridge, Coventry, York, Gloucester, Leicester, London and Westminster, Northampton, Nottingham, Sarum and Winchester. One of the first of these MPs was Sir Thomas Foljambe (the third) in 1302 in London and a relative, Sir Henry Foljambe[65], represented the county in 1305. Thomas (the third) was an MP again in 1308 and 1309 in London and Thomas (the fourth) was an MP in 1315 in York.

In 1324 Sir Thomas Foljambe (the fourth) died and was succeeded at Wormhill by his 7 year old son Godfrey (1317-1377) – the ninth generation at Wormhill. Sir Godfrey was to become the most famous of the Foljambe dynasty, representing the county as an MP in the 1339 Parliament at Northampton, the 1341, 1365, 1370 and 1372 Parliaments at Westminster and again in 1372 at Winchester. In due course Sir Godfrey became Master of the Household to the Duke of Lancaster (John of Gaunt), and his Baro Scaccarii (Baron of the Exchequer). In the latter role he would have been responsible for holding the accounts of royal expenditure and the income from knights' fees (often called the pipe rolls), arranged by county for each financial year – a position of great power and influence.

John of Gaunt (1340-1399) (colour plate 8) was the third son of Edward III and was born at Ghent. He was created Duke of Lancaster in 1362. During the last years of Edward III and before Richard II came of age he acted as head of government and provoked protests from parliament for the corruption of his rule. The Lancastrian Kings ruled England from 1399 to 1461, starting with Henry IV, the son of John of Gaunt, in 1399 and ending with the weak and mad King Henry VI who was deposed in 1461 and murdered in 1471. In 1351 the Duchy of Lancaster became a county palatine with its own courts outside the royal jurisdiction but these rights have been attached to the Crown since 1399.

Sir Godfrey Foljambe married first Anne, from whom he had no children and second Avena, the second daughter and heiress of Sir Thomas Ireland from Hartshorne, Kent. Avena gave him five sons (Godfrey, Thomas, Richard, Alvaredus and Robert). The eldest, Godfrey (the second) (1344-1376), died a year before his father aged 32.

Godfrey (the second) married Margaret de Villiers of Kinoulton, Nottinghamshire in 1367 when she was aged 15 and produced a son Godfrey (the third) (1367-1388) and a daughter, Marjory (born 1369) who married Sir Nicholas Montgomery. The latter was an MP for Derbyshire in 1390 at Westminster and again in 1411 and 1415. In 1432 he became High Sheriff of the county.

---

[65] Son of Thomas, grandson of Roger (brother of Sir Thomas (the first)), and great grandson of Sir John. See Joseph Foster's *Pedigrees of the county families of Yorkshire* Vol 1 London 1874

Sir Godfrey Foljambe, Member of Parliament and holder of the judicial appointment of Puisne Justice of King's Bench before his elevation to Master of the Household to the Duke of Lancaster, founded Bakewell Chantry in 1344. Sir Godfrey was buried at Bakewell in recognition of his foundation of the Chantry when he died in 1377 at the age of 60. In Bakewell church (*colour plate 9*) there is a stone wall memorial carved in 1385 of Godfrey and Avena both at prayer under a double canopy showing the Foljambe shield, he wearing armour and helmet and she with an ornate headdress.

Sir Godfrey Foljambe (the third) – tenth generation at Wormhill – succeeded to the manor in 1377 at the age of 9½ on the death of his grandfather, his father having died the previous year. He married in due course Isabel[66], the daughter of Sir Simon Leeke[67] but by the time he died in 1388 aged 21½ he had a daughter, Alice (1386-1416), but no male heir.

Sir Godfrey Foljambe (the third) died on 9th September 1388. His daughter Alice was only aged 1½ at the time. On 18th November the dower[68] was granted to his widow Isabel in the presence of Sir John Leeke, her brother. Isabel thereby retained ownership of the manor as the eleventh and final member of the Foljambe family at Wormhill but Sir John Leeke was permitted to farm the land.

On 16 February 1389 King Richard granted to Sir John Leeke for the sum of 50 marks the right to marry off the heiress Alice and hence to sell the ownership of the manor once Alice reached marriageable age.

The Leeke family went on to acquire large estates in Derbyshire in the 1400s. Sutton, Sandiacre and Kirk Hallam came to them by marriage to the Greys and they acquired further manors from the Deincourt family. Their fortunes peaked in the 17th century when Sir Francis Leeke was created Earl of Scarsdale (1645) and were then to collapse a century later with the bankruptcy of Nicholas, the fourth and last Earl.

The ownership of the Wormhill manor by the Foljambe family came to an end when Isabel's dower was transferred to Sir William Plumpton of Plumpton Yorkshire. The deal was that Alice would be married to Sir William's son and heir, Robert (1383-8 Dec 1421). Sir William paid 100 marks[69] for the transaction and agreed to pay Alice an annual allowance until she was 15. This marked the end of the Foljambe dynasty at Wormhill, though another branch of the family continued as owners of the Tideswell manor until they too died out in 1468.

Thus ended, at Wormhill at least, the lineage of a very distinguished family, several of whom had held high office in England as well as in the local area. They had been deeply involved in the country's internal and external wars and in its wider political developments and intrigues during the reigns of thirteen Kings

---

[66] Born 1371 in Bakewell.
[67] Born 1345 in Tideswell.
[68] The widow's share of the estate for life.
[69] About £66.

from William I to Richard II. We know of them principally through the research of genealogists such as Joseph Foster whose 1874 history of the family is the most authoritative. There is however no physical record of them in the village which is unsurprising. If they were buried in the churchyard, their graves would have had no enduring memorial because it was uncommon to have headstones before the 17th century. Indeed they may not have been buried at Wormhill at all where the first chapel was built in 1273 in the time of Sir Thomas (the first) as a minor concessionary outpost of the parent parish church which was at Tideswell. All major church ceremonies had to be celebrated at Tideswell and it is therefore quite possible that the early lords of the manor were buried there too. Members of the Tideswell branch of the family can certainly be found in the church there but there is no trace of the Wormhill Foljambes there either.

THE ROYAL FOREST OF HIGH PEAK

The chief attraction of the local area for the Norman and Plantagenet Kings was the hunting in the Royal Forest of High Peak. There were herds of wild ponies, many wolves and, according to one writer using colourful exaggeration, 'the number of red deer was so great that they trampled men and dogs to death in their wild flight'. Red deer were plentiful in the district until the 17th century.

The Kings of England had owned land in the area before the Norman Conquest. In the time of Edward the Confessor (1042-1066) the eastern side of the forest including Hope, Edale and Tideswell provided an annual payment to the Crown of £30 in cash, 8 pints of honey and 5 cart-loads of lead. The western side including Chapel-en-le-Frith and Wormhill paid £2. But this is not

Stag Hunting

evidence that the Anglo-Saxon Kings kept the forest as a game reserve and it is much more likely that this only happened with the arrival of the Normans. In

Anglo-Saxon times anyone wishing to hunt could do so and there were no restrictive laws.

It was King William I who claimed the monopoly of hunting in England and set up a number of game reserves throughout the country, of which the Macclesfield Forest, Sherwood Forest, the Forest of Dean and the New Forest in Hampshire are examples. In Norman times up to a third of the land space of England is said to have been reserved for the King's hunting. The Anglo-Saxon Chronicle records of King William:

> *He set up a vast deer preserve and imposed laws concerning it.*
> *Whoever slew a hart or hind*
> *Was to be blinded.*
> *He forbade the killing of boars*
> *Even as the killing of harts.*
> *For he loved the stags as dearly*
> *As though he had been their father.*
> *Hares, also, he decreed should go unmolested.*
> *The rich complained and the poor lamented.*

The Norman Kings hunted whenever the opportunity arose but routine culling was left to professional huntsmen. Much of the game from the royal forest was delivered to the King for feasts and major ceremonies. In the time of Henry III up to 1260 the King's annual requirement for feasting was listed as 607 fallow deer, 159 red deer, 45 roe deer and 88 wild swine. From 1066 onwards the Forest, of which only the name of the village of Peak Forest remains to indicate its status and topography from the 12th to the 17th century, was administered and

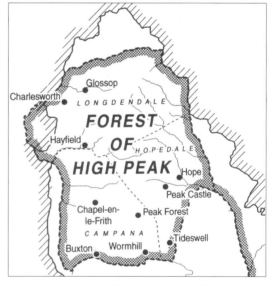

Boundaries of the Norman Forest of High Peak

managed solely to provide game for the King's sport. Despite being called a 'forest', the area is unlikely to have been heavily wooded. The name 'forest' merely indicated that it was a royal game reserve and, although timber and scrub was probably more prevalent than today, there would also have been large areas of open pasture and moorland. The 'wildwood' would have consisted of predominantly ash, wych elm, small-leafed lime and hazel, on which the population would have relied for building, implements and fuel.[70]

The Royal Forest, which covered an area of about 180 square miles, was sub-divided into Campana (including Wormhill), Hopedale and Longdendale. Peveril Castle at Castleton was the administrative centre with subordinate head-quarters at Chamber, Peak Forest[71]; Chapel-en-le-Frith; and Hope. Where the three Forest wards met on the slopes of Kinder Scout there is the Edale Head Cross which doubled as the boundary marker between the Edale and Hayfield parishes. Chamber Farm was the designated Hunting Lodge for the Forest and there are records of various gifts and furniture being allocated to it by the Bailiff for that purpose. A special chapel was also erected at Peak Forest which the King placed outside the jurisdiction of the Bishop of Lichfield. These special privileges attached to the Forest Chapel were exploited subsequently by ministers in the 17th century to grant marriage licences at their own discretion. Peak Forest thus became a Gretna Green of the Peak District and the 'special register' was only finally closed down in 1804. The bounds of the Forest as set out in 1286 were described as follows:

The metes and bounds of the Forest of the Peak begin on the south at the new place of Goyt, and thence by the river Goyt as far as the river Etherow; and so by the river Etherow to Langley Croft at Longenhead; thence by a certain footpath to the head of Derwent; and from the head of Derwent to a place called Mythomstede Bridge; and from Mythom Bridge to the river Bradwell; and from the river Bradwell to a certain place called Hucklow; and from Hucklow to the great dell of Hazelbache; and from that dell as far as Little Hucklow; and from Hucklow to the brook of Tideswell, and so to the river Wye; and from the Wye ascending up to Buxton, and so on to the new place of Goyt.

The Campana[72] ward which included Wormhill provided the best grazing in the Forest and, where there were no rivers to form the boundary, was enclosed by a wall and ditch (known as a deer leap) which was enough of an obstacle to prevent deer from jumping out of the reserve but did not deter other outlying deer from leaping in. Where however the boundary was formed by a river, this would not have represented any obstacle to deer moving in either direction. Some local accounts refer to the fact that the remains of a deer leap can be found in the grounds of Wormhill Hall but this is unlikely because the boundary of the Campana ward was the river Wye half a mile to the south.

Animals sacred to the Norman and Plantagenet monarchs were red deer, fallow deer, roe deer, wild boar, bears, wild bulls and wolves. Stag hunting started at the

---

[70] Sycamore was not introduced until the 15th century and horse chestnut did not appear before the 16th century.

[71] Mr Hadfield's farm is called Chamber Farm.

[72] Meaning open fields, derived from the Norman French *campagne* or open countryside.

Feast of St John[73] and ended on Holyrood Day[74]. Hind hunting began on Holyrood Day and finished at Candlemas[75]. Bears were hunted from Christmas to Candlemas. Foxes, hares and pine martens were also beasts of the chase but rabbits were classed as beasts of the warren[76]. Otters were plentiful but there is no mention of badgers. Pheasants, partridges, quail, wild duck and herons were beasts of warren. There are also records of 'cornilu', thought to be black game. Wild boar became extinct in the Forest by the late 13th century. Originally the only dogs allowed to be kept in the Forest were mastiffs but sheep and cattle dogs arrived later and there was an order that these had to be disabled from hunting deer by having their claws cut off[77]. In the early Norman period there were herds of wild ponies which were hunted but, by the time of King John, studs had been established to improve and domesticate the wild horse stock.

Nevertheless keeping horses in the Forest was a contentious issue, even for members of the royal family, because they competed for forage with the deer. In 1284/5 the Queen Consort[78] of Edward I was reported to the Swainmote for having in her Equitium[79] in Campana 115 mares and foals 'to the great detriment of the Forest'. Furthermore, it was said, other people were also keeping horses in the Forest and pretending that they belonged to the Queen. One such offender, a forester-in-fee called Peter de Stratton, had 11 horses and mares feeding in Campana. He was fined and ordered to remove them.

In the following century around 1350 the wife of King Edward III, Queen Philippa of Hainault[80] had 100 stallions and mares at stud in Campana. In 1352 the Assize Rolls noted that her stud farm suffered a bout of vandalism when her 'parks and closes in Tideswell and Wormhill were broken by evil doers'.

In the 1165-66 accounts of Gervase de Bernake, Bailiff of the Peak, is a charge of 76s 8d for keeping the King's bears at Peak Castle. Wild bears are thought to have become extinct in England in the 10th century. It is not known whether the King's bears were kept at the Castle and released for hunting or whether they were kept to amuse the King through the practice of bear baiting, though the latter is the more usually accepted explanation.

---

[73] Around Midsummer Day, 21st June.
[74] 14th September.
[75] 14th February.
[76] Animals to be taken by the owner/occupiers where they were found rather than hunted with royal authority over long distance in the open countryside.
[77] A practice known as *lawing*.
[78] Eleanor of Castile.
[79] Stud Farm.
[80] Who died in 1369.

There was a distinct hierarchy of Forest officials who were appointed to administer the Forest and its laws. There were 9 principal offices:

- The High Steward, who was appointed by the King by letters patent. This was an honorary though very powerful position which was unassailable by any law.

- The Master Forester, also an honorary position.

- The Receiver, who was a paid official. His duty was to enforce payment of the forest rents and fines. He had 2 assistants called the bailiff of the franchise and the bailiff of the winland.

- The Constable of the Castle (Peveril Castle). An appointment nominated by the King. The first occupant in 1191 was Hugh de Novant, Bishop of Lichfield. Later Constables included William de Ferrers in 1232, Prince Edward in 1250, Simon de Montfort in 1263, Piers Gaveston[81] in 1307, John of Gaunt in 1372. Because of the enormous receipts which went straight into the Constable's pocket, this was a highly lucrative job and one used by the mediaeval Kings to repay their favourites or buy off the loyalty of powerful warlords who might otherwise have posed a threat to the throne. The appointment transferred to the Dukes of Devonshire when they acquired the manor of Castleton in the 1700s and remains with them to this day.

- The Ranger. An appointment nominated by the King. The Ranger was responsible for collecting all the Forest rental income. His office also comprised the appointment of Bowbearer. In 1626 Francis Tunstead[82] was recorded as the Bowbearer and he claimed a pension of £50 per annum for carrying out this office. He was Bailiff of the Forest in 1632

---

[81] Gaveston was the gay lover and favourite of King Edward II and this appointment in 1307 coincided with the accession of Edward II to the throne. Gaveston was later seized and killed by the barons in a manner which defies description in a decent family production like this.

[82] He lived at Tunstead and the settlement is named after the family.

and his son James Tunstead was Bailiff in 1650 – one year after the end of the Civil War. He must have been one of the last appointees of the Royal Forest before it was finally dissolved at the end of the 17th century.

- The Beremaster, appointed by letters patent from the King. This official was responsible for the weighing of all mineral ore extracted in the Forest. He was paid either by a percentage of the ore weighed or by a percentage of the proceeds of sale.

- The Woodmaster, a paid official nominated by the King. The Woodmaster or Woodward[83] was responsible for seeing that the timber was not interfered with to the detriment of the deer

- The Bailiff of the Forest[84]. This was also a King's appointment but one for which the appointee paid for the privilege – unsurprisingly because the occupant's job was to collect (and keep) the Forest fines. In the 'Hundred Rolls' of 1274 Sir Thomas Foljambe of Wormhill is recorded as paying 400 marks for the post which entitled him to the Forest fines for the next 9 years[85]. Under the Bailiff were four Verderers[86] who held inquests into all forest crimes. Further officials called Regarders, normally 12 or more knights, were appointed to supervise the forest officials and held inquiries every 3 years into offences committed by them. This was a fairly sophisticated form of justice referred to subsequently in English Law as 'Quis custodiet custodies – Who keeps an eye on the custodians?'.

- The Foresters in Fee. These were hereditary offices which granted the owners land in perpetuity. Foresters[87], responsible for preserving the 'vert[88] and venison', were appointed for each ward. Answerable to the Foresters were the Agisters who collected rents for the feeding of cattle

---

[83] Symbol of office a small hatchet.
[84] Tilley refers to two bailiffs working to the Receiver – the bailiff of the franchise and the bailiff of the winland. It is possible that they carried out the same function of enforcing and collecting rents and fines and that the two posts had been merged into one by the end of the thirteenth century; or that the terms 'bailiff of the franchise' and 'bailiff of the winland' were superseded by the terms 'bailiff' and 'ranger'.
[85] In fact Sir Thomas was promoted to the post of Constable in 1281 which brought in even more income.
[86] Symbol of office an axe.
[87] Symbol of office a hunting horn.
[88] The landscape and infrastructure.

and pigs in the Forest and the Wolf-hunters who were particularly well rewarded, receiving an extra fee of 25 shillings per year in 1160. In 1167 the King paid 10 shillings for the travelling expenses of two Peak wolf-trappers to cross the Channel to kill wolves in Normandy.

The penalty for destroying any of the protected game was castration and loss of eyesight under William I, death under William Rufus, loss of a limb under Henry II, and torture 'too barbarous for description' under Richard I. Poaching any of the protected animals was described as 'more heinous than murder'. King John prevented any of his nobles from hunting feathered game without his permission and ordered all hedges and fences near his forests to be levelled so that the deer could feed on the farmers' fields wherever they chose. Needless to say, the royal restrictions on hunting, the adverse implications for the livelihood of local farmers and the brutal penalties for poaching were greatly resented. It is worth noting that both King William II (Rufus), who died in 1100, and his elder brother Richard, who died in 1075, were killed 'by stray arrows' whilst out hunting. One such incident might well be attributed to an unfortunate mistake but two members of the royal family killed in the same way within 25 years begins to look more than accidental. Indeed William Rufus is known to have been deeply unpopular and a predatory homosexual.

There were four types of courts. The court of 'Attachment' met every 40 days for the presentments[89] of the Foresters to the Verderers. The presentments were then forwarded to the 'Swainmotes' which were held at Wormhill or, more usually for the Campana ward, Chapel-en-le-Frith. Swainmotes, composed of the Steward of the Forest and not less than 20 Foresters, adjudicated on all the issues in contention within the Forest boundaries and delivered the verdicts and punishments for Forest infringements. It is not known where in Wormhill the Swainmotes might have been held but it is probable that they would have taken place in the largest and grandest building in the village – almost certainly the manor house. The site of the original manor house is also a matter of contention, some claiming that it was at Old Hall Farm and others that it was at an earlier building long since demolished on the site of Wormhill Hall.

There were various standard offences which appear regularly in the records of the Swainmotes. 'Stable Stand' referred to a poacher found with his bow drawn back or his dog in a leash. 'Dog Draw' occurred when the poacher had wounded a deer and was caught following it with a dog. 'Back Bear' meant that the poacher was carrying a dead deer on his shoulders and 'Bloody Hand' indicated that he had been caught literally red-handed after killing a deer.

The court of Regard was run by the Regarders who investigated offences by the

---

[89] Statements on Oath.

forest officials and their findings were forwarded to the court of the 'Justice Seat'[90] which sat every 3 years. The so-called Forest 'Eyres' were held in 1212, 1216 and 1251 at Nottingham and in 1285 at Derby. These courts tried some very senior offenders. The 4th Earl of Derby was tried for illegally taking 2000 deer with his associates during his tenure as Bailiff from 1216 to 1222. The Earl of Arundel and Ralph Bigod, brother of the Earl of Norfolk, were also tried for illegal hunting during the years of the Barons' Revolt when the King's attention was distracted elsewhere.

Under King John the High Steward had more authority than a Chief Justice of the Kingdom. Everybody, whether noble or commoner, had to obey him. The Forest Laws had become so harsh that they became one of the great causes of the Barons' Revolt of 1173 and eventually the King was forced to sign the Forest Charter on the same day as the second edition of Magna Carta in 1217, ending the absolute power of the monarch over the forests and decreeing that nobody should lose life or limb for killing deer. Instead the punishment was restricted to a fine or imprisonment for a year and a day.

This did not put an end to complaints about the high-handed actions of the High Stewards of the Forest. In the early 1400s Robert Bagshawe, one of the King's tenants in the Peak, complained to the Earl of Suffolk that 'Roger Clark, servant to Sir Richard Vernon (the High Steward), came with seven armed men with jacks and salets, and forcibly took him and imprisoned him for three days in the Castle of the Peak without cause. The said Roger also made a warrant to the bailiffs of the Peak to raise diverse assessments on him.' A 'jack' was a strong leather jerkin and a 'salet' was a basin-shaped helmet with a projection at the back to protect the neck. In other words the men were wearing military uniform.

The Foresters who policed the forest laws on behalf of the High Steward were powerful men and were often rewarded with the grant of land. Some local land-owners can trace their ownership back to the appointment of their ancestors as foresters. By about 1225 the foresters and deer-keepers had bought a portion of the Crown land held by William de Ferrers and built themselves a chapel which they called Chapel in the Forest (Frith), around which the village grew.

There are a number of records in the Court, Forest and Assize rolls of the 13th and 14th centuries of offences committed in the Forest and of the findings of the courts.

In the Court Rolls of 1280 recording the cases brought before the Swainmote at Chapel-en-le-Frith there is an account of deer poaching at Wormhill. William Foljambe reported Henry de Meadow for taking a doe with a certain black grey-hound called 'Collyng' at Combs Head. Henry promptly accused William Foljambe and his servants in return of killing 100 deer in Martinside[91], Wheston and Wormhill. The court found both parties guilty of poaching, though William

---

[90] Also known as Forest Eyres
[91] Martinside is the name of the hillside between Dove Holes and Chapel, neither of which would have existed in 1280 as definable locations.

was convicted of killing only 20 deer. Henry was fined 100 shillings and William 20 marks[92]. Twenty marks was a very substantial fine – a century later the same sum was enough to buy 12 houses and 200 acres, as recorded in the King's licence of 1383. It must also have been a cause of intense embarrassment to his father who was Bailiff of the Forest at the time and about to be elevated to the even more distinguished post in the Forest hierarchy of Constable.

According to the Forest Rolls of 1285 another deer poacher from Wormhill was convicted by the Swainmote:

Thomas Bozun, Bailiff, presented Michael son of Adam de Wormhill of killing fawns in the Forest and selling their skins at Bakewell, and he was convicted.

There are records of a Forest Inquisition at Wormhill in 1318 which debated the ownership of tithes claimed by the Chapel in the Frith. The freemen who sat on the Inquisition were William de Stafford, Hugh de Bradbury, Richard de Clough, William le Ragged, Richard de Bagshawe, William del Kyrke, Robert le Taylour, John de Chinley, Richard de la Ford and Thomas Martin. Nicholas de Bagshawe was quoted as a witness. Note that most of these surnames are identified by the places from which they came, though one is identified unenviably by his appearance (le Ragged) and one by his trade (Taylour).

A case of murder was recorded at Wormhill in 1330. The Assize Rolls for that year contain the following entry:

At Wormhill one John, son of Henry of Hokelow[93] struck Robert, son of William del Hull[94] with a gode[95] whereupon he forthwith died and after the deed he fled and is suspected. Therefore let him be exigent and out-lawed. He has no chattels[96]. He was in Frankpledge[97] to John Carleys who now hath him not. Because this happened by day, and the village of Wormhill hath not taken him, therefore it is in mercy[98]. The first finder is dead[99]. No Englishry is presented[100]. Judgement : Murder upon the Wapentake.

Royal visits must have been a regular occurrence during the hunting season. In 1275 King Edward I used Tideswell as his base from which to go hunting in the

---

[92] £13-40 in the Sterling equivalent of the age. By comparison the stipend of a priest at the time was £2 per annum and priests were relatively well paid. The fine amounted thus to about 7 years' salary.
[93] Hucklow.
[94] The del Hall family was linked to the Bagshawes by marriage.
[95] A cattle prod.
[96] Belongings.
[97] A form of pledge for good behaviour of all citizens over the age of 14 and an undertaking that they will be available to answer any infringement of the law.
[98] Otherwise the whole village would have been in trouble for allowing him to escape.
[99] The first person to find him is authorised to kill him on sight.
[100] There are no special provisions in English law which affect this finding.

Forest. An order was sent to the Sheriff of Lincoln to *'cause ten tuns*[101] *of wine of the right price from the King's wine merchant at Boston to be carried without delay to Thydwell near the Peak, there to be delivered to the King's bailiff.'* The King spent several days at Tideswell during the summer during the stag-hunting season and visited again in September and October 1290 for hind-hunting. There are references to Tideswell as the King's venison larder, from which salted game was delivered to the King's larder at Westminster. Edward I was hunting again in Campana in the summer of 1295 when he was witness to a particularly brazen piece of poaching:

> *In the year 1295 when King Edward I made his chase in Campana upon a Wednesday next after the Feast of the Assumption of the Blessed Virgin*[102] *William son of Rankill of Hucklow came, and when the King's hounds had got a stag at bay beyond the bounds of the Forest, William shot the stag and killed the King's hounds, upon which the King's hunters coming up, they cried him and he fled, and they took the venison to the King's Larder.*

At least three other Kings in the following century used Tideswell as their hunting lodge – Edward III for 3 days in September 1331 and Henry IV first in 1382 when Benedict Tatton presented him with a greyhound 'value twenty pence' and again from 1st to 7th August 1402 on his way north to the battle of Homildon Hill where he defeated the Scots on 14th September. In 1483 King Edward IV visited Tideswell with his son while out hunting in the Forest. By the 14th century Tideswell may have offered more comfortable lodgings than the windswept and increasingly derelict Peveril Castle. Of all the mediaeval monarchs, Kings Edward I, Edward III[103] and Henry IV appear to have had particularly strong links to the Forest of High Peak, helped no doubt by the fact that in some cases their wives also had interests in the Forest. Queen Eleanor of Castile (married to Edward I) rented Peveril Castle and both she and Queen Philippa of Hainault (married to Edward III) ran an extensive stud farm for their horses in Tideswell and Wormhill.

The Forest records of 1285 indicate that the Foresters holding hereditary serjeanties in the Campana ward were: Archer, Daniel, Foljambe, Forester, Gomfrey and Wolfhunt.

The Archers were a family of long standing fame as forest officials. Robert the Archer witnessed a deed dating from before 1214. Thomas the Archer held four

---

[101] Barrels. Ten tuns was the equivalent of 2520 gallons – enough for quite a party!

[102] 18th August.

[103] Kings Edward I and III were the red-blooded warrior kings who were big into hunting. Edward II (reigned 1307-1327) was a limp-wristed gay in a severely homophobic age who was eventually deposed by his wife Isabella and her lover Edward Mortimer. He was killed in gruesome fashion at Berkeley Castle by the barons.

bovates of land in Hucklow in 1285 valued at 3 shillings per annum as a forester in fee. Ralph the Archer held a dwelling and land in Great Hucklow in the reign of Edward I 'by the service of keeping the King's forest with a bow and arrows'.

John Daniel held one bovate of land in Wormhill and one of his family, Daniel Pincerna (the King's ex-butler) held the mill at Blackwell. The Daniel coat of arms, like that of the Foljambes, contains the six scallops denoting the family of a former crusader. In due course the Daniel forest serjeanty passed by marriage to the Meverells and then to the Eyres. John Daniel had a close shave with a deer poacher in 1283, as recorded in the Forest Rolls:

Radulf Cotterill in 1283 came into Campana ... with his bow and arrows hidden and shot at a herd of deer, and upon him came John Daniel forester-in-fee and cried him, and would take him, but he resisted and shot two arrows at the said John. He was however captured.

A horrible fate no doubt awaited Radulf for this heinous crime but the silence of history has mercifully spared us the details. The Cotterill or Coterel family have had a curious history of ending up on the wrong side of the law in this part of Derbyshire. In 1335 one Nicholas Coterel, described variously as an outlaw or gangster, was offered the chance of making good by being appointed the Queen's bailiff for the High Peak. The queen in question would have been Philippa of Hainault, wife of Edward III, who had a prominent stud farm in Tideswell and Wormhill which might have fallen within Nicholas's management responsibilities. However, within 2 years of his appointment, Nicholas Coterel was accused of interfering with tax collection and 'having been guilty of many other oppressions by the pretext of his office'. A case of once an outlaw, always an outlaw?

At one of the Forest Inquisitions John Daniel was asked what rights attached to his appointment as a Forester. He replied that he had the right of *'housebote and hogbote* (right to take spare timber for the repair of his house and pig sties) *out of the woods of the Lord our King for the repairs of the house in which he dwelt, and for the repairs of the other houses of the serjeanty by view and delivery of the Chief Steward of the Forest, viz of oaks for the repair of his house and other houses and also of Boulic and Alret* (decayed wood and alders).' He went on to claim that *'he had the right to have his pigs fed in the same serjeanty free of pannage* (payment for the right to pasture pigs in the lord's woods), *and also pasture for his cattle in the King's pasture in the bailiwick when that pasture is sold or allotted by the Bailiff of the Peak. And at the time of masting* (when the beech seed dropped) *when the King had agistment* (pasture) *in the said bailiwick, he and his fellow Foresters had the right to take a pig of their own choice from the lord's quota. Furthermore he had the right to a deputy to perform his duties as Forester when he was absent on the duties of his bailiwick and a servant under him at his own expense who should make oath concerning Vert and Venison before the Bailiff.'* One might guess that John was pushing his luck a little far here but *'it was agreed by the Ministers of the Forest, by 24 of the jury, and by the ancient rolls, that his ancestors possessed these rights from the time of the enfeoffment* (the time when these rights had been entrusted to his forebears), *when they had paid 3 shillings for the privilege.'*

The Meverells were a famous Tideswell family and, for a time, lords of the manor. Sir Sampson Meverell is buried in the centre of the Chancel in Tideswell Church. Some controversy is attached to the origins of this tomb – the top, marked with crosses in the corners and centre, is thought to have been an altar slab (possibly from the 12th century chapel) and may have been 'misappropriated' from the Founder's Tomb which was but is no longer at the top of the chancel. Sampson (1388-1462) was a distinguished soldier in the Hundred Years War with France, fought in 11 major battles in 2 years and was knighted at the siege of Orleans by the Duke of Bedford before Joan of Arc succeeded in relieving the town and driving off the English Army. He also achieved some notoriety as a jury-knobbler. In 1423 he was taken to court for allegedly seizing some land in Tideswell. Just before the case was to be heard he gathered together a band of 'divers malefactors and outlaws' who assaulted the jurors and 'had chased and captured Henry de Longesdon, one of the jurors, and compelled him to swear on the book that he would find a verdict for the said Sampson and Isabella' (Sampson's wife). He threatened to kill any jurymen who gave a verdict against them. None of the jury-men appeared at court but eventually Meverell was fined two marks and those that had carried out the assault 10 shillings each. Meverell was constantly in dispute with his neighbour Ralph Basset of Blore for allowing his cattle to stray into Ralph's hay, and with the vicar of Ilam about tithes. Basset got his own back when Meverell returned from the wars by indicting him for depriving the vicar of Ilam of 8 marks and getting him confined to the Marshalsea prison until such time as he had paid. None of this stopped Meverell in his later years from becoming a JP for Staffordshire!

The Foljambe mentioned as a Forester in the records of 1285 was Sir Thomas Foljambe (the second), lord of the Wormhill manor.

Adam Gomfrey shared a bovate of land in Wormhill with Sir Thomas Foljambe until he died in 1305/6. He was succeeded by a son of the same name who was living at Wormhill in 1318.

Other families were forest officials in the 14th century, including the Bagshawes in the Longdendale ward and the Needhams of Thornset[104]. In 1306 it was recorded that Walter de Neville died possessed of 30 acres of land in Wormhill in exchange for his services as a King's Forester. In 1402 William de Needham held

---

[104] Thornset is claimed by some to be a 'lost' location close to Great Rocks in the parish of Wormhill. Some 19th century county directories refer to 'the district in the liberty of Thornsett between the villages of Great Rocks and Tunstead' which could indicate a parcel of land controlled by the parish of Thornsett. It is equally possible that it could have referred to the still extant village of Thornsett itself between Hayfield and New Mills which would have been in the Longdendale ward.

a messuage and 32 acres in Wormhill and was a Forester in the Campana ward. This office passed to Robert Middleton in 1448. In 1525 Hugo Needham was a forester in Campana and in 1527 William Needham of Thornset was also a forester.

In 1285 John de Wolfhunte held a house and land in Wormhill for 'chasing and taking all wolves that should come into the King's Forest of the Peak'. He and Thomas Foljambe are said to have shared a bovate of land at Wormhill for their services. Wolves had caused serious problems by killing domestic stock since the establishment of the Forest. Gervase de Bernake, the 12th century bailiff, reported on one occasion that a colt had been strangled by wolves in Edale and that two sheep had been killed by wolves in another part of the District. At an inquest in 1285 it was stated that the wolf-hunters went through the forest twice a year, in

March and September, to take wolves in places they frequented, and that at the Feast of St Barnabas when the wolves had young, they went out with a mastiff and a servant carrying traps and armed with hatchet, spear and hunting knife to kill wolf cubs. In the 14th century surnames started to be used describing people's occupation – hence John the wolf-hunter. By this time they had obviously started to control wolves as vermin, rather than hunting them as game.

Old Hall Farm has a high walled enclosure next to the farmhouse which includes a 'loup-hole'[105] in the wall facing the road, from which wolves used to be shot by bow and arrow or cross-bow as they approached to raid the livestock inside. The wall is about 8-10 feet high but would originally have been surmounted by a wooden palisade to keep the wolves out.

The origin of the name 'Old Hall Farm' is unknown but it is conceivable that it marks either the site of the original Norman manor house occupied by the Foljambes before the present Wormhill Hall was constructed in 1697 or, more likely, of the home farm which went with the manor. This latter explanation is made more plausible by the fact that the farm was known simply as 'Hall Farm' up to 1881 when Thomas Eley was the occupant. The present Old Hall Farm is a mixture of 16th and 17th century building with the original mullioned windows and is distinguished by having a cellar with a barrel-vaulted ceiling and the original mediaeval meat salting benches and ale stands. It is the oldest remaining building

---

[105] *Loup* comes from the Norman-French word for wolf.

Loup-Hole – Old Hall Farm

in the village but not old enough to have been the original twelfth or thirteenth century manor house, unless it had been rebuilt on earlier foundations. The loup-hole however must have been constructed and used some time before the last wolf was killed in the parish in the winter of 1490. On the other side of the road Elm Tree House is built on top of another similar 17th century cellar.

The church, first built in 1273, was likely to have been constructed as close as possible to the manor house which tends to suggest that the Hall has always been on the same site. The earliest known reference to a Wormhill Halle is in 1346 in the Wolley Charters in the British Museum. The original Norman Hall would typically have been a large single room structure made of timber walls reinforced with clay and possibly with a thatched roof. Its fragile construction would have meant that it was never a permanent structure and may have been added to or rebuilt several times in the centuries down to the Elizabethan age when the Hall was built for the first time in solid stone.

Apart from the fines for Forest offences, there were other receipts for the King's treasury, some of which no doubt found their way into the pockets of the higher level

Forest officials. The fullest but, even so, perhaps not complete account comes from Sir Thomas Wensley, Bailiff of the Forest, who set out receipts from the Forest in 1391 as follows: £130-5-10½ in rents from the villages of Litton and Wardlow, and from the wastes of Chapel-en-le-Frith and elsewhere; £6-10-8 for winter herbage rents at Edale, Castleton, Thornhill, Hope, etc; £64-17-4 for summer herbage rent at Fairfield, Wormhill, Maidstonefield, Tideswell, Wheston, Edale, Combs, etc; £10-13-0 rent from the mills at Castleton, Maidstonefield[106], Tunstead, Hayfield, Chisworth and Beard, with their fisheries; £30-13-4 for lead ore; £6-13-4 for passage, stallage and toll for cows at Chapel-en-le-Frith; 25d for pannage of pigs; and 37s 6d for agistment rents. The exploitation of grazing rents within the Forest put pressure on the deer, a situation which came to a head in the 16th century.

Sir Thomas Wensley was later killed at the Battle of Shrewsbury in 1403 where Henry IV defeated the rebels led by Harry Hotspur (Henry Percy), son of the Earl of Northumberland. His tomb is in Bakewell Church. After his death Lady Wensley became a nun.

The Forest remained in being through to the end of the 17th century, its lands being redistributed and the remaining deer killed after the Civil War, and then only after much contention and dispute. The demise of the Forest will be covered later in this history.

PROPERTY

As we have seen earlier, the pattern of feudal society had been established long before the Norman Conquest by the Anglo-Saxons and the Normans continued with a similar system. The King was at the top of a pyramid of landowners and below him came the barons and the knights who owned the manors. King William I had taken care to distribute land in such a way that he could reward those who had been of service to him in the wars whilst seeking to ensure that none of his barons became too powerful by ownership of land that they could mount a challenge to his authority or his throne. It was also within the King's gift to exercise patronage by granting confiscated land to new favourites or by distributing lucrative appointments in, for example, the Royal Forest where generous income from fines and rents could buy off the loyalty of local warlords. Licences were issued by the King which stipulated in some detail the conditions under which local warlords could build their castles, including the height of the walls and whether or not they were permitted battlements and crenellations. One such licence was issued to the Vernons at Haddon in 1190. By the beginning of the 13th century however interference by the King and the arbitrary nature of property hand-outs had become a severe bone of contention and a cause of

---

[106]   The former name of Chinley.

rebellion rather than a means of containing it.

One example came in the Reign of King John (1199-1216) when he granted to his former butler, Daniel Pincerna[107], a mill at Wormhill to which the inhabitants of Buxton and Fairfield had to take their corn for grinding – a highly profitable and much sought after concession. In these times the local mill was an essential institution for survival. Corn stocks were vital in providing the staple diet of unleavened bread which, along with gruel soup made from vegetables, kept the population alive. Corn stocks would run low in the months preceding the next year's harvest and July was often a hard month when people relied on the last of the mouldy grain for food. The new crop was celebrated at the Feast of Lammas in the first week of August. Examination of teeth from people who died in the 11th and 12th centuries reveals that they were often ground down by the effect of fragments of mill-stone in the bread.

The Wormhill mill operated by Daniel Pincerna is most likely to have been on the river Wye at Blackwell Mill next to Meadow (which is close to the corn-growers of Buxton and Fairfield and where there is a record of a mill in 1391). The mill at Millers Dale would still have been owned and operated by the monks of the Monks Dale grange.

The Daniels progressed to ownership of Tideswell in the 13th and 14th centuries and they had some land in Wormhill as well. An entry in the Forest Rolls of 1251 records that Richard Daniel held one bovate in Wormhill value 3s; William de Wormhill half a bovate value 1s 6d; and Thomas Foljambe one bovate value 3s. By 1317 another charter shows that the same or perhaps a later Richard Daniel had joined the ranks of the royal foresters and had increased his property ownership – Richard Daniel held a messuage and 30 acres of land in Wormhill, by the king (ie granted by the monarch) by 'serjeantry' (through his appointment as a forester) and he and Johanna his wife held land in Tideswell, of the Castle (ie part of the estate of Peveril Castle) and 60s rents (a small fortune at the time). This is a clear illustration of the benefits that royal patronage and Forest appointments could bring.

Another example of arbitrary royal patronage was in 1207 when King John granted the tenancy-in-chief of Tideswell to Thomas Armiger (also known as (aka) Lameley) on payment of 60 shillings a year. 'Armiger' was the title often given to a person allowed to bear heraldic arms[108] and not necessarily a surname. Thomas's daughter and heiress Joan married Paulinus de Bampton. It was Paulinus who was granted, in 1250/51, the right to hold a market in Tideswell on Wednesdays and to hold a two day fair at the Festival of the Decollation (Beheading) of St John the Baptist.

---

[107] Daniel was the family name and *pincerna* is derived from the Latin word for a butler. John had been, for a time, the custodian of Peveril Castle when he was a young prince in the reign of his elder brother King Richard I which might explain why he acquired a local man as his butler.

[108] In the Latin inscriptions of church memorial tablets the word 'armiger' is sometimes used to denote one of the younger sons of a noble family who did not have a title himself.

A year later in 1208 King John granted the tenancy-in-chief of Wormhill to the same Thomas Armiger (aka Lameley), though the Foljambes remained lords of the manor. Tenants-in-chief (often synonymous with Barons) were the highest rung on the feudal ladder beneath the King and above the knights as lords of the manor. Their privileges were entirely within the gift of the King and could be withdrawn[109] either when the existing tenant-in-chief died or when he fell out of royal favour. A century earlier the tenancy-in-chief of Tideswell and Wormhill had been awarded to the Ferrers family, as confirmed by the Domesday Survey, and it is therefore probable that King John chose to reallocate it in 1207/08 because one of the Ferrers descendants had either died or fallen foul of royal approval. The timing however does not coincide with any of the Barons' Revolts in which the Ferrers were involved. On the other hand John had been custodian of Peveril Castle in the years before he came to the throne and this award to Lameley may have been recognition of loyal service to a local favourite.

King John had a habit of making grants of land and property, regardless of existing ownership. This caused much confusion and controversy. As a response to his demands for excessive feudal dues and attacks on the privileges of the Church, Archbishop Langton proposed to the Barons in 1213 the drawing up of a charter (Magna Carta) which John was forced to accept at Runnymede on 15th June 1215. Magna Carta reaffirmed the rights of the Church and guarded against infringement of feudal customs. In particular the King was prevented from demanding any grant beyond those customary without the consent of his tenants-in-chief. This would have reinforced the authority of the Foljambes and Thomas Armiger and put an end to arbitrary royal grants like that given to Daniel Pincerna.

In 1215 King John gave the chapel at Tideswell[110] to the canons at Lichfield. This royal gift to the Church occurred in the year that the King signed Magna Carta and may have represented one of the first 'legitimate' property transfers by royal charter.

Soon after the signing of Magna Carta we begin to see the first evidence of property becoming freehold and being bought and sold. The records are in the form of so-called Charters which were the first legal documents and were held by a combination of the Church and some of the great families of the land. In 1906 I H Jeayes of the British Museum was commissioned to collate all the known charters referring to Derbyshire from a wide range of public and private collections. His work is an invaluable source of early property transfers and agreements.

There are, for example, records of Robert de Tunsted buying land at Great-rakes[111] in 1216 and again in 1221. The family subsequently bequeathed their name to the hamlet of Tunstead and were resident there for at least the next 450 years. In 1251-52 Nicholas de Tunsted and Richard de Tunsted were building houses

---

[109]   A process known as *escheat*.
[110]   Noted as part of the royal demesne or ownership in the Domesday Book.
[111]   Great Rocks.

there in the King's domain of the Peak Forest by licence of the Bailiff (*colour plate 10*). In 1330 Ralph de Tunsted was a juryman at Derby Assizes. In 1568 Robert Tunsted was appointed as a Roman Catholic servant to Mary Queen of Scots during her visits to the spa at Buxton. In 1632 Francis Tunsted was Bailiff of the Forest and his son James succeeded him as Bailiff in 1650. The same James Tunsted was a Captain of Dragoons in Rowland Eyre's Royalist Regiment in the Civil War.

Much of the land in the village however was let by the lord of the manor to his tenants. The rent in some cases was hardly punitive. In 1277 Sir Thomas Foljambe allowed Nicholas Stanedon and his wife Letitia to hold 10 acres in the manor for the rental of one rose payable at the nativity of St John the Baptist. However, from the 1277 Calendar of Fines, it would appear that the Stanedons' tenancy did not come without penalty. It looks as though the Stanedons had been foolish enough to dispute the ownership of the 10 acres; Sir Thomas Foljambe had won the dispute, been awarded 8 marks for his trouble, but had then been generous enough to rent the land to the Stanedons for a peppercorn sum. The Calendar records:

Between Thomas Foljambe plt[112] and Henry son of Nicholas de Stanedon and Letitia his wife defts[113]. Grant on a plea of warranty of charter and in consideration of 8 marks of silver, of 10 acres of land at Wormhill.

Thomas de Wormhill held 15 acres on the same rental terms in the same year.

A record of the ending of a tenancy during the reign of Edward I (1272-1307) reads as follows:

Quitclaim from Thomas fil. Ade de Herdewykewall to the Dean and Chapter of Lichfield, of a certain 'placia tofti inarii de Tidiswell' and of other lands, etc in Tydeswell and Litton. Witn Dom. John Daniel, knt., William Foliambe, William Martin, John Martyn, Ralph Coterel, etc., Temp Edw. I. (Lichfield. B. 16)
Derbyshire Charters I H Jeayes 1906.

This is a notice by Thomas son of Ade of Hargate Wall to give up the tenancy of land in Tideswell and Litton (Wormhill and Hargate Wall were part of the parish of Tideswell). 'Placia tofti inarii' is a form of mediaeval Latin used in legal documents and can be translated as 'a place of the unploughed or fallow hillock'[114]. This notice would have absolved him from continuing to pay dues to the Foljambes as lords of the manor and to the Church. It would have been recorded by the Dean of Lichfield. The Wormhill manor and the parish of Tideswell were

---

[112] Plaintiff.
[113] Defendants.
[114] *Toft* in mediaeval English meant either a hillock or a homestead.

then part of the diocese of Lichfield and did not come under the diocese of Derby until it was created as a separate see in 1927. The diocese kept all the property records. Note that Thomas has no attributed surname. In the centuries after the Conquest and down to the Middle Ages people lived in such small and enclosed communities that it was unnecessary to give them a second name because every-one would know them by their first. If people needed to be identified more explicitly than by their first name, for example in a legal document or to avoid confusion with someone else with the same Christian name, reference was made to the name of their father. Hence Thomas 'fil' (son of) Ade. Surnames were intro-duced in the Middle Ages, often referring to the owner's trade – Miller, Baker, Wheelwright, Cooper, etc – but the practice of using the father's name as secondary identification was perpetuated by using surnames with the suffix 'son' – Peterson, Stevenson, Thomson, Robertson, etc.

Another example of a 'Quitclaim' record is in 1337:

Quitclaim from Adam Cadas de Wormhull to Richard fil Ade Forestarius de Wormhull of a messuage and an acre and a half in Wormhull. Witn. Richard Foliamb, Alan del Hull, Ralph fil Nicholai de Tiddeswall, Roger fil Radulfi, Henry fil Radulfi. Dat. Tideswall, S.b. Assumption of B.V.M.[115], II Edw. III
Derbyshire Charters I H Jeayes 1906.

Through this deed Adam Cadas formally hands over a house and 1$\frac{1}{2}$ acres in Wormhill to Richard son of Ade the Forester. At the end of the previous century the Ades had been living at Hargate Wall, as shown in the previous quitclaim during the reign of King Edward I. Richard Foljambe, recorded as a witness, was the son of William Foljambe of Wormhill and nephew of Sir Thomas Foljambe (the first).

Transfers of ownership as well as tenancies start to show up in the records in 1346:

Grant from Richard Foliamb of Wormhill to John fil Ricardi Foliamb, etc, of 32 acres of land in Wormhull. Witn. Simon del Halle, Robert fil Willelmi del Tunstedes, Robert de Hope,etc. Dat. F. of Ass. of B.V.M 20. Edw. III
Derbyshire Charters I H Jeayes 1906.

Richard Foljambe, one of Sir Godfrey's oldest relatives by this date (Richard was the son of William the poacher and nephew of Sir Thomas (the first)), hands over two bovates/one virgate of land in Wormhill to his son John.

The first record of a church at Wormhill came in 1273 when Ralph de Sempringham, rector of Tideswell and later dean of Lichfield, gave permission to the inhabitants of Wormhill to build a chapel, finding their own chaplain. However

---

[115] 15th August.

it was stipulated that the villagers had to attend all the major religious festivals at the parent church at Tideswell. This is the origin of St Margaret's Church. Only the base of the Norman Tower remains. Wormhill continued to be part of the Tideswell parish until it became a separate and independent parish in 1859.

Taxation details start to appear in the 14th century. In 1327 under Edward II all parishes were taxed on the basis of one twentieth of all 'movables' (the total of all annual produce in the parish). Wormhill's movables were valued at £60 which was a high figure in relation to the assessment on other local manors.

It is unusual to find early records of individual houses within the village but just occasionally a reference can be found in the proceedings of the courts. The Assize Rolls of 1330 refer for the first time to a Hall at Hargate Wall – *Herdwykhalle* – which tends to suggest the existence of a sizeable house on the site by that date.

Despite the 1273 concession allowing the building of a chapel at Wormhill, the village remained part of the parish of Tideswell and it was to the church there that the inhabitants of the village would have trooped on foot in all weathers for the major church festivals and events. Construction of the present church of St John the Baptist at Tideswell began on the foundations of the former 11th and 12th century chapel in 1330. The building programme was delayed by the Black Death which ravaged the country in 1348/9 and its reconstruction took 50 years before completion in 1380.[116]

The Cathedral of the Peak at Tideswell

The Black Death or Plague entered the country via Weymouth in August 1348 and spread to the north of the country before it died out in the autumn of the following year. The epidemic destroyed between a quarter and a third of the population of England. The terror which this virus must have inflicted on a

---

[116] The current notice-board outside the church erroneously states that the period of construction spanned the years 1350-1399. The error, I suspect, stems from references in Pevsner and elsewhere to the church being built 'in the second half of the 14th century'.

population which had no understanding of disease or modern medicine and no means of counteracting a lethal and highly contagious epidemic can only be imagined. Nothing is known of the local impact, except that 50% of the clergy in the High Peak succumbed because priests were obliged to deliver the last rites to the dying, but Sir Godfrey and his wife survived it. After further epidemics in the 1360s and 1370s England's population, reduced to around 3$\frac{1}{2}$ million, stood at just over half its level in 1300.

As a result there were fewer mouths to feed and fewer men to produce the food. The value of land and the price of grain fell dramatically. As a consequence some lords of the manor reduced the amount of land under the plough, thus keeping grain prices higher and labour costs low. The untilled fields were usually transferred to sheep-rearing which was less labour-intensive and more profitable. Other landowners gave up farming their estates for profit and leased them out for fixed rents. Others still attempted to continue the feudal system of agriculture and persuaded the government to fix a ceiling on wages. Most controversial of all were attempts to reimpose certain compulsory unpaid services on the peasants which, in the past, had been performed by the serfs and villeins who were permanently bound to the manor and its lord. Dissatisfaction with serfdom and low wages led to the Peasants Revolt in 1381. This was triggered by the introduction in 1380 of a Poll Tax under which every man and woman over the age of 15 was obliged to pay a tax of one shilling. Wat Tyler gathered a mob of 60,000 from the villages of the Home Counties and marched on London (population 40,000) where they sacked large parts of the city. The rebellion was dispersed after the 14 year old King Richard II personally addressed the mob at Mile End and Wat Tyler was killed by the Mayor, William Walworth.

Soon after the rebuilding of the church at Tideswell was completed we start to see records of new endowments designed to support the running of the much larger and more expensive building. The creation of what we now call the 'Cathedral of the Peak' also signified the grandeur and status of Tideswell as one of the 6 market towns of Derbyshire and the principal town of the High Peak Hundred. In 1383 we find:

Licence from King Richard II in confirmation of a similar licence from Edward III now cancelled, to Nicholas de Stafford, chiv, James Foliaumbe, John Larcher of Highlowe, Wiliam de Hokelowe, Robert Jowesone of Tunstides, Henry Alisaundre, chaplain, Richard le Machon of Tiddeswelle, and Henry atte Tounesende de Lytton, and John fil. Henrici de Monyassh, in consideration of 20 marks received in the King's Hanaper[117], to convey for the support of two chaplains celebrating divine service at the altar of the Blessed Mary in the church of St John

---

[117] A round wicker case or small basket in which documents were kept.

Baptist Tiddeswell, twelve messuages, and two hundred acres of land in Tiddeswelle, Litton and Wormhille. Dat. 20 Nov anno 7 (Wooley XI, 27) Charters British Museum.

Derbyshire Charters. I H Jeayes.
Assistant Keeper of Manuscripts, British Museum 1906

This is an example of generous royal patronage – 20 marks which was enough to buy 12 houses and 200 acres for the support of two chaplains at Tideswell – and may well have been a handout from John of Gaunt, who was running the country on behalf of the infant King Richard II who was only 16 at the time. The grant arrived 3 years after completion of the new and larger church at Tideswell and, no doubt, ensured that it was properly endowed to support its increased size and responsibilities. The main recipient, Nicholas de Stafford, is noted as a 'chiv'[118] – a member of the knightly classes and guardian of the code of gallantry and honour that the knights were supposed to observe. In 1392 a subsequent grant from Nicholas de Stafford refers to him formally as 'knt' or knight. There are references to other members of the Foljambe family in this and other records from the British Museum. There were several branches of the family which owned the manors at Tideswell and a total of 12 manors in the county. James Foljambe, mentioned in the licence above, died *in vita patris*[119] and was the son of Roger, Lord of Tideswell, and the grandson of John Foljambe who died on 4 August 1358.

Nine years after receipt of the royal grant the more wealthy members of the local community took it upon themselves to further underpin the financial viability of the Tideswell Church. In 1392 there is a further grant:

Grant from Nicholas de Stafford, knt., James Foliaumbe, Robert Jewesone of Tunstede, Henry Alisaundre, Robert Sharpe, chaplains, Roger Machon of Tiddeswell, and Henry del Tounesende of Litton, to John Smyth and John Redymone, chaplains, of lands in Wormehill, Tiddeswell, and Litton, to found a chantry at the altar of the B.V. Mary in the church of St John Baptist of Tiddeswelle, for prayers for the souls of King Edward (III), of King Richard II, of Anne, Queen of England (Anne of Bohemia) and of John Duke of Aquitaine and Lancaster[120,] of William de Astone, his chancellor, of John Foliaumbe, of John, son of Henry de Monyasshe, Henry de Tiddeswelle, John Alisaundre, Elizabeth, wife of the said Nicholas de Stafford, Roger Foliaumbe, Thomas, son of Godfrey Foliaumbe, knt., John de Stafford, sen., Thurstone de la Boure, and Margaret, his mother. Dat. Tiddeswelle. S.6. F. of St Michael (29 Sep) 16 Ric. II. (Wolley XI 26)

Derbyshire Charters. I H Jeayes 1906.

---

[118] The Court of Chivalry endured from Edward III's reign through to 1737.
[119] In his father's lifetime – ie he did not inherit.
[120] John of Gaunt.

In about 1364 John Foljambe of Tideswell had founded a chantry in the church. A chantry was an endowment to provide for either laymen or priests to say a mass daily or weekly for the souls of the benefactors. It was often accompanied by the gift of a separate altar. Amongst the highly charged superstitions of the Middle Ages, and especially after the devastating attacks of the Plague in the 1300s, was a firmly held belief that the gift of a chantry reduced the time spent by sinners in Purgatory after their death. Naturally the Church did nothing to discourage such a belief.

By 1392 John's endowment had proved to be inadequate to keep the chantry going in the new and more extensive church completed in 1380. So his grandson James Foljambe, Sir Nicholas Stafford and others clubbed together to renew it and donated land in Wormhill, Tideswell and Litton to provide the necessary income. The charter for this new endowment went on to stipulate that the two lay cantarists[121] were to be present in their surplices and black copes to assist the priest at mattins, mass and other services on pain of a 1d fine for alms if they were absent without reasonable excuse. At the Feast of All Souls they were to hold special services and distribute 40d to the poor. If either cantarist misbehaved he could be removed from office by the priest with the consent of the aldermen of the gild. The first two cantarists appointed to the chantry were Christopher Lytton and Christopher Synderby who had free use of a house valued at 4 shillings per annum. The gild (guild) was a society of the wealthier members of the community who came together to facilitate mutual welfare, trade, business and investment as well as the funding of religious endowments. The Old Gild Hall where the members met was on the site of the present National Westminster Bank. Once a year on Good Friday the charter was to be read out in public in Tideswell church. The altar dedicated to this chantry was in the north transept.

Thurstan de la Bower (*Thurstone de la Boure*)[122] is listed here as one of the people for whom prayers were to be said. Thurstan was a well known local 14th century industrialist (lead-smelter) and a dedicated benefactor of Tideswell Church. Interestingly there is a large stone tomb in the south transept of Tideswell Church, called the 'de Bower Tomb'. A paper handout (20p), written by a Warwickshire descendant in 1994, claims that he was a knight with special royal privileges, Shield-bearer to the Treasurer of England Thomas Neville, veteran of the Scottish campaign of 1402 and of the Battle of Shrewsbury in 1403 and that the effigies in the transept are of him and his wife Margaret. Apparently he was nothing of the sort! Not only was he never knighted (as claimed on the inscription round the tomb on its restoration in 1873) but there are many authorities who doubt that the tomb represents the Bowers at all. The Foljambes and the Lyttons have

---

[121] Men who conducted the prayers.
[122] The name Thurstan usually indicates Norse ancestry from the Viking invasions but the surname de la Bower is distinctly Norman. The Vikings did however invade Normandy as well as England.

both claimed it as one of their ancestral tombs.

The historian John Pym Yeatman[123] maintained that one of the figures was of the Black Prince, a memorial erected by the Staffords as lords of the manor. This would seem to be possible as the effigies are two separate sculptures and the faint inscription on the headband of the knight in armour could be 'The Prince'. Edward (1330-1376), Prince of Wales, eldest son of Edward III and known as the 'Black Prince' from the colour of his battle armour, was one of the greatest national heroes of his day. He served at Crecy; captured the French King at Poitiers in 1356; ruled Aquitaine from 1362 to 1371 and conquered Castile in 1367, restoring the throne to the deposed King Pedro the Cruel. On his death in 1376 many English parishes commissioned stone effigies of him to commemorate his exploits.

So these curious stone effigies, knocked about and defaced with carved initials over the centuries could in fact be anyone. The only common agreement is that no-one but the Bowers thinks they were Thurstan and Margaret.

It should come as no surprise to find that not all grants and transfers were as proper and above board as the establishment of the Tideswell chantry. In 1388 there is the following record

Lease, for life, from Mag. Edmund de Stafford, Canon of Lichfield, afterwards Bishop of Exeter, Richard, vicar of Alstonefeld[124], Nicholas Rotour, chaplain, to Nicholas de Stafford, 'chyvaler', and Elizabeth his wife, of the manor of Throwley and Frodeswall[125] and Tyddeswell with land in Tyddeswell, Wormhyll and Spondon and in the bailiwick of the Forest of High Peak, at a rose rent. Dat. Lycchesfeld, 1 Oct, 12 Ric. II
Derbyshire Charters I H Jeayes 1906.

This lease, drawn up by Edmund de Stafford for the benefit of Sir Nicholas de Stafford, looks suspiciously like nepotism. Large tracts of Staffordshire and Derbyshire, including the manor of Tideswell with some land in Wormhill, are leased to him for life on payment of one rose per annum. The clerk who drew up

---

[123] John Pym Yeatman was an antiquarian eccentric who published between 1886 and 1907 five volumes on the *Feudal History of the County of Derby*. The relevant piece on Tideswell is in Vol V Section IX. Pym Yeatman was an odd character who sought to debunk most other historical accounts, including for example putting forward a proposition that the Foljambe family were never resident at Tideswell and never the owners of the manor. He was firmly convinced in 1907, amongst other things, that the Church of England would voluntarily reverse the Reformation and return its loyalty to the Church of Rome. He claimed to have access to ten times as many charters as those published in the excellent volume by I H Jeayes in 1906 and he eventually went bankrupt before completing the work as a result of failing to repay the publication costs to his subscribers. One copy of a limited edition of only 50 is in the Buxton Library.

[124] Alstonefield, Staffordshire.

[125] Fradswell, Staffordshire.

the lease seems to have been confused by the title chevalier, writing it in inverted commas as 'chyvaler'. In due course the Tideswell manor passed by marriage from the Staffords to the Meverells.

TRADE AND INDUSTRY

By the beginning of the 13th century the inhabitants of the High Peak were involved in more than subsistence agriculture and hunting. Many of the old mineral industries started by the Romans and continued by the Anglo-Saxons were continued and expanded. In 1200 Derbyshire was England's main source of lead. Lead mines in the area were owned by the Crown. The industry flourished until about 1350 and then gradually declined before being pursued again vigorously in the 18th century. Derbyshire lead was used in royal building work at Westminster and for monastic buildings at Rouen in France. The first lead seams were discovered close to the surface and lead was extracted by open cast mining, leaving long scars or 'rakes' on the landscape. Deeper seams had to be accessed by sinking shafts into the rock. The entrance to one of these lead mines remains at the top end of Monks Dale and the spoil-heap of stone flowing down to the bottom of the dale is testimony to the huge labours of removing the rock by candle light to get at the small seams of lead. Records from 1195 reveal that the Tideswell mines (including perhaps the one in Monks Dale) produced 2600 loads of lead ore in that year – about 650 tons.

Separating the lead ore (galena) from the rock was done by crushing using a heavy mill-stone as a roller drawn by horses over a circular track. Once the ore had been separated, it had to be smelted (*colour plate 11*). Up to about 1590 smelting took place in furnaces built at the top of 'Bole' hills, one of which over-looks the Sitch. Boles were sited at 900 feet above sea level or more because wind was required to increase the temperature of the burning fuel. It required a wealthy man to finance the operation because everything had to be hauled up to this level including timber for the bole's construction, charcoal and the ore itself. There would usually be only two smelts per year, always providing that the wind continued to blow throughout the smelt. Inevitably those who lived and worked with lead suffered short lives from progressive poisoning.

In 1392 Thurstan de la Bower, yeoman of Tideswell and a 'brenner'[126], paid his annual rent of 12d at Baslow manor court for a licence to have his boles within the manor. Thomas, son of Henry de Litton paid 6d, Roger de Wormhill 3d[127] and Ralph le Barker 3d. Thurstan de la Bower was a major benefactor of Tideswell

[126] Or lead smelter – derived from the Anglo-Saxon word meaning 'burner'.
[127] Perhaps he might also have been responsible for the smelting site at Bole Hill on The Sitch.

Church and, in the charter of the 1392 chantry, is quoted as one of the people for whom prayers were to be offered.

Lead was such a valuable commodity that strict penalties were enacted for theft. King Edward I drew up a law that anyone who stole from the lead mines of Derbyshire was to be severely punished. The first offence attracted a fine; the second offence a double fine but a third offence was punished by having one hand nailed to a table or the winding gear of the lead mine and being left without food or drink. The thief could only release himself by cutting off one hand with the other :

> *For ſtealing oar twice from the Minery,*
> *The Thief that's taken fined twice shall be,*
> *But the third time that he commits ſuch theft,*
> *Shall have a Knife ſtruck through his hand to th'haft,*
> *Into the Stow[128], and there till death ſhall ſtand,*
> *Or looſe himſelf by Cutting looſe his hand;*
> *And ſhall forſwear the franchiſe of the Mine,*
> *And always loſe his freedom from that time.[129]*

8oz Lead Weight Wormhill 1195-1340

Amongst the numerous curious customs associated with lead mining is a prohibition on whistling inside the mines. Whistling was forbidden because it was supposed to frighten away the ore – 'However many may sing or hallo when at their work, no man or boy is to whistle'.

More elaborate processes for lead mining and smelting were developed in the 18th century. The last major lead mine in Derbyshire, the Magpie mine near Sheldon, closed in 1958.

Markets were needed to buy and sell the produce of the mines and the farms and Tideswell was well placed to be selected as a centre for trade. In 1251 Tideswell was granted its first

---

[128] The wooden winding gear at the top of a lead mine shaft.

[129] Part of the poem in which Thomas Manlove, a Barmoot Steward, wrote down the mining laws in verse in the mid-1600s. His original manuscript is in the Peak District Mining Museum at Matlock Bath.

market charter and major fairs were held five times a year. Cattle and sheep markets, the sale of cheese, wool and lead brought population growth and wealth to the village. Traders' measures were standardised and stamped. An 8 ounce lead weight, decorated with the 3 leopards[130] of England and in use between 1195 and 1340, was found in Wormhill and is now in the Buxton Museum. It was probably part of a set of weights used for official business.

Three years later in 1254 similar privileges were extended to Bakewell. A weekly market and 15 day fair (the longest Peakland mediaeval fair) was granted to William Gernon, lord of the manor of Bakewell. These were the forerunners of the Monday market and Bakewell Show.

So, by the end of the 1300s our village had been under the rule of the Norman and Plantagenet monarchs for 300 years and the Foljambes had been lords of the manor for the same period of time. Many of the Foljambe squires had been wealthy and powerful men who would have helped to bring patronage and prosperity to the local scene. Few people other than the squire would have been aware of events beyond the parish boundary – of crusades taking place at the furthest distance of the known world, of rebellions by the barons in the 13th century, of minor wars with the Scots, or of the 100 Years War with France which had begun in 1337. There had been no invasions and no violent takeover of property by a foreign power and people. Other manors nearby which fell under the authority of the Ferrers and the Peverils would have been at the mercy of the misfortunes to befall those families but the inhabitants of Tideswell and Wormhill had the good fortune to be governed by an extended family of Foljambes who consistently backed the winning side and hence contributed to a sense of relative stability. The Royal Forest brought further kudos and privileges to the parish as well as lucrative employment and royal investment. Agriculture and industry were thriving to such an extent that Tideswell had become one of the main trading centres of the county with one of the biggest and most prestigious churches. Life for the average villager would nevertheless have been hard – unswerving subservience to the lord of the manor, reliance on unpredictable crops and harvests, harsh and even brutal punishment for poaching and other offences. There was a severe and nation-wide famine in 1315-17, for example, caused by adverse weather and disease of farm animals, and there are records of people having to make bread from ferns and bracken because of the shortage of corn. Great fear would have been inflicted on all by the repercussions of virulent and incurable epidemics which they called ominously the 'Black Death' and which had halved

---

[130]   In 1194 King Richard I was freed from captivity in Germany after being arrested in Austria on his way home from the Third Crusade. He returned to England with his mother Queen Eleanor of Aquitaine and quickly saw off the threat posed by his younger brother Prince John. It was at this point that he added the third leopard (sometimes erroneously called a lion) to his coat of arms before returning to France, never to be seen in England again.

the population inside the past century. Whether they recognised that they had been living in a period of relative stability and prosperity and whether they felt any benefit from the experience is therefore improbable. What we do know is that the next century was going to be very different – an absentee lord of the manor living in Yorkshire and executed for treason, rebellions in Scotland and Wales, the climax of the 100 Years War and a very divisive Civil War called the Wars of the Roses.

YORK v LANCASTER

The Wars of the Roses were fought out between two royal families, each of them vying for the throne of England. The House of Lancaster, whose crest was a red rose, was promoted by John of Gaunt (1340-1399) and ruled England from 1399 to 1461. When the Lancastrians were defeated at the battle of Towton in 1461, Edward IV of the House of York (white rose) assumed the throne until he was deposed temporarily in 1470-71 by the Lancastrian King Henry VI. The House of York gained the upper hand again after victories at Barnet and Tewksbury until 1485 when Henry of Richmond restored a branch of the House of Lancaster after the battle of Bosworth. As King Henry VII he married Elizabeth of York, thus uniting the two competing Houses and bringing a degree of peace and reconciliation, even though Yorkist rebellions continued through to 1497. The 15th century was thus a complete bloodbath for the ruling classes of England – three Kings, one Prince of Wales, eight royal or semi-royal dukes died in battle, by murder or execution, together with a third of the peerage and countless members of the gentry. And we think we live in dangerous times!

In 1392 the ownership of the Wormhill manor by the Foljambe family came to an end when Isabel's dower was transferred to Sir William Plumpton of Plumpton Yorkshire. Robert Plumpton married Alice Foljambe on 16th January 1393 in accordance with the rights purchased by his father. Robert would have been only 10 and Alice only 7 when they entered into this arranged marriage but it appears to have survived. Alice gave birth at the age of 16 to their first child William and the Plumpton family went on to own the manor for just over a century until 1498. Alice gave Robert another son (Godfrey) and daughter (Alice) in due course. The eldest son and heir, Sir William, was eventually the father of Sir Robert Plumpton who married Elizabeth, daughter of Thomas, Lord Clifford. It is not known whether any of the Plumpton family came to live at Wormhill but, as most of their property was in Yorkshire, it seems likely that they would have stayed there. There is certainly some evidence that the head of the Plumpton dynasty remained Yorkshire-based during the 15th century.

On 8th June 1405 for example Sir William Plumpton, owner of Wormhill at the time, was executed for his part in the rebellion against King Henry IV by Richard Scrope, Archbishop of York, who was his uncle on his mother's side of the family. His severed head was displayed on the battlements of Micklegate Bar in York. Richard Scrope had joined Thomas Mowbray, the Earl Marshal, and Henry Percy, Earl of Northumberland, in rebellion. They called out the citizens of York and many others and had manifestos nailed to the doors of churches and monasteries in the city. They were deceived into laying down their arms by the Earl of Westmorland. An amnesty was proclaimed but not observed. When the King came to York, the archbishop and the earl marshal were both beheaded. Sir William Plumpton was executed at the same time. King Henry aroused widespread opposition for executing an archbishop. To many of his subjects the mysterious illness which overtook him soon afterwards, rumoured to be leprosy, seemed a judgement from God for his misdeeds. Sir William Plumpton's son Robert, by then 22, and his wife Alice, then 19, took over the manor.

Henry IV, son of John of Gaunt, took an active part in politics under Richard II and was banished in 1398. He returned in 1399 when his father died, headed a revolt and was accepted as King by parliament. His reign lasted until 1413 but was beset by rebellions by the barons, the bishops and by the rising of Owen Glendower in Wales. In order to survive as King, he had to conciliate the Church by introducing a law for the burning of heretics and by making many concessions to parliament.

Sir Robert Plumpton died on 8th December 1421 and was succeeded by his 17 year old son William (7 Oct 1404-15 Oct 1480). William had married Elizabeth Stapleton in 1415 and could not have been more than 11 at the time.

Despite the turbulence of these years, the existence of charters transferring property in the village shows that life otherwise went on as normal. An early example in the 15th century dated 1402 reads as follows :

Grant from Thomas Alynson of Herdwyckewalle, within the township of Wormelle, to Roger Alynson his brother, called Thomas, of land in 'le Ware Slacke' adjoining land of St Mary of Tyddeswalle, within the said township of Wormhill. Dat. F. of Tr. of St Thomas (7 July) 3 Hen. IV.
(Public Record Office. c. 606)
Derbyshire Charters I H Jeayes 1906.

This transaction took place in a year when King Henry IV was fighting rebellions in Scotland, where Henry Percy defeated a retreating Scottish army at Homildon Hill, and another rebellion in Wales. There is still a field called Wire Slack[131] on the right (south) of the little 3-cornered copse beside Cow Lane (*colour plate 12*). It has therefore retained this name for at least 600 years. There is a theory that 'Wire Slack' refers to land that is prone to subsidence – 'Slack' is a name commonly given to slight hollows – and there are some small pits in this and surrounding fields which may have given rise to the name. These so-called 'sinkholes' are not uncommon on land overlying limestone where underground springs and water channels can gradually erode the rock and overlying soil until

---

[131] Ordnance Survey Number 579.

subsidence occurs at the surface. The Alynsons clearly were freeholders of a house and land at Hargate Wall other than the Hall, which remained in the ownership of the Plumpton family, and may have occupied either Dakins or the farmhouse in what is now Number 4 Hargate Cottages.

On top of all the instability and rebellions at home, the 100 Years War with France continued unabated. There were some famous English victories at the start of the century in which local families took part. Edward Foljambe for example, son of John and Isabel and grandson of Roger, Lord of Tideswell, was knighted at the battle of Agincourt by King Henry V on St Crispin's Day 25th October 1415 after the famous victory over the French who had a numerical superiority of between 3 and 5 to 1. Edward married Cecilia, daughter of Sir Philip Leeke of Sutton-en-le-Dale. The Foljambes appear to have married into at least two branches of the Leeke family.

Sampson Meverell of Tideswell was also knighted at the siege of Orleans in 1429 by the King's brother, the Duke of Bedford. English history tends to focus on the famous victories and conveniently forget about the defeats, just as French history tends to do the reverse. The unpalatable truth is that the War went badly for the English after defeat at the battle of Patay in 1429 and Formigny in 1450 which led to the loss of Normandy. When it ended with the French victory at Castillon in 1453, the English had lost all their possessions in France except Calais and even that was lost in January 1558.

Back at home The Wars of the Roses between the competing dynasties of York and Lancaster did not begin before 1422 but the Plumptons and the Foljambes had a long history of support to the House of Lancaster. A descendant of the Plumptons, another Sir William, was captured after the battle of Towton in 1461 where the Lancastrians were heavily defeated and had to buy his pardon from his Yorkist captors. He had fled to Cumberland along with the Earl of Wiltshire and was arrested by the Sheriff Richard Salkeld who took them to King Edward at Newcastle. The King had already executed 42 captured Lancastrian knights on the battlefield at Towton and gave orders for Wiltshire to be beheaded on the spot. Plumpton was lucky therefore to survive but, although spared on that occasion, he was later executed for further acts of subversion. The map of England (*colour plate 13*) shows the allegiances of the English estates to York and Lancaster in the second half of the 15th Century. Derbyshire was largely Lancastrian but there were pockets of Yorkist loyalties as well. This must have made for difficult relationships, not to mention open hostilities, between neighbours. The Vernons of Haddon were Lancastrian supporters and several Vernons were involved in clashes which led to murder. Long periods passed when the House of York was in the ascendancy and it would have been suicidal to have shown any Lancastrian sympathies. Some families like Warwick and Stanley switched their loyalties as each side gained or regained power; others lay low waiting for the strife to be resolved.

In the midst of this Civil War the Tideswell branch of the Foljambe family now reached crisis point with no male heir to secure the succession. A concession however provided some leeway for the last of the family, as this charter from 1468 shows:

Power of attorney from John Grysley and Thomas Stathum, knts., Will. Babyngton, Richard Willughby, John Casson, Nicholas Longford, Ralph Pole, and Nicholas Fitz-herbert, esqrs. and Thomas Babyngton, to John Stathum and John Coke of Walton, to deliver to Godith Foliambe, widow of Roger Foliambe, esq., seisin[132] of the manor of Tyddeswall, and of all other lands, etc., in Tyddeswall, Huklow, Wormehyll, etc., which they had of the demise of John Spondon, abbot of Dale, and others, etc for the use of the said Godith for life. Dat. 5 Apr., 8 Edw. IV (Foljambe Charters)
Derbyshire Charters I H Jeayes 1906.

Roger Foljambe died in 1447, leaving 3 daughters but no male heir. He was the last direct descendant of the Tideswell branch of the family – the Tideswell manor had been handed down from Sir Thomas (the fourth) to John to James to Sir Edward and thence to Roger. His widow, Godith, was the daughter of John Statham of Tideswell. In 1447 the Tideswell manor and other pieces of land in the local area had passed indirectly to Thomas Foljambe, a descendant of Sir Godfrey's younger brother, but Thomas had died in 1451 and his son had died in 1468 without male heir, thus leaving no Foljambe at all to inherit the Tideswell estate. Godith however was still alive with her 3 daughters and sought a life interest in the estate.

This concession, allowing Godith to retain the freehold of the manor for life, came during a particularly turbulent power struggle for the throne of England during the Wars of the Roses. Edward IV, son of the Duke of York, occupied London in 1461, throwing out the last of the Lancastrian Kings, and was proclaimed King by a council of his peers. His position was secured by the defeat of the Lancastrians at Towton in Yorkshire in 1461 – by far the bloodiest battle of the Wars of the Roses with up to 28,000 killed on both sides[133] – and by the capture of Henry himself. However Edward quarrelled with the Earl of Warwick, his strongest supporter, who temporarily reinstated Henry VI as King in 1470-71 before Edward recovered his throne by his victories at Barnet and Tewkesbury where Warwick himself was killed. For the Foljambes and Plumptons, who had strong affiliations with the Lancastrian dynasty, these must have been difficult times.

---

[132] Owner of the freehold.
[133] The Lancastrian Army turned under the pressure of superior numbers and it is said that, on the line of their retreat, the snow was stained red over an area 3 miles wide and 6 miles deep.

The fact that inheritance of land and property could be such a contentious issue is evidenced by the practice at this time of drawing up conveyances and trusts. One such document, dated 1483, saw Nicholas Eyre of Castleton leaving his various pieces of land, including some at Hargate Wall, in trust.

Feoffment[134] by Nicholas Eyre of Redseats to Richard Gernon of Hasylbadge, Henry Columbell of Darley, Walter Holly and Hugh Nedham, of all his lands in Redseats, Castylton. Bradwall, Herdikwall and Sterndale in High Peak, in trust for the said Nicholas, with remainder to his sons Nicholas and Martin, etc. Witn. John Marchington, Ralph Downes, etc. Dat. Th. a. F. of St Martin[135] 1 Ric III.
Derbyshire Charters I H Jeayes 1906.

These small insights into local events in the 15th century can give only a flavour of what life must have been like for the inhabitants of Wormhill and then only for the hierarchy rather than the mass of ordinary villagers. But it seems probable that no-one could have been immune to the chaos and confusion, fear and hardship caused by the combination of external and internal wars. There had also been serious famine throughout the country in the middle of the century as a result of poor growing seasons leading to failed harvests, particularly during the period 1438-41. These preoccupations would have taken the shine off the prosperity and stability of former times. Farming, the mineral industries and the hunting in the Forest no doubt continued but would have been over-shadowed by the power struggles raging elsewhere. Some semblance of stability and hope would have been restored by the ascendancy of Henry Tudor in 1485 but the 165 years of the Tudor and Stuart times brought trials and tribulations of a different kind.

[134] Conveyance.
[135] 11th November.

TUDOR AND STUART ENGLAND

On the death of Edward IV in 1482 his brother Richard III seized the throne and did away with his nephew princes Edward and Richard who were imprisoned in the Tower of London. The reign of Richard III was however short. He was killed at the battle of Bosworth in 1485, the last of 14 Plantagenet Kings, to be replaced by the victor Henry Tudor. This marked the end of the Wars of the Roses and the start of the Tudor dynasty.

The Tudor Age heralded a change in agricultural practices which would have affected our village as much as any other. Until the fifteenth century feudal landowners pursued the patriarchal system of farming their own property, then called demesnes, by the labour services of their dependants and local villagers who were prevented from moving away from the manor, or at least from the local Hundred. After 1485 landowners became receivers of rent. Home farms were cultivated not by lords of the manor through bailiffs and labour-rents but by free-holders, leaseholders, copyholders and hired labourers. Tudor farmers sought to make agriculture more than self-sufficient. They aspired to be sellers and not just consumers, to raise from their lands profits as well as food. Pasture replaced tillage, sheep replaced corn and wool replaced meat as the demand for cloth increased. Reduction in the requirements for labour led to the depopulation of rural districts and the progressive growth of the towns.

Even though the rural population declined, the overall population of England doubled in the 16th century and increased by 50% during Elizabeth's reign alone. This was despite the terrible ravages of disease – a flu pandemic in the period 1557-59 for example killed up to 10% of the population – and hunger caused by the stagnant output of grain at a time of rapid population increase. In addition there were bad harvests from 1594-98 and again in 1600, all of which contributed to a 300% inflation of the price of grain in the 16th century. Famine was widespread and unusually high mortality rates were noted in the parish registers – the national death rate jumped by 6% during the crop failures of 1596-98. Barley, oats and rye were the main corn crop in the Peak District and bread was made with either rye or rye and wheat. Cattle were often slaughtered in the autumn months and either salted down or smoked because there was insufficient feed to keep them through the winter. In 1584 land in Derbyshire was fetching the surprisingly high figure of £5-10-0 per acre on the open market in recognition of the spiralling demand for food.

In 1563 the Privy Council ordered a census of the number of households in each parish. The return for Wormhill showed 66 households and 4584 acres of land. Two hundred years later the number of households had nearly halved to 35 in reflection of the flight of population from the country to the towns and it was not until quarrying restored the need for labour in the mid 19th century that numbers returned to those of 1563.

Sir William Plumpton (the second) had died in 1480. His only child was a daughter, Agnes, who was married to Richard Aldborough on 12th October 1460. Ownership of the manor by the Plumpton family continued for another 18 years (possibly by the dower being transferred to William's wife until her death) but came to an end in 1498 after four generations and 106 years. The Plumptons sold to Catherine Eyre, wife of Stephen Eyre of Hassop in order to pay off expenses incurred in a very expensive bout of litigation against Empson, the villainous lawyer of King Henry VII. Further litigation against the Plumpton family, brought by an illegitimate daughter laying claim to the Yorkshire fortunes, severely depleted the Plumpton estates. The Eyres[136] held the manor on an annual payment of 3d and knight service to the Crown.

Nevertheless it appears that some sales and leases of other property within the manor had taken place by this time as this charter of 1525 shows:

The 'Hill' March 2006

---

[136] In mediaeval times an 'Eyre' was a travelling judge who went about the country dispensing justice for the king – a possible origin for the family name.

Counterpart of Lease from James Denton, Dean of the Chapter of Lichfield, to Christopher Jamys of Tyddeswall, yeoman, of 'omnes domos' of the Rectory Farm of Tideswell for 25 years. Dat. 1 Mar 1525(6)

Attached to the above is another lease between the same people and of the same date for the tithes of corn and hay at Hardwykwall and [Wormhill] Hill

In addition to leasing the Rectory Farm at Tideswell for 25 years, Christopher James was entitled to some tithes on crops at Hargate and Wormhill which presumably went with the Tideswell Rectory.

As shown in the 1483 charter quoted earlier, some land at Hargate Wall had been owned by one of the Eyres at Castleton during the Wars of the Roses and a further conveyance of 1536 seems to show that the same family continued to own property there when John Eyre, also of Redseats, established a further trust.

Grant of John Eyre, late of Redsettes, to Adam Barbur of Pyndall, John Marshall of Lytton, and Roger Wryght of Herdycwall, of all his lands in Castylton and elsewhere in co. Derby, in trust for the said John Eyre and his heirs, in tail male.[137] Dat. 17 Nov 28 Hen VIII.

Derbyshire Charters I H Jeayes 1906.

The Eyres, especially the Hassop family, were prolific purchasers of property throughout Derbyshire during the period 1470-1640 and they continued to buy further property in the village. Amongst the schedule of purchases is one on 2nd September 1597 when they bought 'messuages,[138] etc' in Hardwickwall for £600 from William Frost of London, who was the mortgagee of a Mr Needham.[139]

On 10th April 1602 the Eyres bought the 'Capital Messuage of Hardwickwall' (Hargate Hall) from Raphe Blackwall of Dethick, who was acting on behalf of Mr Needham. The purchase price is not recorded.

At some stage during the early 17th century and possibly soon after it was purchased by the Eyres in 1602 Hargate Old Hall was built in the typical Jacobean form in which it remained until 1909. It may then have been a new building but is more likely to have been rebuilt on the site of the previous dwelling sold by Mr Needham (and recorded as a Hall in the Court records of the 1300s). Either way the construction of the Hall must have been effected by the Eyre family of Hassop who were the owners of the property from 1602 through to about 1670. Construction must have been completed before 1655, at which point it was already referred to as a 'messuage' or mansion in the rental agreement that year between

---

[137] In the male line.
[138] Dwellings.
[139] Almost certainly a forebear of John Needham who repurchased Hargate Hall in 1760.

The Original Jacobean Hargate Hall

Rowland and Thomas Eyre and Humphrey Wilson. The latter was already the occupant of the house in 1655 and may have rented it for some time before that date. It is thus not possible to pinpoint the exact year when the Eyres built or rebuilt the Hall but it seems likely to have been part of the extensive building programme carried out by the Eyre family during their tenure of the manor in the 16th and 17th centuries.

During the reign of Henry VIII (1509-1547) one of the most dramatic developments, affecting this community as much as any other, was the King's break with the Church of Rome, enforced adherence to the new Church of England and the consequent persecution of Catholics.

On the orders of King Henry VIII, Thomas Cromwell his 'vice-regent, vicar general and special commissary' set about proving that all the minor religious institutions in the country were corrupt and should be abolished. He undertook a series of 'visitations' to prove that this was the case. The real purpose was to raise revenue for the King who did not have enough money and that purpose was realised by 1540 when the royal revenues had increased from £100,000 to £140,000 a year. Property and rights which were confiscated at the Dissolution were bought up by local landowners. Sir Francis Leeke of Sutton bought up two thirds of the lead tithes formerly owned by the Monks Dale Grange and Ralph Gell of Hopton bought the other third. It is not known what happened to the grange and chapel but the standard practice was to remove the roofs and staircases to make the buildings uninhabitable and allow the weather to complete the destruction. In due course no doubt local farmers would have removed the usable stone to make their own buildings and enclosures.

There was a nunnery at Buxton to which Henry III in 1235 had given land in the Goyt Valley, Combs and Dove Holes. This was searched during the Reformation by one of Lord Cromwell's minions, Sir William Bassett of Meynell Langley, who wrote to his master:

'According to my bounden duty, and the tenor of your Lordship's letters lately to me directed, I have sent your Lordship by this bearer, my brother Francis Bassett, the images of St Anne of Buckston and St Mudwen of Burton-on-Trent, which images I did take from the places where they stood, and brought them to my house within forty-eight hours after the contemplation of your Lordship's letters, in as sober a manner as my little and rude will would serve me. And for that there should be no more idolatry and superstition there used, I did not only deface the tabernacles and places where they did stand, but also did take away crutches, shirts and shifts, with wax offered, being things that allure and entice the ignorant to the said offering; also giving the keepers of both places orders that no more offerings should be made in those places till the King's pleasure and your Lordship's be further known in the behalf. My Lord, I have locked up and sealed the baths and wells of Buckston, that none shall enter to wash there till your Lordship's pleasure shall be further known; whereof I beseech your good Lordship that I may be ascertained against your pleasure, and I shall not fail to execute your Lordship's commandments to the utmost of my little wit and power. And my Lord, as touching the opinion of the people and the fond trust they did put in those images, and the vanity of the things, this bearer can tell your Lordship better at large than I can write, for he was with me at the doing of all this, and in all places, and knoweth good Jesus, whom ever have your Lordship in his precious keeping. Written at Langley with the rude and simple hand of your assured and faithful orator, and as one and ever at your commandment, next unto the King's, to the uttermost of his little power, – William Bassett, Knight.'

In other words the fawning little creep had pillaged the convent at St Anne's Well and hoped that his master would approve!

An Act of 1585 had ordered that all Catholic priests were to be deported but inevitably many remained in hiding, often in so-called 'priest holes' in the homes of Catholic supporters. Nicholas Garlick, who had previously run a 'free' school in Tideswell, and Robert Ludlum, having become Catholic priests in France, were arrested at Padley Hall in Grindleford and found guilty of high treason. They were hanged, drawn and quartered at Derby Gaol on 24th July 1588. This was four days after the first sighting of the mighty Spanish Armada ploughing its way up the Channel off Plymouth with the intention of picking up a Spanish Army in Flanders before invading England and returning the country to the old religion with the

1 *Wind Low Tumulus*

2 *Arbor Low*

3 Site of the Roman Fort at Navio

4 Knotlow

5 *Anglo-Saxon cultivation strips at Chelmorton*

6 *9th century map of Englnad*

8 *John of Gaunt*

7 *Peveril Castle Castleton*

10 *Tunstead March 2006*

9 *Sir Godfrey and Avena Foljambe*

12 *Wire Slack 2004*

13 *Map of England during the Middle Ages*

11 *Lead ore*

14 *Chatsworth*

15 *Wormhill Hall*

16 *Oatcake making*

17 *The Brindley Memorial*

18 *Ashford black marble*

19 *Blue John Vase in Buxton Museum*

20 *Litton Mill 2001*

21 *The Crescent at Buxton*

22 *Aquatint of Chee Tor 1769 by P. Scotin after Thomas Smith*

23 *Enclosure*

24 *The Pinfold*

25 *The village stocks*

26 *High Peak Harriers at Wormhill February 2006*

27 Former School House Wormhill

28 Former Post Office

29 *The Cutting*
30 *Monsal Dale railway viaduct*

31 *St Margaret's Church*

32 *Wormhill well dressing*

33 *Hargate Hall 2005*

34 *Chapelsteads 2006*
35 *Bateman Farm*

Pope's blessing. On 20th July the alarm was spread throughout England by the lighting of beacons. The citizens of Derby would have undoubtedly understood the threat on the day of Garlick and Ludlum's execution, though whether this had any influence on the gruesome fate of the priests is not known. By the first week of August the Spanish fleet had been attacked by English fire-ships at its anchorages off Holland and then pursued relentlessly by the Royal Navy right round the coasts of the British Isles before returning with massive losses and humiliation to Spain.

One account[140] suggests that there was an ulterior motive for Nicholas Garlick to set up a school in Tideswell. He had, apparently, fallen madly in love with the daughter of Richard Stafford, Lord of Tideswell but stood no chance at all of marrying such a high born girl.

And one evening as he wandered through Monks Dale he entered the old oratory (of which there are a few stones remaining) and before one of its deserted altars he vowed to put aside the passions of his heart and devote himself to the service of God.

The owner of Padley Hall, John Fitzherbert and his family were arrested at the same time for harbouring the priests and narrowly escaped hanging which was the standard penalty for such an offence. John Fitzherbert was however incarcerated in Derby Gaol for 2 years – a filthy institution at the time and known for the stench of the open sewer which ran though it. He was then sent to the Fleet prison where he died on 8th November 1590.

Chantries and gilds like those endowed by the Foljambes at Tideswell and Bakewell were dissolved. The Tideswell chantry is said to have been finally dissolved and its revenues confiscated in the time of Edward VI (1547-1553).

The High Peak was notorious for its high number of 'Recusants', people who refused to attend Church of England services and who were suspected of being secret Catholics. One of the consequences of the dissolution of the monasteries and other religious foundations was the loss of many local schooling facilities previously provided by the priests and monks. In 1559 Bishop Robert Pursglove ceased preaching and founded Tideswell School as a charitable endowment funded by both the laity and the clergy. Tideswell School is still named after him today.

The Tunsteads, the Eyres and the Alleynes were amongst the recusant families and ran the constant risk of fines or imprisonment. Fines for persistent non-attendance at a Protestant church in the space of any one month could be as high as 1/- and for deliberate recusancy over a longer period as much as £20. The

---

[140] By Tilley and hence not 100% reliable.

Alleynes had a secret chapel at Wheston Hall which was eventually registered for Catholic worship under the Act of Toleration in 1791 before it was superseded by a new Catholic chapel at Tideswell in 1830.[141] The Eyres also kept a clandestine chapel at Hassop which was searched for priests in 1611. Some evidence but no priests were found; Rowland and his sons Thomas and Gervase were arrested but later released. Rowland Eyre suffered further as a result of his Catholic and Royalist loyalties in the Civil War and did not even escape persecution after his death. His memorial in the church at Great Longstone, where he and his wife are buried, was defaced during the years of the Commonwealth.

The date stones at Dakins Farm Hargate Wall reveal another story about religious persecution. They read:

GT(A?)T   HTAT :
16(2?)..   REFD1623

These two date stones are above the front door of the farmhouse and the left hand one has faded. It is conceivable however that this one is the earlier of the two, though it also appears to date from the 1620s. If so, GT-T would refer to the generation preceding HTAT. HTAT are the initials of Humphrey

---

[141] Other Non-Conformist churches proliferated in Tideswell in the 19th century – the Congregational Church in 1877; the Wesleyan Methodist Church in 1888; and the Primitive Methodist Church in 1893.

Thornhill[142] and Ann Thornhill, his wife. The letters REFD are probably an abbreviation for 'Reformed', indicating that 1623 was the year when they transferred their religious allegiance to the Reformed (Protestant) Church. The English Reformation began under Henry VIII who repudiated the authority of the Pope in 1534 and dissolved the monasteries. Under Edward VI Protestantism was established and, after a temporary Counter-Reformation under Queen Mary up to 1558, the process was completed by Elizabeth I who died in 1603. Persecution of Catholics and recusants continued under the reign of Stuart Kings James I and Charles I even though the Stuarts had distinct Catholic sympathies, and Protestant neurosis increased as a result of the Gunpowder Plot of 1605 and fears that the Crown secretly favoured restoration of Catholicism. Thirty-six Derbyshire recusants were fined a total of £443-18-4 in the year 1610.

The Thornhills may therefore have come relatively late to adoption of the Protestant faith, having waited for many confusing years to see where the religious allegiances of the country would end up. Eventually they may have become all the keener to make a public display of their conversion out of fear of being accused of recusancy which carried a penalty of a severe fine or imprisonment.

The Parish Constables were required to keep account of suspected recusants and report them to the County Sessions. In 1634 the village policeman had no less than 19 names to report:

Gervas Torr, constable of Wormhill, doth present these popish recusants following their absence from the church for one month past, viz John Greatworks of Tunstyde yeoman and Elizabeth his wife, Margaret Buxton widow, Elizabeth Greatworks widow, Ralph Stadon labourer, George Bagshawe of Wormhill yeoman and his wife, Anne Chadderton widow, Joan Tompson spinster, Francis Tunstyde gent and Thomazin his wife, Joan Redfern widow, Anne Longden wife of Richard Longden the younger, Elizabeth Torr spinster, Elizabeth Ridge spinster, James Tunstyde of Tunstyde yeoman, Joan Hayward widow, Grace Kirke widow, Emma Whildon widow.

Thus failure to attend the Protestant village church for four Sundays in a row gave rise to a minor inquisition and a fine for those who could not offer a satisfactory explanation. Just imagine the village bobby standing outside the

---

[142] Humphrey was recorded in 1633 as the only freeholder at 'Hardwicke Wall' in that year. The significance of recording freeholders was that they were the only people who could be selected for jury service. All other occupants of Hargate at the time were therefore tenants or leaseholders. Humphrey and Ann Thornhill were also mentioned in the will of a John Hadfield, yeoman, in 1668 – 'Humphrey Thornehill of Hardwickwall, Yeoman; Ann Thornehill his widow; Thomas Thornehill'. A Humphrey Thornhill (perhaps the son of HT) was still living at Hargate Wall in 1670, as evidenced by the appearance of his name in the Hearth Tax Return for that year. A probable descendant, George Thornhill, was recorded as living at Hargate Wall in 1773.

church door with his mill-board and ticking off those who appeared and then working out who hadn't! Some of these defaulting families like the Tunsteads and Haywards may well have been genuine recusants but others like the old widows and spinsters may just have been ill or house-bound and unable to get to church. It also seems probable that the village policeman was informing on one of his relatives (Elizabeth Torr). This is a good example of the political and religious intolerances of the 17th century, reminiscent of the worst practices of a police state.

Before the establishment of a County Police Force in 1856 the Parish Constables were the sole guardians of law and order and held an important position in the community. If there was no-one willing to take on the duty, the job fell to the local landowners in rotation. The Constable had to execute all warrants issued by a JP; take anyone committing a breach of the peace to the village stocks until they could be transferred to a proper lock-up or jail; and they were further responsible for surveying, building and repairing bridges in their parishes.

The anti-Catholic persecution continued into the 18th century, as shown by the fine of £58-17-0 imposed in 1715, the year of the first Jacobite rebellion, on another Gervase Torr, yeoman of Wormhill, for refusing to take the oath of Protestantism to King George I. The average annual income of a yeoman at the time was £2.

The Forest of the Peak continued to be run as a royal hunting reserve but the Tudor and Stuart monarchs had nothing like the same enthusiasm for hunting as their Plantagenet predecessors. It seems likely that the Forest enjoyed less and less royal patronage and was coming increasingly into conflict with the interests of local agriculture.

At the start of the Tudor dynasty wolves had been hunted almost to the point of extinction and the last wolf was killed in this parish during the winter of 1490.

By 1526 there were serious concerns about over-stocking within the Forest of the Peak and an inquiry was held. It found that in the Campana ward there were five herds of cattle amounting to 960-980 head, a flock of 4000 sheep and 320 horses. The commissioners noted that some 360 of the deer were in very poor condition and would be unlikely to live through the coming winter. They recommended that sheep should be kept out of Campana, as indeed they used to be. This led to continuing disputes between the forest officials and tenants of grazing rights about the number of sheep which could be pastured in the forest.

Pressures exerted by local landowners and farmers seem to have gained a steady ascendancy over the waning royal interests in maintaining the Forest as a hunting reserve as the 16th century progressed. In 1579 the deer were confined to a park based around the chamber at Peak Forest and contained by a tall deer fence. It is thought that the boundaries of the deer park corresponded approximately to the modern parish boundaries of Peak Forest village. If so, the construction of a 10-12 ft deer fence presumably in timber over a distance of several miles round the circumference of the parish would have been a major and expensive undertaking.

J Speed 1610   *R Morden 1722*   *J Tuke 1798*

It would also have signified a considerable change of attitude to the royal prerogative over hunting. Two centuries earlier the King had ordered the demolition of fences so that his deer could graze wherever they wished. By the late 16th century the number of deer had been reduced to some 100 head. Part of Longdendale was then sold by the Crown to George, Earl of Shrewsbury and removed from the Forest.

Early mapping of the area was notoriously inaccurate until the middle of the 18th century but the map made by John Speed in 1610 purports to show the boundaries of the Forest at that time. If he was correct, this would indicate that the Forest had indeed been confined to the much smaller deer park based on Peak Forest village and, interestingly, his map appears to show the paling deer fence constructed in 1579. The King's Forest of the Peak continued until Charles II's time and the royal rights were only finally abolished by Parliament in 1674. The final Forest Court was held in the time of Charles I who was the last monarch who tried to penalise and fine people for alleged encroachment on Forest lands. This was one of the first grievances to be addressed by the Long Parliament. So Speed's map of 1610 may have accurately reflected the progressive reduction in the size of the Forest which had begun in the 16th century. R Morden's map of 1722 appears to be a copy of the 1610 version, even though by then the Forest had been dissolved and was in the process of being enclosed by its new owners. By the time J Tuke produced his more accurate version in 1798 (which also showed the new turnpike roads), there was no longer any reference to Forest boundaries at all.

Early in the reign of Charles I the Duchy of Lancaster gave part of the Forest (the 'Old Lands') to the freeholders and in 1634 the freeholders and tenants petitioned the Crown to disafforest the rest and to enclose the remaining wastes and commons (the 'New Lands'). They complained about the iniquities of the Forest Law which had been increasingly used to extract more revenue and of the damage done to their crops by the deer. Commissions were set up in 1634 and 1639 and negotiations began. The High Peak was officially disafforested and the remaining deer were either destroyed or removed.[143]

The Civil War of 1642 then intervened and it was not until 1673 that the legal processes began again. It did not help that the Civil Wars had encouraged many people to make encroachments on the land remaining within the Forest and there were many long drawn-out disputes. Eventually by the early 1700s the legal entitlements had been settled and the freeholders and tenants began the division and enclosure of their own portions, a process which was not completed until the following century. Enclosure of common land by private owners was however contentious, particularly amongst the lead miners, many of whom joined the 'Levellers' movement in the 18th century.

Another sign of the demise of feudal customs was the change in the way that the nation's armies were raised for overseas operations. By the 16th century the obligations on the lords of the manor to provide men for military service had lapsed, to be replaced by a system of paid mercenaries, of which each county and Hundred was expected to meet a quota. Tideswell, as the principal market town in the High Peak Hundred, was the recruiting centre for pressing men into military service for the King. In 1552 no less than 1,124 men were assembled there from across the District to join the levies. Amongst them were:

64 archers with horse and harness
148 billmen without (horse and harness)
300 billmen with horse and harness
612 archers without

The mounted men were to receive 8d per day for their services.

As recorded in the 'commonplace book' of Roger Columbell, 13 men from Wormhill joined the levies in 1566. These men were *furnished with bylles and yewe bowes.*[144] The levies were extremely unpopular and people did whatever they could to escape the call-up. In 1599 the Earl of Essex had an army of 18,000 fighting in Ireland, of which 100 had been levied from Derbyshire. On 10th March of that year a John Brocklehurst of Wormhill was listed as a deserter.

At Buxton the wells and chapel had been plundered and closed down during the

---

[143] All types of wild deer have been absent from the local area from that time until only recently. Now however, in the 21st century, red deer have re-established themselves in the Macclesfield Forest and the Goyt Valley to the west of Buxton (the Campana ward) and on the Pennines to the north (the Longdendale ward). Roe deer likewise are steadily making their way back and are known to have re-colonised areas less than 30 miles away. A roe was killed on the Chapel bypass in Oct 04 and others can be seen in the wild at Stanton. A lone muntjac appeared briefly at Hargate in May 1999 but there have been no sightings since. There is a fallow deer herd in Chatsworth park and a sika herd in Stanton park.

[144] Bill(hook)s and yew bows.

Dissolution of the 1530s but were in use again by 1553 under the control of the Cotrell family who seem to have been the first to exploit the commercial advantages of the site. However there were problems controlling the behaviour of the bathers and preventing hooliganism. Roger Cotrell was bound over at Derby Assizes for £100 in 1553 to maintain good order at the wells and to prevent *'youthful persons from washing and bathing in the wall called Saint Anne's well, not only to get tipple and drunk within the said chapel on the Sundays and holidays, but most irreverently also to pipe, dance, hop and sing within the same to the great disturbance of the inhabitants of Buxton'*. Clearly this was the 16th century equivalent of the Anti Social Behaviour Order but it was imposed on the owner of the premises rather than the offenders.

The Cotrells sold the wells to George Talbot, the 6th Earl of Shrewsbury, who was to make Buxton the principal tourist centre of the Peak. The treatise published in 1572 by Dr John Jones on the beneficial effects of the Buxton waters had acted as prime publicity. By 1573 the high reputation of Buxton for its medicinal springs and baths was resurrected for the first time since the departure of the Romans. The charges for use of the Buxton Baths were by no means uniform and varied according to a person's ability to pay. In 1572 the charges were: for an Archbishop £5; a Duke £3-10-0; a Duchess £2; and a Yeoman 12d.

George Talbot, Sixth Earl of Shrewsbury (1528-1590) married Bess of Hardwick in 1568 (her fourth husband) and became the custodian of Mary Queen of Scots a year later. He built the Hall[145] in Buxton as a safe house to allow the Scottish Queen to take the waters at Buxton. Mary Queen of Scots stayed at the Hall on at least 5 occasions between 1573 and 1584, usually for several weeks in the summer when she was allowed by Queen Elizabeth to escape her confinement at Sheffield Castle where she was effectively kept in house arrest. However house arrest should not be compared to hardship and poverty. Mary was said to have enjoyed a permanent retinue of 60 servants and two physicians; and was allegedly offered a choice of 32 dishes for each meal. She was also allowed to pay seven visits to Chatsworth over the same period, where Queen Mary's Bower was built in formal gardens beside the river to commemorate her presence there. In 1580 it took Mary two days to travel the 24 miles from Sheffield to Buxton on horseback. On that occasion she had fallen when mounting her horse at Sheffield, though whether a resulting injury or the state of the almost non-existent roads or an overnight stay at Chatsworth (or all three factors) was the cause of the prolonged journey is not known (*colour plate 14*).

Elizabeth was nevertheless very suspicious of Mary's contacts at Buxton and kept close tabs on her, complaining at one point to the Earl of Shrewsbury when she was reported to have spoken to a beggar outside the baths. Mary was followed

---

[145]   Now the Old Hall Hotel.

by notable members of the Court including Lord Burleigh the Lord Treasurer, Sir Thomas Smith Secretary of State, Lord Gilbert and Lady Mary Talbot, and the Earl of Leicester. Catholic supporters of Mary also followed and Buxton became a centre of some plotting and intrigue at this time, provoking visits by Richard Topcliffe, the Catholic persecutor.

Alongside the growing popularity of the spa, other industries were again starting to thrive. Lead output in Derbyshire became the basis for the wealth of many local landowners and it continued to increase throughout the 17th century. An output of 3000 fothers a year in 1600 had risen to 10000 fothers a year by 1675. Prices also rose, fuelled by the demand for lead shot during the Civil War. The price of a fother[146] of lead in 1544 was £3-6-8; in 1580 was £8-10-0; in 1630 was £8; in 1640 £10 and in 1661 £15.

The Eyres who owned much of the village by 1600 were one such family who owed their wealth to lead mining. They were a Catholic, Royalist and Jacobite family and it is known that they and the parish had come under severe pressure during the Reformation and the dissolution of the monasteries in the 1530s. Rowland Eyre made his money from lead-mining which provided the funds for building new houses at Hassop and Wormhill. In the mid 1500s English lead from Derbyshire and the Mendips flooded the international market and effectively closed down competition from Europe. Derbyshire output was half of the European total and the profits rolled in.

Then, as now, a favourite subject for conversation in this part of the world was the weather and, in particular, any extreme climatic condition. One of the records for the beginning of the 17th century takes some beating. In 1615 one of the heaviest snows on record lasted from January through to Whitsun. The Youlgreave parish register described it as follows:

This yeare 1615 Jan 16 began the greatest snow which ever fell upon the earth, within man's memorye. It covered the earth five quarters deep upon the playne. And for heapes or drifts of snow, they were very deep; so that passengers both horse and foot, passed over gates, hedges and walles. It fell at 10 severall tymes, and the last was the greatest, to the greate admiration and feare of all the land, for it came from the fowre parts of the world, so that all entrys were full, yea the South parte as well as these mountaynes. It continued by daily encreasing until the 12th day of March (without the sight of any earth, eyther upon hilles or valleys) upon which day (being the Lorde's Day) it began to decrease; and so by little and little consumed and wasted away, till the eight and twentieth day of May and then all the heapes or drifts of snow were consumed, except one upon Kinder's Scout, which lay till Witson week and after. There fell also ten lesse snowes in Aprill, some

---

[146] About a ton.

a foote deep, some lesse, but none continued long. Uppon May day in the morning, instead of fetching flowers, the youths brought in flakes of snow, which lay above a foot deep upon the moores and mountaynes.

This was followed by four months of the great drought of 1615 which provided the first recorded example of well dressing at Tissington[147] in gratitude for the fact that the wells of the village continued to flow:

No rayne fell upon the earth from the 25th day of March to the second day of May, and then there was but one shower. Two more fell between then and fourth day of August, so that the greatest part of the land was burnt up…

The custom of well dressing is thought by some to be of Celtic origin but there is no real knowledge of how far back it can be traced. Certainly it had been a Celtic practice to worship the local water gods and the Celts were responsible for other ceremonies which have survived such as garland festivals, corn dollies and may-pole dancing. But whether wells were decorated in the Iron Age is impossible to establish.

In Tudor and Stuart Wormhill there can be little doubt that crime and punishment went on much as before, though specific records for the village are thin. In 1636 however there is a record of an unnamed Wormhill man becoming the victim of a brutal murder elsewhere in the county. He was found with his throat cut by robbers in Earnshaw Clough near Cutthroat Bridge on the A57 Snake Pass on the Sheffield side of Ladybower. He died some days later at the house he was taken to in Bamford and his murder gave rise to the place-name of the bridge where the incident took place.

So at the start of the Civil War in 1642 the Stuart King Charles I was on the throne and most, though not all of the village was owned by the Eyres of Hassop – a family of strong Royalist and Catholic sympathies. Subsequent events would show that their sympathies were shared by others in the village despite the penalties for recusancy and the history of Catholic persecution. The rural population was smaller than in 1485 and patterns of agriculture had changed. The interests of farming predominated over the interests of the Royal Forest which had been all but abolished. Other industries – especially lead mining – were proving particularly profitable. The ordinary villager was a freer man than he had been 150 years previously but he was still liable to be roped in for some pretty unpleasant military adventures a long way from home. Indeed the period of the mid-1600s was one of interminable internal and external wars: 1640 The Bishops' War; 1641

---

[147] There is an unproven claim that the first well dressing at Tissington occurred during the Plague of the 14th century which the village escaped ostensibly because of the purity of its water.

The Irish Rebellion; 1642-1648 the three phases of the Civil War; 1649 Execution of Charles I and War in Ireland; 1650-1652 War in Scotland; 1652 War with the Dutch Republic; 1655 War with Spain. Arguably it was the outcome of the forth-coming Civil War which was to shape the future of Wormhill more than any other factor.

THE CIVIL WAR

On 22 August 1642 King Charles I raised his standard at Nottingham to assemble his subjects for military service. In doing so, he was making a declaration of war, not against a foreign country but against his own people to determine whether the monarch or Parliament should dictate how the country was to be governed. Neither Nottinghamshire nor the adjacent counties were very keen to answer the call to arms. Derbyshire, a county with mixed Royalist and Parliamentary sympathies, did not produce much manpower for the King's armies and some of its arms were confiscated. The Earl of Devonshire, the Lord Lieutenant, was ordered to raise the county militia for the King but knew that they would be reluctant to answer the call, and so hesitated. In response the House of Lords ordered his arrest. The Earl of Rutland at Haddon, a lukewarm supporter of Parliament at the best of times, was ordered to raise the county militia for the Parliamentary forces and hesitated also. Some did answer the King's call to arms including large numbers of High Peak lead miners who were persuaded by being absolved of their duty to pay lead tithes to the Crown. The lead miners then tested their new-found rights by occupying and expropriating part of the Earl of Rutland's estate at Haddon and digging up the ground in search of lead. This led to a number of clashes between landlord and miners and a long-running dispute which was not resolved before the end of the Civil War.

Christopher Fulwood of Middleton by Youlgreave and Sir Thomas Bushell, the Master of the King's Mines, raised 1000 men at Tideswell of whom many were lead miners for service in the King's Life Guard. Fulwood himself was eventually cornered and mortally wounded by the Roundheads behind a rock in Bradford Dale which is still known as Fulwood's Rock. He died at Culton in Staffordshire a few days afterwards where his captors had taken him on the way to Lichfield. The Tideswell contingent of the King's Life Guard included Captain John Statham[148] of Tideswell who supplied a troop of horse for the King at the start of the Civil War. A tablet in Tideswell Church records: *John Statham, captain of a troop of horse which he raised at his own charge for the Royal King Charles I and was afterwards a patient sufferer of the tyrannies and sequestrations of those impious regicides.* Clearly the Stathams, like the Eyres, paid dearly for their royalist loyalties during the Civil War but they would have been unable to erect a

---

[148] A descendant almost certainly of the Stathams mentioned in the grant of 1469.

tablet containing this sort of wording before the Restoration in 1660.

Others pledged their allegiance to Parliament. Captain Edward Bagshawe of The Ridge, Chapel-en-le-Frith remained loyal to the Roundheads. He became captain of a company of foot under Sir John Gell and was killed in an assault on Tutbury Castle on 20th April 1646.

During the three phases of the Civil War from 1642 to 1660 Derbyshire remained mainly in the hands of the Parliamentarians but contributed forces from time to time to both the Roundhead (Parliamentarian) and the Cavalier (Royalist) armies. Many villages and even families were split down the middle in their loyalties to one side or the other. Skirmishes and sieges took place at Stockport, Newark, Nottingham, Lichfield and elsewhere in the surrounding counties but no major battles took place in Derbyshire itself.

A number of local families however held out for the Royalist cause. One of these was the FitzHerbert family of Tissington where Colonel FitzHerbert garrisoned the Hall and was lucky that it wasn't demolished in reprisal. In February 1644 a Royalist gathering in the neighbourhood was dispersed near Tissington by Roundhead cavalry under Major Sanders with the loss of 170 prisoners and a number of killed and wounded. FitzHerbert had intended to take Sanders by surprise at his home base in Ashbourne but Sanders was obviously alerted to the threat and reacted in good time.

The Eyres,[149] who owned most of Wormhill by this time, were another exception to the county's Parliamentarian loyalties. They were supporters of the King, garrisoned Hassop Hall and fought the Roundheads at its gates. On 6th July 1644 Colonel Eyre and his Royalist regiment were surprised at dawn by the same Roundhead cavalry under Major Sanders, who caught them asleep without sentries in Boylestone church between Ashbourne and Sudbury. They had just returned from the battle of Marston Moor (2nd July 1644) where the Regiment consisting, as they then did like a modern day Battle Group of Horse, Foot and Dragoons, had fought with Frescheville on the left wing under Goring. Despite the initial successes of the left wing, the Cavaliers had taken a hammering, fled the battlefield and were no doubt trying to recover. The whole regiment of 300 men was taken prisoner without a shot being fired. Major Sanders marched the prisoners from Boylestone and from another engagement at Burton to Gell's stronghold at Derby with the Colours of six royalist Regiments of Foot and one Regiment of Horse.

At least two men from Wormhill fought in Rowland Eyre's Regiment and

---

[149] Another Eyre married Lady Mary Radcliffe, whose father and brother, persistent supporters of the Stuarts and the Jacobite cause even after the Civil Wars, were both captured at Preston in the 1715 Rebellion where her father was beheaded. The brother was imprisoned at Newgate from where he escaped, only to be recaptured at sea off the Dogger Bank during the Jacobite Rebellion by Bonny Prince Charlie in 1745 and he too was then beheaded. In the 17th century the Eyres owned 20 manors in the county and 20,000 acres including Wormhill. Through Mary Radcliffe the Eyres were for 40 years Earls of Newburgh, one of whom built the Roman Catholic church at Hassop in 1815.

probably went into the bag at Boylestone before being marched off to Derby Gaol and purchasing their freedom in due course. Henry Hayward of Tunstead and Hargate was the Quartermaster to Lieutenant Colonel William Eyre in the cavalry part of the regiment. All Henry's worldly goods were seized later in 1650 for taking the royalist side. And Captain James Tunstead of Tunstead was a captain of dragoons in the same regiment. For reasons unknown he emerged from the Civil War rather better, becoming one of the last Bailiffs of the Royal Forest in 1650. Maybe, like many others, he was persuaded to 'compound' or pay a fine, in which case he would have been forgiven but still regarded with some suspicion during the years of the Commonwealth under Oliver Cromwell.

Like all the Midland counties Derbyshire suffered from progressively harsher taxation during the war in order to fund the prolonged operations and at times both sides in the conflict demanded a share of the dues. This came on top of some highly contentious forms of taxation imposed by the King before the outbreak of war. It had been the custom for many years to raise so-called 'ship money' in coastal counties for the maintenance of warships and protection against piracy. But in 1635 King Charles demanded the same from inland counties and set his sheriffs the task of collecting it. John (later Sir John) Gell of Hopton succeeded in raising £3681-11-8 in the county that year against a demand for £3500, £514-8-4 coming from the High Peak Hundred. When ship money was demanded again in the following year, it became apparent that the tax was a permanent one and it was no surprise that the Sheriff in 1636 John Milward managed to collect less than half the reduced figure of £1300. From 1638 onwards the ship money assessments provoked ever increasing resistance and correspondingly reduced revenue.

The significance of Derbyshire during the Civil Wars was that the Trent Valley was an essential corridor for the Royalist forces between their supporters in Newark and Lincolnshire in the east and the Royalist heartlands in Staffordshire, Shropshire, Worcestershire, Hereford and Oxford in the west and south. The Cavaliers had to keep the corridor open and this led to a number of battles and sieges at Lichfield, Burton, Wingfield Manor and Newark. The Eyres were very much involved but they were not the only supporters of the Royalist 'Cavalier' cause fighting the Parliamentary 'Roundheads' led by the Earl of Essex, Fairfax and Oliver Cromwell.

Bolsover Castle near Chesterfield, home of the Cavalier commander William Cavendish[150] and regarded as impregnable during the 1600s, was held by the Royalists until William and Prince Rupert lost the battle of Marston Moor 7 miles west of York on 2nd July 1644 and with it the King's influence in the North of England. The Royalist Army was completely defeated by the Parliamentarians and Scots under Cromwell and Lord Leven, with Cromwell's cavalry charges being decisive.

---

[150] William Cavendish also owned Welbeck Abbey in Nottinghamshire.

William Cavendish 1618 (later Duke of Newcastle)

Bolsover was briefly besieged by Parliamentary forces thereafter but surrendered in 1645 and was quickly rendered incapable of mounting resistance. William Cavendish went into exile at Antwerp and did not return until the restoration of King Charles II in 1660 even though his brother had 'compounded' or paid the fine for William's role in the Civil War. His loyalty to the King was rewarded with his elevation from Earl to the Marquess of Newcastle, and finally in 1665 to the Dukedom of Newcastle. William was fortunate to be able to restore Bolsover to its former state and even extend it further up to his death aged 83 on Christmas Day 1676. His dukedom however survived only to the death of his son Henry in 1691.

Chatsworth was another Royalist stronghold, home of a cousin – another William Cavendish, the 3rd Earl of Devonshire (1617-1684). The Earl himself, after being threatened with arrest by the House of Lords, went into exile abroad for the duration of the war but in October 1645 Chatsworth was attacked and held for a time by Colonel Shalcross on the orders of Sir John Gell[151] of Hopton, a tough Puritan colonel. The house was garrisoned with 300 horse and dragoons from the Welbeck garrison. The gates of Chatsworth were broken up and breaches were made in the walls to ensure that the house could not subsequently offer resistance.

When the Earl returned at the end of the war, he 'compounded' like many Royalist supporters but he got off lightly with a fine of £5000 because he had taken no part in hostilities. After the Restoration of the monarchy in 1660 he was re-appointed Lord Lieutenant of the county.

His son, the 4th Earl, was not the only one to exploit the Grand Revolution of 1688 when William of Orange was invited to assume the English throne but the Dukedoms of Devonshire, Rutland, Newcastle and Portland[152] all stem from this time.

Sir John Gell fought throughout the Civil War as a Roundhead Colonel, achieving some notable successes and receiving only one rebuke for arriving a day late for the Battle of Naseby! He was unusual in that he was one of the few members of the county gentry and nobility to be commissioned by Parliament and support the Roundhead cause and he appears to have been some-thing of a rough diamond.[153] He had a notoriously sharp temper and was not averse to some earthy language and behaviour. He also had well known political ambitions. Many of his troops mutinied from time to time, usually because they had not been paid but also when they had not been issued with arms and ammunition. Nominally under the orders of the County Committee, he co-ordinated all military activity in the county on behalf of Parliament but he was for-ever in dispute over his chain of command – at loggerheads with Fairfax, resisting transfer to the Northern Association and constantly petitioning Essex for support and supplies which rarely arrived. Despite this he appears to have been an

Sir John Gell

---

[151] A descendant of the same family, Sir Philip Gell, built a road from his lead mines and quarries at Hopton to Matlock in 1791. This was and is still named the Via Gellia. The Gell family has since left Hopton Hall which is being developed as a model garden and much of the estate has been submerged under the reservoir of Carsington Water.

[152] Their ownership of major estates in Derbyshire, Nottinghamshire and Leicestershire gave rise to the term 'The Dukeries' which is sometimes used to denote that part of England

[153] See *Man at War: John Gell in his troubled time* by Ron Slack 1997.

effective leader, inspiring confidence from his troops through good communication and example on the battlefield.

His base at Derby remained under his control throughout the war and he conducted some successful raids into Nottinghamshire, Leicestershire and Staffordshire with his regiment of grey-coats. These territorial forces were usually no match for the professional Royalist armies before Cromwell and Essex created the New Model Army but Gell inflicted a notable reverse on the Earl of Northampton at a skirmish on Hopton Heath near Wirksworth on 19th March 1643. Gell's cavalry was quickly scattered and it was only Gell's personal leadership which prevented an impending rout of his infantry:

Our Collonel (Gell) quitt his horse, and went to the foote, being then in great feare and disorder, many of them readie to rune, and standing with their pykes advanced; the Collonel, with his owne hands, put down theyre pykes, encouraged both them and the musquetyers, who were all disorderly crowded together; he speedily gott them into order and gave the enemie such a vollie of shott upon theyre chardge, that they first wheeled, and much discouraged by the death of the Earle of Northampton and Captaine Middleton, with dyvers other gentlemen and officers, they all presently fledd.

This Roundhead account of the battle is apparently a little wide of the truth. After being unhorsed, the Earl of Northampton was indeed killed by a halberd blow to his head while he was fighting on foot. The Royalist cavalry charge did however succeed in capturing all of Gell's artillery. That evening Gell refused to return Northampton's body unless the parliamentary cannons were returned to him in exchange. The Cavaliers declined to accept the deal, since cannons were more important than an earl's corpse, but the incident did add to Gell's reputation for lack of chivalry.

After the war Gell ended up in a quarrel with Parliament over his remuneration. His many enemies from the days of the Civil War (including Major Sanders who had regularly rebelled against his command) accused him of embezzlement and tried to have him impeached. That resulted in him changing his loyalties to supporting the royalists, being convicted of treason and being sent to the Tower for life on 27th September 1650. However he was released in 1652 and pardoned the following year. He died in 1671.

The Earl of Devonshire's son, Charles Cavendish, was killed in battle fighting for the Cavaliers near Gainsborough on 28th July 1643 after he had been unhorsed. His body was pickled in a barrel of brandy before it could be buried in the family vault. In 1657 his mother, Christian Countess of Devonshire built a chapel at Peak Forest in his memory. It was dedicated to St Charles, King and Martyr. A window in the present church (rebuilt in 1876-1877) shows the King beside a crown, an execution block and an axe.

Cavaliers and Roundheads had a brief skirmish on Hartington Moor, leaving behind lead pistol bullets and the corpse of a Royalist leader called William de Rossington of Rowsley. He was killed in the fighting but was wanted by the Parliamentarians dead or alive. His lover was determined to deny the Roundheads their prize and when night fell after the skirmish, she secretly buried his body close to where she lived in woodland near Cressbrook. His remains were discovered complete with his sword and armour two centuries later.

In the last phase of the Civil War a Scottish Army under the Duke of Hamilton and Sir Marmaduke Langdale marched south to challenge the Parliamentarians but they were resoundingly defeated by Oliver Cromwell and Lambert in a series of engagements near Preston on 17th and 18th August 1648. After the battle the Scots scattered into the Peak District where they received rough treatment from the locals. A group of Scottish soldiers loyal to the King were imprisoned and starved to death in Derwent church and 1500 Scotsmen were rounded up, marched to Chapel-en-le-Frith and locked up for 16 days in the church. Forty-four of them did not come out alive and more died after being released.

After the final victory of the Roundhead armies and the execution of the King in 1649, Parliament ordered that the personal and real estates of the 'Delinquents' and 'Malignants' (Royalist and Catholic supporters) should be seized. Rowland Eyre of Hassop was obliged to forfeit his entire estate which was to be put up for sale. Cunningly however he managed to buy back most of it through nominees at a cost of nearly £15000 by arranging loans and contracts for future sales amongst his neighbours and friends. His troubles were increased in 1655 by the introduction of the 'Decimation Tax', a 10% tax on the value of estates imposed on all who had fought for Charles I. His resulting tax bill for 1655, 1656 and 1657 came to £178-19-10½. Despite their cunning ruses to avoid losing their estates, the Eyres appear to have lost most of their property by 1715. During the first Jacobite rebellion that year lists were drawn up of all papist landowners and the value of their estates. The Eyres were valued then at a mere £1115. A close watch was kept on them again during the 1745 Rebellion when their arms and horses at Hassop were seized and they were effectively confined to the house.

One of the beneficiaries of Rowland Eyre's misfortune was William Bagshawe of Litton (1598-1669) who was a small farmer made rich by revenues from lead mining. His personal estate in 1662 was said to be £5000. He bought part of Rowland Eyre's forfeited estate in Tideswell in 1652, secured the Earl of Newcastle's forfeited estate at Hucklow for £2400 in 1657 and finally the Ford Hall estate at Chapel for £1300 in 1662 which the family occupied for the next three centuries.

On 25th March 1655 Rowland Eyre was also forced to lease his property at Hargate Wall:

Counterpart of Lease for 24 years.
1) Rowland Eyre of Hassop, esq., and Thomas Eyre, his son, to
2) Humphrey Wilson of Hardewickwall, yeoman
'All that theire messuage – in Hardwickwall afforesaid containinge by estimation 14 acres, be it more or less Together with a dwelling house and other buildings uppon the same now in the tenure and occupation of the said Humphrey Wilson
Consideration : £17.14.0
Rent :   £8.17.0 per annum
att the hannuntiation of the Virgin Mary and St Michall Marck Angell
And a fatt Goose at Christmas and also the keepinge of a Spaniell yearly during the sd. terme.[154]

This lease of Hargate Hall may well have been another device used by Rowland Eyre to hide the true value of his estate after Parliament had ordered it to be sold 6 years earlier. It may also have been a means of avoiding the Decimation Tax which was imposed in the year that the lease was drawn up. When converted to currency values in 2000, the consideration of £17.14.0 would have amounted to about £1330 in today's terms and the rent of £8.17.0 equates to about £670 per year. The fat goose at Christmas and the keeping of a spaniel for the owner were small but pleasant bonuses and a reasonable means of tax avoidance in the face of otherwise horrendous pressure from a victorious and vindictive Parliament.

These then were among the dire consequences of a terrible Civil War which had divided the whole country and affected every parish in the land including our own.

---

[154] Manuscript note in the handwriting of Margaret Mackenzie of 3 Summerfield, Ashdell Road, Broomhill, Sheffield.10 – a local history enthusiast with whom my mother corresponded in 1966.

AFTER THE RESTORATION

The Restoration and coronation of King Charles II in 1660 were widely welcomed throughout the country. 'All over the country the maypoles were set up again, loyal toasts were drunk immediately, Puritanism was repudiated and derided.' Even today this event is commemorated on 29th May (Garland Day/Oak Apple Day/ Royal Oak Day) in the village of Castleton. A procession of Morris dancers led by the 'King' on horseback, hidden beneath a 'garland' of flowers and followed on horseback by his Lady (both in Stuart costume), parade through the village to the market place, where the Garland is lifted off the King's shoulders and hauled up to the top of the church tower. This has happened every year since the Restoration.

The expropriation of the Eyres' Derbyshire estates continued as the penalty for their support of Charles I in the Civil Wars. Ownership of the manor of Wormhill passed from the Eyres and the Earl of Newburgh[155] to the Bagshawe family. The Bagshawes had owned some property in the village since at least the 15th century but Adam Bagshawe (1646-1724) was the first of the family to own the Hall and the manorial rights. Adam was the eighth child of William Bagshawe of Litton (1598-1669; 6 sons and two daughters by two wives). Some accounts claim that the Bagshawes acquired Wormhill Hall in 1646 but this is questionable because Adam was only born in that year and 1646 was in the midst of the Civil War. The Eyres were not obliged to sell off their estates before the anti-Royalist act of Parliament in 1649. Furthermore Adam Bagshawe is listed on the 1670 Hearth Tax return for Wormhill Hall (4 hearths)[156] when he would have been 24 years old but there is no record of him on the earlier return in 1662.

A house containing 4 hearths in 1670 would have been considerably smaller than the present building, even though it had more hearths than any other in the village at that time. What is beyond question is that Adam Bagshawe rebuilt Wormhill Hall in 1697 (colour plate 15). This date and his initials B AA appear on many of the lead downpipes of the present Hall. Adam would have been the first resident lord of the manor since the demise of the Wormhill branch of the Foljambes 300 years previously. It was a brave decision to rebuild in that year. Thomas Beverley, a self-professed prophet, had forecast that the world would come to an end in 1697. When he was pressed for an explanation in 1698, he

---

[155] A title inherited by the Eyres.
[156] Four other Bagshawes – George, Henry, Nicholas and Robert – were listed in the 1670 Hearth Tax Return for Wormhill with one hearth each.

explained that it had in fact happened but somehow no-one had noticed!

Wormhill Hall in the early 1900s

The Bagshawe family have a long history in the parish and the local area. They were resident at Ridge Hall near Chapel-en-le-Frith as early as 1141 and 12 generations of the family lived there in succession until the 18th century. The name of Bagshawe appears on an Inquisition held at Wormhill in 1318 by which time they had been hereditary foresters in fee since the reign of Edward I (1272-1307) and held the manor of Abney on that account. They owned some land in Wormhill since at least the time of Nicholas Bagshawe who married Alicia Hall of Hucklow in 1449. Roger Foljambe, the last of the Foljambe dynasty at Tideswell, had died in 1447 without a male heir and some of the Foljambe property in Tideswell, Hucklow and Wormhill was dispersed shortly thereafter. Nicholas Bagshawe is thought to have acquired some of the Wormhill property at this time. His great grandson Edward Bagshawe of Wormhill, Abney and Hucklow married Elizabeth Greatorex of Great Rocks and Edward's son Nicholas married another Wormhill girl called Isabell Benbridge. The initials WB 1637 RB[157] appear above a farm-house door lintel at Wormhill Hill.

The name Bagshawe is thought by some to mean 'a small wooded glen' whilst others ascribe its origin to the word 'Baggensaw' meaning a 'badger copse'. Other parts of the extended family lived at Abney, The Ridge, Ford Hall, Hucklow, Litton, Bagshaw, Bakewell, Farewell near Lichfield and Castle Bagshaw County Cavan at various times from the 14th to the 18th centuries.

---

[157] Perhaps Adam's father William and uncle Robert Bagshawe. In 1637 William was living at Litton but his brother Robert was listed on the 1670 Hearth Tax Return as a resident of Wormhill and they may have been joint owners of the property.

Adam's eldest brother William Bagshawe (1628-1702), was the famous Apostle of the Peak. He was born at Litton Hall and, as the first born son, infuriated his father by insisting on going into the Church rather than running the family estates. William preached his first sermon in Wormhill in the midst of the Civil War in 1646 at the age of 18 after completing his studies at Cambridge University and remained in the village for 3 months. Following the second Act of Uniformity in 1662 about 1700 clergy including William were ejected from the Church of England and many were imprisoned and persecuted during the reigns of Charles II and James II. Much of the religious argument revolved around the enforced adoption of the newly introduced Book of Common Prayer and the doctrinal authority of the King over that of the bishops and clergy. William abandoned his church at Glossop and became a dissident and underground preacher, travelling the district on horseback to preach in disguise. He was reinstated after the 1689 Act of Toleration and continued to live in the family home at Ford Hall. His will dated 15th October 1701 stipulated that the proceeds of his property in Wormhill should go to charity:

As for my worldly goods I dispose thereof as follows: Seeing that justice is everyone's due I desire that my debts and heriots[158] be paid; item, seeing that our charity should in some sort outlive us, I charge as a rent charge on those closes, enclosures and fields, lying within the precincts of Wormhill, now in the tenure of the children of Thomas Alsopp or Edward Torr as their guardian, the sum of fifty shillings yearly or year after year for ever to be paid out in pious and charitable purposes; to wit five shillings yearly for the poor of Litton where I first breathed, five shillings for the poor at or near Glossop and Chalsworth[159] where I most exercised my most public ministry.

Another Bagshawe ancestor had written tracts against the Anglican hierarchy, was imprisoned in the Tower and died in Paris. Another was the famous puritan MP for Southwark. One took part in the puritan march to Naseby and was mortally wounded at Tutbury; and another fought with the Cavaliers at Oxford during the Civil War – a further example of how the Civil Wars divided not just neighbours but even members of the same family.

In 1732 Richard Bagshawe (the younger) married and lived at Wormhill Hall. Both he and his father were Deputy Lieutenants for the county during Bonnie Prince Charlie's 1745 Rebellion and contributed towards the £6000 raised for the local militia which disgraced themselves by fleeing at Derby at the first sight of the Scottish Army. Richard's more lasting contribution to the village came from his extensive tree-planting schemes around the Hall and along the avenue which runs up the hill.

---

[158]   Feudal dues paid to the lord of the manor on the death of a tenant.
[159]   Charlesworth.

In the same century Colonel Samuel Bagshawe[160] (1713-1762) of Ford Hall had a distinguished military career, losing a leg from cannon fire in Brittany in 1746, serving in India from 1754-1756 where he lost the sight of an eye, and thereafter in Ireland, retiring on grounds of ill health on the point of being promoted Major General.

The family owned the living of St Margaret's Church in Wormhill and provided a succession of local curates[161]. One of them, Rev William Bagshawe of Banner Cross[162] and Ford (born 6 Jan 1763) took up the curacy of Wormhill and purveyed an austere form of Puritanism, disapproving even of the local children playing football. In his diary for 3rd February 1794 is the following entry :

Preached at Wormhill on the vanity of human pursuits and human pleasures – to a polite audience an affecting sermon. Rode in the evening to Castleton, where I read three discourses by Secker. In the Forest[163] I was sorry to observe a party of boys playing at football. I spoke to them but was laughed at, and on my departure one of the boys gave the ball a wonderful kick – a proof of the degeneracy of human nature.

Moving on to the 19th century, one of the Bagshawe owners of Wormhill[164] became embroiled with poachers on the river in Chee Dale on the night of 19th July 1854 and was murdered at the scene. The squire had become fed up with the constant poaching of the river and laid a trap with his keepers and workmen. In the ensuing punch-up two guns were discharged by the poachers and the squire was hit, dying the following day. Seven men were later charged but acquitted of murder. The judge's[165] verdict was that the men were not just resisting arrest but a savage attack and were within their rights to retaliate. One of the men, Benjamin Milner aged 33 and a fearsome character known as 'Big Ben' was described as 'a man not soon to be forgotten'.[166] The judge's reputation was savaged by local landowners after this verdict and he never again took a case in the county. The seven acquitted poachers however were greeted as heroes on their return to Tideswell and paraded through the streets behind the band.

It seems probable that, either when the Eyres sold the manor around 1670 or soon thereafter as part of their punishment for backing the wrong side in the Civil Wars, Hargate Wall was also sold separately (possibly to the Hague family).

---

[160] Colonel of the 93rd Regiment, MP for Waterford, buried at Chapel 22 Sep 1762.
[161] As the incumbents of an outlying chapel in the parish of Tideswell, they were known as 'curates' and did not become 'vicars' until Wormhill became an independent parish.
[162] In the Eccleshall District of Sheffield.
[163] Peak Forest village.
[164] W L G Bagshawe.
[165] Judge Maule.
[166] From 'All about Derbyshire' by Edward Bradbury 1884.

Certainly the deeds of Hargate Hall in the Sheffield Central Library indicate that ownership of Hargate Wall started to pass through different families from the end of the 17th century.[167]

The Haywards were one family who owned land at Hargate and Tunstead, including the cottage where James Brindley was born. Henry Hayward and 'Widow Hayward' are both listed in the 1670 Hearth Tax Return for the village with one hearth each. They were Royalist supporters in the Civil War and almost certainly Roman Catholics and recusants. Henry Hayward had been the Quartermaster in Rowland Eyre's cavalry regiment and was punished as a 'delinquent' in 1650. This is almost certainly the origin of the name Hayward Farm. There are records of the family farming at Hargate through to 1881 which indicate an association with Hargate lasting at least 200 years. In mediaeval times the 'hayward' was the man responsible for guarding the hay on communal meadowland. He had to ensure that the fences were kept intact during the hay-growing season and that cattle did not get into the grass. Meadowland was there-fore enclosed from 1st February to 1st August or whenever the hay crop had been harvested and it was then opened up for communal grazing. This was un-doubtedly the origin of this 17th century family surname. The lane running past Hayward Farmhouse and down to Cow Lane was a public footpath or highway even in the 17th century. Several farmers owned fields to which they gained access from the Cow Lane, including Town Meadow which belonged at one stage to the owners of Elm Tree House in the village. The lane is shown as Town Gate on the 1822 Enclosure plan, indicating that it was the access for the Town Field.[168]

Hayward Farm

[167] According to Margaret Mackenzie.
[168] Town Fields were invariably arable.

The prevailing circumstances in the country at the end of the 17th century were far from prosperous and Derbyshire was amongst the least favoured parts of it. Gregory King's *State and Condition of England and Wales* published in 1696 estimated the total population at 5,500,000 (the total population of the United Kingdom in 2002 was 60,000,000), of which 1,400,000 were urban and 4,100,000 were rural inhabitants. The total area used for agriculture was 39 million acres, of which 11 million were arable and 10 million meadow or pasture. The total livestock in England and Wales amounted to 600,000 horses, 4½ million cattle, 11 million sheep and 2 million pigs. The 7 poorest counties were Cheshire, Derbyshire, Yorkshire, Lancashire, Northumberland, Durham and Cumberland. Average annual incomes were quoted as follows:

40,000 freeholders of the better sort	*£84-0-0*
140,000 freeholders of the lesser sort	*£50-0-0*
150,000 farmers	*£44-0-0*
364,000 labouring people and out-servants	*£15-0-0*
400,000 cottagers and paupers	*£6-10-0*

So poverty was endemic in the North of England at the end of the 17th century and took time to eradicate after the trauma and destruction of the Civil and other external Wars. As an example of what a farm in the village in 1676 might have been like, we get some idea from Robert Maples of Barlborough who described a typical small mixed farm in the High Peak:

'Six horses and mares, 6 oxen, 5 cows, a heifer, a bullock, 6 calves, a bull, 25 sheep, 10 pigs. Crops of wheat, barley, peas, oats and hay. Three ploughs, 3 harrows and assorted farm carts, implements, saddlery and other gear were on the farm.'

National wealth and revenue had been exhausted by the wars and had to be restored by new forms of taxation which would have added to people's real and perceived sense of poverty. In 1670 there is a comprehensive record of all the householders of Wormhill paying the 2 shillings a year Hearth Tax[169] which had been granted to King Charles II by Act of Parliament in 1662. The tax required all the hearths and entries (external doors) to be recorded. The return for Wormhill in 1662 listed 82 hearths and 70 entries. However people quickly got wise to this and reduced the number of fireplaces and doors to reduce the tax, so that by the time the same return was recorded for 1670, Wormhill had mysteriously reduced in the space of 8 years to 67 hearths and 54 entries! The Hearth Tax came to an end with the revolution of 1688 and was abolished by William III in 1689. In due course it

---

[169]   Based on the number of fireplaces in a dwelling.

was followed by the equally unpopular Window Tax under which householders had to pay tax according to the number of windows in their homes. In some cases people walled up some of their windows rather than pay excessive taxes. Clearly local taxes were as unpopular then as they have remained!

Even more unpopular must have been the periodic extra taxes needed to fund the nation's wars. A tax assessment drawn up on 20th March 1695 as a one-off levy in support of funding the war with France, raising 4 shillings in the £ for one year, shows that a total of £22-2-6 was raised in the village for this purpose. Thomas Eyre was taxed £2-0-0, Rowland Eyre £0-7-6, Charles Heaward (No 4 Cottage Hargate Wall) £0-4-2 and Humphrey Thornhill (Dakins Farm at Hargate Wall) £0-1-10.

The Church Register at Wormhill started in 1674 under the direction of the Bagshawes who provided a number of the parish curates and vicars over the next 200 years. The first Register was kept by Nicholas Bagshawe who describes himself at the beginning of the first volume as 'clerke and schoole master for want of a better'! The Bagshawes have since remained the owners of Wormhill Hall for over 300 years. From the end of the 17th century therefore we have, for the first time, an almost comprehensive (though sometimes barely legible) record of all baptisms, weddings and burials in the village and thereafter it is possible to deduce much useful data about individual families, life expectancy and birth and mortality rates.

By the late 17th century travel from Derbyshire to London by horse took four days. The first night would be spent at Nottingham, the second at Market Harborough, the third at Dunstable, arriving in London on the evening of the fourth day. The condition of the roads was so bad that they were often impassable from November through to April. Not that this would have worried most of the inhabitants of Wormhill because few would have had any reason to travel outside the district in their lives and few could have afforded to do so even if they had wished to.

Their diet would also have been different from today. In 1693 it was noted that oatcakes were the form of bread on which the northern part of the county relied. Oats were easier to grow at the higher elevations of the Peak District than wheat which is the more usual ingredient of white bread. Quarrymen were said to survive on a diet of oatcake and cheese. Oatcakes are still a Peak District speciality and are made by some of the local butchers (*colour plate 16*).

Medicine would still have been primitive by modern standards and such doctors who carried out their trade in the local area would have relied on bleeding and other useless herbal cures, some of which undoubtedly worsened rather than improved their patients' condition. Protection against disease and epidemics would have been equally rudimentary. Major epidemics like the plague had not been seen since the 14th century but it was to recur in a particularly harrowing way in a nearby village. It arrived in Eyam, supposedly in linen sent up from London. The epidemic lasted from September 1665 to November 1666. The village went into voluntary isolation and quarantine for 12 months, during which time a quarter of the population (259 people in all) died. Food was brought from other villages and left at outlying places, one being a little brook to the north of the village. This is known as Mompesson's Well in memory of the vicar who sustained the inhabitants during their ordeal. Mompesson, who was only 28 years old and recently arrived in the parish in 1664, decided to co-operate with his dispossessed and staunchly Puritan predecessor Thomas Stanley. They set aside their religious differences and, after an initial meeting in the rectory, came up with the idea of quarantining the village. They then had to sell the idea to the villagers but, by presenting a united religious and moral front, they succeeded in persuading the community to accept their plan. They agreed that there would be no more organised funerals or burials. Instead people were encouraged to bury their dead in their gardens or the surrounding fields in an attempt to restrict the spread of the disease. A cordon sanitaire would be imposed round the village boundary to halt the spread of infection to the outside world. And the church would be locked until the epidemic had passed. Church services were held instead in the open air at Cucklet Delph, a natural limestone amphitheatre just below the village, where a commemorative service continues to be held on the last Sunday of August every year.

Memories of the Plague are preserved in the children's nursery rhyme :

Ring-a-ring o' roses
(the purple rash or 'macula' which appeared on the chest of plague victims)
A pocket full o' posies
(pomanders or nosegays of sweet-smelling herbs and spices which were carried by women because they were thought to prevent the inhalation of the plague spores)
Atishoo! Atishoo!
(the first symptoms of the disease)
We all fall down
(and then we all die)

The ravages of diseases like the plague are hardly surprising when we consider the poor understanding of the principles of hygiene, the absence of any form of immunisation and the relative ease with which contagious disease would have spread. Even in the better houses set aside for visitors and travellers the standards were pretty basic. Celia Fiennes, in her journal of travels through the Peak District in 1697, lamented the poor state of accommodation in Buxton in the days before the building of hotels for the visitors to the spa.

The house that's call'd Buxton Hall which belongs to the Duke of Devonshire is where the warme Bath is and Well, its the largest house in the place tho' not very good, they are all entertaining houses and its by way of an Ordinary, so much a piece for your dinners and suppers and so much for our Servants besides; all your ale and wine is to be paid besides, the beer they allow at the meales is so bad that very little can be dranke, you pay not for your bed room and truly the other is so unreasonable a price and the Lodgings so bad, 2 beds in a room, some 3 beds and some 4 in one roome, so that if you have not Company enough of your own to fill a room they will be ready to put others in the same chamber, and sometimes they are so crowded that three must lye in a bed; few people stay above two or three nights it's so inconvenient: we staid two nights by reason one of our Company was ill but it was sore against our wills, for there is no peace nor quiet with one Company and another going into the Bath or coming out; that makes so many strive to be in this house because the Bath is in it.

So, at the dawn of the 18th century, life in our village was hard; incomes were low and taxation was high; some diseases were rife and most were incurable; some families had suffered from divided loyalties in the course of a protracted civil war which had killed over 11% of the male population of the country and impoverished those who remained. Other families had suffered forced confiscation of property because they had ended up on the losing side and other families still had benefited by buying up the property of the dispossessed. The next century was to bring a welcome change and a return to prosperity.

The Industrial Revolution

James Brindley, who became a nationally famous engineer and designer of canals, was born in the parish at Tunstead in 1716. He and his family lived here until 1726 and James would have received some early education from the local vicar who doubled as schoolmaster. He is said to have worked for a time (even before the age of 10) at Old Hall Farm leading the horses drawing grain carts to the corn mills and to have been inspired by his visits to the local mills at Blackwell and Millers Dale. It has sometimes been claimed that Brindley was illiterate – 'he could not read and wrote only with difficulty' – and it is said that he carried the designs of his canals and mills in his  head rather than on paper, often retiring to his bed to think the problems through. Difficult though this may be to believe, it was a common feature of the age that the greatest engineers, including his friend the great Josiah Wedgwood who left school at the age of 9, learned more by their apprenticeships and trial and error than by study. In 1726 the Brindley family moved to Lowe Hill Farm near Leek where his father was described as a yeoman or small land-owner. At the age of 17 James apprenticed himself to a mill-wright at Sutton near Macclesfield and set up on his own as a mill-wright in 1742. His greatest achievements in canal design and construction ran from 1759 through to his premature death from pneumonia complicated by diabetes on 27th September 1772. He stayed at the spa in Buxton for 2 weeks in August 1767 in an attempt to cure his illness but diabetes was un-diagnosed and untreatable at that time. He was also so mobbed by his fellow patients who desperately wanted to engage the famous Canal Engineer in conversation that he went home early, feeling that he might have been better off resting at home.

Brindley married Anne Henshall in December 1765 when he was 49 and his bride was a mere 19. They had two daughters – Susannah who later married and emigrated to Australia and Anne who remained a spinster. At the time of

Brindley's death, his wife was only 26. Three years later she remarried and went on to produce another 7 children.

James Brindley is commemorated by the well in Wormhill village, (*colour plate 17*) built in 1875, where the annual Well Dressing takes place in August and by a plaque set into a stone at his birthplace at Tunstead. The original cottage is long since demolished but the plaque reads:

James Brindley
1716-1772
Mill-Wright and Civil Engineer
Here stood the cottage in which James Brindley was born
Of humble birth, he became famous as the pioneer builder
Of the great canals of England

The Brindley Stone at Tunstead

In addition to being a surveyor and builder of canals he was also famous for the construction of watermills and steam engines. The principal canals for which he was responsible were: The Bridgewater Canal, The Trent and Mersey, the Coventry Canal, the Droitwich Canal, the Birmingham Canal, the Leeds and Liverpool, the Oxford Canal and the Chesterfield Canal. Some of these were colossal construction projects which Brindley did not live to see completed. The Trent and Mersey Canal, for example, when finished in 1777 included 76 locks, 5 tunnels, 160 aqueducts and 213 bridges.

The advent of Brindley's canals revolutionised the transport of lead and coal and vastly expanded the scope and pace of the Industrial Revolution. Economic acceleration led, within 25 years, to a trebling of the population of the Staffordshire Potteries which many of the canals served. The Duke of Bridgewater commissioned Brindley to build a canal from his estate at Worsley to Manchester and was able to reduce the cost of coal carried on this new route to a quarter of its former level. This particular canal was all the more notable for its revolutionary achievement of carrying the canal over the river Irwell by means of an aqueduct. The proposal was at first ridiculed but it was a success and became one of the sights of the time. Arthur Young wrote in 1768:

'The effect of coming at once onto Barton Bridge, and looking down upon a large river, hung in the air, with barges sailing upon it, form altogether a scenery somewhat like enchantment. The numbers of foreigners who have visited the Duke of Bridgewater's present navigation is surprising.'

Caldon Canal near Leek, surveyed by Brindley but not completed before his death

The Scottish author Thomas Carlyle (1795-1881) wrote of Brindley: *'The English are a dumb people. They can do great acts but not describe them. Whatever of strength the man had in him will be written in the work he does. The rugged Brindley had little to say for himself. He has chained seas together. His ships do visibly float over valleys, and invisibly through the hearts of mountains; the Mersey and the Thames, the Humber and the Severn have shaken hands.'*

A more recent author, Chrichton Porteous, has ascribed these qualities to the climate of the Peak District:

'The climate induces a certain hardiness, a self-reliance, which is the essence of endeavour ... Not only do conditions draw out fine qualities of men now;

through the ages these conditions have operated. Here men continually have fought and won or failed, and the evidence of this fighting remains more prolifically than anywhere else that I know.'

The same author quotes an example of typical Derbyshire earthy and pragmatic humour: Children in a farming district, after being told the parable of the lost sheep, were asked why the shepherd who after all still had 99 sheep was so concerned by the one that was lost. A farmer's son answered 'Appen it were th'tup' (Perhaps it was the ram)!

Other types of communication and travel were also transformed in the course of the 18th century, not least the road network. The road from Buxton to Manchester was turnpiked in 1724, followed in 1749 by the Buxton to Ashbourne road. Tolls were collected at tollhouses, with a toll bar placed across the road. The turnpikes progressively improved the quality of the roads and hence the relative speed of travel. In 1742 the travelling time from Derbyshire to London had been reduced from 4 days to 3; and by 1760 to one day.

Nevertheless the new roads were not necessarily of the highest quality. In the days before the development of the spa by the Dukes of Devonshire, not all of the visitors from London found their trips to Buxton to their liking. In July 1755 an anonymous London gentleman and his companion rashly travelled to Buxton in a light carriage called a post chaise. They found the roads hazardous for their light vehicle and better suited to 'the vast number of pack horses travelling over the hills of which we counted 60 in a drove'. Their chaise was damaged on three occasions, on the last of which they lost four spokes on one wheel. Once at Buxton, they were not impressed by the town's amenities:

The walks are adjoining the well and are contained in a field of about an acre, almost circular; bounded on one side by a pretty river; on the other by the afore-said dirty lane; the walks are not of grass or gravel, but of pure natural earth, strew'd over with fine ashes to prevent the soil from sticking to the ladies' shoes; on the side next the river stands a large temple, dedicated to the goddess Aoacina; in the middle a mount is cast up and planted with trees and shrubs; and to enliven the scene, a number of tame rabbits run scuttling about, hiding themselves among bushes and nettles, to the high amusement and entertainment of the company. Finding but few ladies on the walks (six or eight at most), we returned back to our inn, disappointed in our expectation of finding Buxton a grand and brilliant place.

By 1760 the road[170] running above Hargate and down the dale to Tideswell was

---

[170] Noted as a 'new road' in 1758.

one of the main turnpikes in the county, linking Macclesfield, Buxton, Tideswell and Sheffield, with a toll-bar at Fairfield. Stage-coaches operated every second day on this route. The houses at Hill Green acted as a staging post where horses would be exchanged and additional horses[171] provided to haul coaches out of the Dale in both directions. The lane from Hill Green via the dale to Tideswell had a rough stone base and was only converted into a tarmac-surfaced road in the 1960s. There was an old turnpike milestone on the south side of the road beside Hargate Hall which is now damaged but which originally showed the distance to Buxton and Sheffield. There was originally another turnpike milestone in the bottom of the Dale but this had 'disappeared' before the end of the 18th century.

Before 1758 there had been only an old packhorse 'green' road[172] running from Green Fairfield via Great Rocks Dale[173] to Tunstead to Hargate Wall and then Tideswell, ie a track suitable for individual horses and packhorse trains but not for coaches and carriages. The packhorse road came up the slope from Tunstead to the Wind Low tumulus, down past Haywards to Hargate Wall and across Dakins farm to join Tideswell Lane at what is now the first right-angled corner. The road across the top of Hargate and Hill Green, cutting out the detour to Hargate Wall, was only made when the track was turnpiked. Other local roads, known as 'prime-ways', would have been no more than rough lanes used by farmers' ox-carts. The splayed

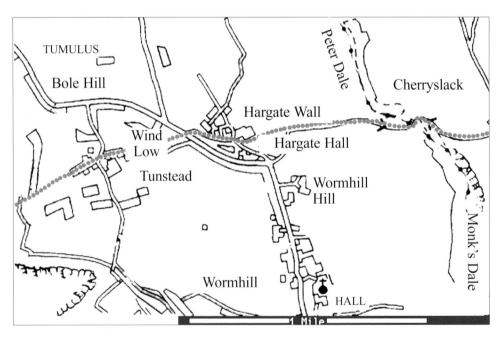

Line of the original Packhorse 'Green' Road running east to west in grey

---

[171] Known as 'cock horses'.
[172] Now a mere public footpath.
[173] Now the Tarmac Quarry.

hooves of oxen gained more traction and caused less surface damage to muddy lanes than the solid hooves of horses.

The packhorse road was one of the 'saltways' on which salt from Cheshire was transported by packhorse to the Eastern counties. Salt was a vital commodity for the preservation of meat in the days before refrigeration. Part of a Roman soldier's pay was in the form of a salt (salis) allowance. This was his salarium from which the modern word salary is derived. On the return journeys the packhorses carried wool and malt from Nottingham or Derby to Manchester. Where the road crossed the valley south of Tideswell used to be known as Saltersford. When it was upgraded by the 1758 Turnpike Trust under the auspices of Mr William Fairbank of Sheffield, there was a preference for re-routeing the road from Buxton to Smalldale, Dale Head, Wheston to Tideswell in order to avoid the steep climbs out of Monks Dale but there was a 'nimby' at Wheston who vetoed this – Mr Farey, writing in 1817, noted:

The tremendous descents into Monksdale valley and others scarcely less formidable, in the road between Tideswell and Buxton, might have been avoided and a very good line of road adopted by passing through the village of Wheston, by Dale-head and Small-dale, but for the opposition of a Mr Robert Freeman, who then resided at Wheston, and did not like a turnpike road through his village. Egregious folly this, very common in the last age.

The switchback ride up Summer Cross, through Monks Dale and Great Rocks Dale was a matter of some alarm to passengers. The Rev Richard Warner, travelling on it in 1801, described it as 'hard as adamant and smooth as a bowling green'. Even a century later Firth in his *Highways and Byways in Derbyshire* of 1920 describes the descent from Tideswell into Monks Dale as a cause of considerable consternation:

Then suddenly the road makes a surprising and extraordinary swoop, a break-neck fall into a ravine which must have caused the 'outsiders'[174] on the coaches to hold their breath as they slithered down. Everything was done to ease the descent but little was possible, for here is a sinuous cleft in the limestone running up out of Millers Dale to Peak Forest.

A diversion was finally made in 1812 by turnpiking the road down Tideswell Dale via Millers Dale to Blackwell Dale to link up with the 1810 turnpike from Ashford via Taddington to Buxton (the modern day A6). A toll gate was set up on the south side of the bridge at Millers Dale. The stagecoach operators found the diversion to be a better route and the Monks Dale road was soon neglected after

---

[174] The coachmen and brakemen who rode on the outside of the stagecoach.

54 years of use, reverting to a parish responsibility and hence progressive deterioration.

With the arrival of more and better turnpiked roads the stage coach companies started to offer faster long distance travel. One 1788 timetable shows a stage coach leaving London at 5am, stopping at Northampton for breakfast (20 minutes), arriving at Derby by 6pm and at Manchester by 11.30pm. A journey which routinely took 4 days a century earlier now took $18^{1}/_{2}$ hours. Stage coaches remained the preferred means of long distance travel through to about 1858 when they were quickly superseded by the railways.

Despite these improvements to the infrastructure of the country which were a necessary precursor to the Industrial Revolution, peace and stability on the political front were far from universal. The Jacobite Pretenders to the English throne, now exiled to France and Scotland, had not given up their claims. In 1745 Bonny Prince Charlie's Jacobite Army marched from Scotland into Lancashire and for a time there were fears that they would invade Derbyshire on the new turnpike road from Manchester via Buxton to Derby. Two regiments of militia were hastily raised by the Duke of Devonshire and Lord Curzon. One of them was sent in haste to dig ditches and other obstacles on the road at Whaley Bridge. But in the event the Scottish Army diverted south via Macclesfield and Leek before entering Ashbourne on December 3rd and Derby on December 4th. The march to London to reclaim the throne for James III was known as the '45 Rebellion'.

The county militia were notoriously poorly trained, paid and motivated and during the eighteenth century their function was steadily taken over by the first true standing Army that the country had seen. The defending Derbyshire regiments did not acquit themselves well and withdrew on every occasion when the enemy was sighted. On December 4th one regiment panicked and fled to Nottingham when movement was spotted on a nearby hill which later turned out to have been a herd of cows! On December 5th and 6th Lord Pitsligo's Jacobite Regiment of Horse took and guarded Swarskeston Bridge, the only crossing over the Trent between Burton and Nottingham. Prince Charlie went to Calke Abbey to seek the support of Sir Henry Harpur. On failing to enlist his support and learning that the King's army was gathering south of the Trent, Bonny Prince Charlie ordered a retreat back to Scotland, thus ending the Jacobite attempt to regain the throne of England. Bonny Prince Charlie was in fact misled about the size and readiness of the three armies which were gathering to block his path to London and much speculation continues to this day about whether he might have succeeded if he had pressed on. It was in fact a finely balanced judgement. The 3500 Highlanders had hoped to generate a mass uprising as they marched south which would in turn have encouraged the French to invade. In the event some recruits were raised in places like Manchester but nothing like the expected numbers materialised and there were no French rein-forcements, not least because the Royal Navy kept them at bay. By early December the game was up – Bonnie Prince Charlie had over-extended his minute

Highland Army; he had an English army following him up from the north (Cope), another preparing to attack him from his right from Chester and a third forming hastily in London; in total ten times the numbers that he had so far succeeded in mobilising. The spontaneous uprising, on which he had relied, had not happened. The choice was to press on in the hope that it might yet happen or to retire to Scotland in the hope that more favourable circumstances might prevail later. In the event the Highland Army withdrew north, signalling failure of the campaign and losing any chance there might have been of further English and French support. They were slaughtered on the moor at Culloden where the famous Highland Charge proved ineffective against English musketeers who could reload three times per minute. Tactical blunders by the Scots and modern English artillery firing four times a minute added to the carnage.

There is however one story which restores one's faith in human nature. On the return march from Derby one of the Highlanders fell out with a broken ankle. There was of course no means of transporting him back to Scotland with the remainder of the Highland Army and he could have expected little sympathy from the local English. But he was taken in by a Derbyshire farmer at Apesford and, after the bone had set, he was returned to the Highlands with a team of Scottish drovers. Who can tell whether incidents like this made the 1707 Act of Union any more acceptable to the Scottish clans?

From the start of the 1700s the details of the village population are much easier to establish from the parish register in the church, from the advent of censuses and directories and from a number of surviving date stones over the door-ways of houses and farm buildings. Here are some examples from my research of people living at Hargate Wall:

Date stone Lambing Sheds: 1728
                      H
                C : A
(Charles and Alice Heaward)

Date Stone above front door No 4 Hargate Cottages: C H 1734 (Charles Heaward)

In 1747 the parish register records the baptism of Jane, daughter of Job Green and Martha his wife of Hargate Wall. The First Paddock at Hargate Wall Farm is referred to as Job Green's Pingle on some old maps.

Hargate Hall came to John Needham[175] when he married Hannah Hague[176] at Peak Forest on 22 Jan 1760. Hannah came from a yeoman family at Hargate Wall and already lived there. The Needham family had owned Hargate in the 1500s and possibly earlier too, when they had been foresters of the Peak in the Middle Ages, but they had sold the Hall to the Eyres in 1602. John was the youngest son of Robert Needham of Perryfoot, Peak Forest, described as a substantial yeoman and three of his sons were sufficiently ambitious and successful to call themselves 'gentlemen'. John Needham was therefore returning Hargate Hall to its former ownership. His third son John's grave is in Wormhill churchyard – a large stone mausoleum between the church door and the back gate leading to Wormhill Hall. It has the family crest on one side and an almost illegible inscription on the other. It can be seen that John, Olive (his wife), Elizabeth and Alice (their two daughters) are buried there.

Hannah Needham died in 1792. Parson Brown was commissioned to write her epitaph, which was displayed on the walls of Wormhill church. The mural inscription was recorded in the 1920s or 1930s and there is a note to this effect in the Needham Papers in the John Rylands.[177] Parson Brown was a well-known figure in the area and accepted the curacy of Wormhill in 1785 on payment of £45 a year plus a house. He also took on the job of schoolmaster for a further £6 a year. Twenty-three children were on the roll in 1790, including some boarders paying £12-£13 a year. The chapel could not be lit during the winter months; so Parson Brown was confined to delivering 'only one sermon' on Sundays from September through to April! Evensong was off for the winter, perhaps, who knows, to the relief of the parishioners. He became Vicar of Tideswell in 1792.

In 1789 Pilkington's *Directory of Derbyshire* provided a mass of data on the county. For Wormhill he recorded 29 houses in the village, 6 at Hargate Wall, 6 at Dale Head, 13 at Wheston, 9 at Tunstead, 5 at Meadow, 4 at Great Rocks and 6 at Upper End. Amongst the benefits of living at the higher elevations of the High Peak he observed that there were no endemic or epidemic illnesses – 'no agues or fevers are known to prevail here.' Tideswell, described as a small market town, with 254 houses and 1000 inhabitants was four times the size of the village of Buxton with 77 houses and 238 inhabitants, though the population of Buxton was said to be three times as large during the season when visitors came to take advantage of the waters. Lodgings and boarding houses had started to be built in Buxton to accommodate the visitors but the numbers of people taking the waters

---

[175] Born 1 Oct 1736 and died 14 Nov 1772.
[176] Born 1736 and died 1792.
[177] Letter from Margaret Mackenzie to my mother.

was so great that some had to be put up in the surrounding villages.

Pilkington's observations about the customs and manners of the people in the High Peak would have caused outrage amongst the locals if they had been able to read them, which was of course unlikely at the time. A quote from Volume II of his history of Derbyshire is pretty scathing:

Accordingly we find that, in the present century, the people of the High Peak are distinguished from the inhabitants of the south of Derbyshire by the rudeness of their manners. However there are several late circumstances and events, from which we may expect a reformation in this respect. They have now from the introduction of manufactures amongst them a more free intercourse with the world. The company who visit the baths and medicinal waters and examine the other curiosities with which the county abounds must also have some influence upon the minds of those with whom they converse. But there is no circumstance which has an equally powerful tendency to refine their manners as the establishment of Sunday Schools. The effect which these institutions have already produced in some situations is very obvious. As the children of the present generation become better acquainted with their duty, they will improve in their reverence for God and religion, in kindness towards each other, in civility to strangers, and to the practice of modesty and decency. Those who have been much in some of the villages of the Peak must know that the inhabitants are greatly wanting in these good qualities. I have not in any other part of England seen or heard of so many instances of rudeness, indecency and profaneness. But in all those places where Sunday Schools are established a great change has been produced in these respects. From hence we may presume that in the next generation these seminaries of knowledge and virtue will have still greater effect and that in the course of a few years the inhabitants of the Peak of Derbyshire will equal those of other countries in the practice of decorum and civility.

One interesting aspect to emerge from the parish register's records of children born in the 18th century is the high rate of infant mortality. Forty-four per cent of the children recorded here appear to have died before reaching maturity, many of them within the first year of life. Diseases and illness, which today would be easily treated with modern medicine and drugs, then proved to be routinely fatal to young children. The numbers of children born per family tended to be higher than in modern times in order to compensate for the expected losses.

Amongst the forms of entertainment practised at the time, cock-fighting was common with cockpits to be found at many inns. Prize money for the larger inter-county contests could reach 200 guineas and admission tickets were one shilling a day. Bull Baiting at so-called bull-rings was also common. Badger baiting was prevalent, particularly during wakes weeks and there is even a mention of bear baiting near Buxton in 1810.

Bare fist prize fighting also went on until late in the 1800s. One account dated 23rd May 1874 reads:

One morning early this week, a set fight, we understand for money, took place near Harpur Hill. Two men employed, it is stated, at the Lime Works, were pitted against each other, and for half an hour did their best to injure each other. The termination was that one man, the smaller, had – to use a sporting term – 'his peepers closed'

Also written down for the first time were some of the local customs. In James Pilkington's *History of Derbyshire* of 1789 he noted a number of High Peak customs, some of which have persisted through to the present day. At Peak Forest, he wrote, it was customary to invite every family residing in the district to funerals and a cake was given to every individual who came to the house of the deceased. Even today many funerals are followed by a celebratory tea held by the deceased's family for all those who attend the funeral service. Another custom was 'Keeping Wakes' – a week of celebration and entertainment held in the summer months. These usually began on a Sunday in July and continued throughout most if not all of the following week. Cottages were thoroughly cleaned and white-washed inside before the festivities and children and parents bought new clothes. Friends were invited to their neighbours' houses and very expensive provision was made for their entertainment. Some people were said to have contracted such large debts that they were scarcely able to discharge them before the next year's event. Wakes weeks continued in Wormhill through to the 1960s with local sports and selection of a Wakes Queen. A third custom was the establishment of 'Sick Clubs' or 'Friendly Societies' in which people in small communities contributed periodically for their mutual support when they were made incapable by illness of continuing their respective employments. They also provided a lump sum to cover funeral expenses. Friendly and Co-operative Societies, often now incorporated into Building Societies, remain a feature of the Northern way of life.

The first theatre in Buxton was situated in Spring Gardens and was described in 1790 by John Byng as a 'mean, dirty, boarded, thatched house; and can hold but few people'. Byng however was notoriously difficult to please and found fault wherever he travelled[178]. A new theatre was built in the 1830s at the foot of Hall Bank, where in 1833 the famous violinist Paganini played to a packed house. This building was in turn demolished in 1854. Eventually a new theatre next to the Pavilion was opened in 1889, to be followed by the Buxton Opera House in 1903.

There is a curious reference by John Byng (later Lord Torrington), in his traveller's journal of 1790, to grouse round Wormhill: 'Round Wormhill grouse are

---

[178] Accusing the Devonshires of bad taste at Chatsworth and complaining that he could find nowhere in Bakewell to offer him turtle for dinner!

upon the hills, and the grey game (black game) they say within a few miles' but he noted 'they were sometimes wantonly destroyed by firing the heath. In hard weather they descend to feed in the roads, and near the cottages.' The only heath, of which I am aware, used to be some heather on Middle Hill on the Sitch before it was ploughed up for barley in the 1960s. My father is alleged to have shot some grouse there in the 1930s but, otherwise, there are no grouse closer than Combs Moss at Dove Holes. The reference to grouse coming down to feed in built-up areas in hard weather is more plausible. My father recalled grouse from the Buxton Moors coming down to feed in the Pavilion Gardens during a particularly hard spell of winter weather in 1904. But round Wormhill?

John Byng also commented on the fishing in Chee Dale: 'The trout and grayling fishing would be exquisite, if poachers were prevented, who destroy more fish in one night, than an angler could catch in a fortnight.' The stark reason for the prevalence of poaching at the time was that so many agricultural workers were living on the edge of starvation that any game would be a welcome supplement to their meagre food supply.

In other respects the 18th century was a period of unparalleled prosperity for the Peak District and many people would have shared in the bounty. Improved infrastructure and transport, new industrial techniques, exploding demand for minerals, fuel and raw materials, and the advent of entrepreneurs ready to take advantage of the opportunities gave rise to what we now know as the Industrial Revolution. The mineral wealth of North Derbyshire was exploited for the first time to the full. There are extensive accounts of feverish extraction of all sorts of minerals as their value became apparent.

Lead was still one of the most precious commodities and large numbers of prospectors went about staking claims wherever they thought there was a chance of striking a rich seam. Miners were allowed to search for lead on anyone's land without permission from the owner to either dig or transport ore to the nearest road. This was the 18th century equivalent of the California Gold Rush. The prospector had three days to set up a wooden windlass on a square frame known as a 'yoking'. With this up, he had fourteen days in which to find ore and notify the Barmaster that he wanted to register a claim. The Barmaster would send two jurymen to inspect and, if enough ore to fill the standard dish had been found, the miner got a 'freeing note'. He then had the right to make a road to the nearest highway, a right to enough land to deposit his waste, to make a dam or puddle in which to wash ore, a right to timber from the nearest wood to protect the sides of his shaft and to burn and split the rock in order to free the ore. The only stipulation was that, if lead was not found within the first 14 days, the land had to be returned to its previous condition. Once lead was found, the prospectors were allocated a stake known as a Meare[179] which

---

[179] Spelt variously Meer, Meere or Meare.

measured 32 yards of vein. Two meares were given to every miner who discovered a new seam. This chaotic process was governed by the Barmasters who spent much of their time adjudicating on the payment of dues which varied from district to district and sometimes from parish to parish. Barmote courts in the High Peak were held at Monyash. In the local area one tenth of the value of lead extracted was due to the Crown and one tenth to the landowner. Much of the wealth of the Dukes of Devonshire relied on mineral dues.

Lead ore was categorised in different sizes – the largest being called Bing, then Pesey, then Smitham which was small enough to pass through a sieve and finally Belland which was the consistency of flour. Before the ore was sold by the miners it was beaten into small pieces, washed and sifted by women who earned about 6 pence per day for their labour. Smelting by bonfires on bole hills was replaced by hearth furnaces where molten lead trickled out through a small channel into a trough in front of the hearth, was then ladled into moulds and cast into half pig blocks.

Eighteenth Century Smelting House in Stoney Middleton Dale

Around 1740 the cupola furnace was introduced, holding up to a ton of ore and, by passing heat along the enclosed furnace and up a perpendicular chimney, the lead could be smelted without coming into contact with the fuel. The task took 6-9 hours to complete. Eight pigs of lead made a fodder. A fodder is usually said to equate to a ton (2235.2 lbs) but, in the ages before standardisation of weights and measures, usage varied from one part of the country to another. A London fodder weighed 2184 lbs and a Derby fodder weighed 2520 lbs, leading no doubt to endless confusion and argument. Sometimes the lead was rolled into sheets near the furnaces. In the 1780s the High Peak mines produced 2000 tons a year. A major problem surrounding lead mining was the draining of subterranean water from the seams. Large tunnels or soughs were driven through the rock from the veins to the valleys. One of these at Hilcar was 2 miles long and cost £20,266-12s-1d, a fantastic investment at the time.

Extraction of other minerals began with a vengeance in the 18th century. In the 1780s 5600 tons of iron ore per year was mined in the county. Iron ore is found mixed with many other kinds of rock. It gives limestone a reddish tinge, as can be seen in some of the houses in the village.

A slender vein of copper ore was found and worked at Great Rocks Dale in the 1750s. Much more prolific quantities of copper were found on the Duke of Devonshire's land at Ecton Hill near Warslow in Staffordshire and these mines were worked from the early 17th to the late 19th century. Vast profits from the Ecton mines in the 18th century enabled the Dukes to develop the Buxton spa.

Lime was burnt in kilns in the Buxton, Peak Forest and Stoney Middleton districts for use as an agricultural fertiliser but its other and more valuable chemical properties were not discovered or exploited until the following century. The Ordnance Survey map is still dotted with the sites of old lime kilns, of which there were several at Wormhill.

Old Lime Kiln

Black marble was mined, polished and inlaid at Ashford (*colour plate 18*), mottled grey marble at Monyash, spar of various colours at Eyam, fluorspars including Blue John at Castleton, where Mr Robert Hall started a business in 1770 making vases and other ornaments (*colour plate 19*). The largest uncut piece of Blue John weighed nearly 5 cwt and was found in 1813. The largest known Blue John vase, currently at Chatsworth, is 2 feet high and with a diameter of 14½ inches.

Hexagonal quartz crystals found in yellowish red earth near Buxton became known as Buxton diamonds. Chert, a flinty substance mined near Bakewell was used for the manufacture of earthenware.

Chert Mine Bakewell

Coal was mined west of Buxton but was of a low quality and described as 'shattery and exceedingly sulphurous'.

Farming was also thriving in the High Peak at this time. Most farmers raised their rents by grazing and breeding of cattle, which were sold at Manchester and Sheffield markets. At Peak Forest large herds were driven from Cheshire and Yorkshire in the spring, put out to grass and driven back again about the end of October. Small quantities of barley and black oats were cultivated. Two thousand tons of cheese per annum was transported from the county to London and the east coast seaport towns for export.

There were a number of farming improvements which were copied throughout England in the 18th century and Derbyshire was no exception. Arthur Young, a renowned agricultural commentator, was pleasantly surprised by what he found in the Peak District during his visit of 1771:

From Chatsworth to Tideswell the country is nine teenths of it enclosed and cultivated; this surprised me, as I expected to find the chief part of the Peak waste land; but such great improvements have been carried on in this country, that even sheep walks too rocky to plough, let at 5s an acre ... Around Tideswell for many miles, has been worked as great improvements as in any part of England : all this country was but a black ling but a few years ago, and common land. It is now enclosed by act of parliament. As this improvement is very curious, and practised I believe in no other country, I was particular in my enquiries, being very desirous to know the means of effecting such profitable undertakings ... The first work was the inclosure, which was done at the landlord's expence, but no more than the ring fence; the subdivisions were made by the tenants; it is all done by dry walling; the stones taken out of pits ... It lasts 20 years before any repairs are necessary ...

These improvements are also carried on all the way to Castleton, and around that town. In the road from Tideswell by Eldon Hole are very many large closes of good grass gained ... from the moors; all of which are full of very large herds of cows fattening ... and it is very remarkable that the grass is equally good to the tops of the highest mountains. At the summit of Mam Tor, which is the highest mountain in Derbyshire, is an excellent pasture ... All these hills have been improved in the manner above mentioned with lime alone.

Horses were used to transport limestone to the kilns and were said to be smaller and lighter than the breeds in the south of the county in order to cope with the hilly terrain. These were almost certainly the standard Galloway packhorses which could carry up to 240 lb each and were the only means of freight transport until the advent of horse-drawn wagons on turnpiked roads. Until that time proper roads simply did not exist. Rough tracks were poorly maintained by the parish communities with each householder responsible for 4 days road maintenance per annum.[180] Ever since an Act of Parliament in 1555 this applied to every parishioner holding land of an annual value of £50 and 'each person keeping a draught of horses or plough in the parish do provide one wain or cart – with oxen, horses or other cattle – and also two able men'. Predictably this arbitrary system was neither effective nor enforceable and the results were pain-fully endured by those who negotiated the potholes in poorly sprung coaches and carriages. The packhorse trains – usually 20-50 horses in line on the single-track cross-country routes – were owned and controlled by 'Jaggers'. The packhorses were finally consigned to history by the construction first of canals, on which a single horse could tow a barge of 30 tons, and then of the railways in the following century when steam power replaced horse power altogether.

Packhorse train carrying limestone and supervised by jaggers

---

[180] This increased to 6 days per annum in 1563.

Dairy cattle were mostly shorthorns and in the 18th century Derbyshire was responsible for developing the breeding of the Shire Horse. The animal had as its ancestor the old English Black Horse or 'great horse' which, up to the early 1700s, had been kept exclusively for knights and battle. The great horse was a weight-carrier because a knight in full armour was heavy. But in the Civil Wars when armour started to go out of use to be replaced by pistols, muskets and artillery, the warriors began to want lighter horses, and so the great horse was at last allowed to pass to the farmers. It was a lumbering animal and, to improve it, Lord Chesterfield imported 6 mares from Zealand in Denmark. Derbyshire led in the careful breeding from this stock and Leicestershire and other Midland counties followed. The last working Shire horse in Wormhill was worked by Robin Taylor of Old Hall Farm in the 1960s.

Judging shire horses Wormhill Wakes Week early 1900s

The textile industry began in the 1700s with the manufacture of worsted stockings spun on hosiery frames which were let out to cottage workers in the local villages, particularly Litton and Tideswell. The workers obtained the raw materials on Mondays from warehouses in the larger towns like Belper and Derby, to which they returned the finished goods on the following Saturday afternoon. The weekly rent of a hosiery frame in 1780 was 9d; in 1812 one shilling. This cottage industry proved to be a popular way of supplementing the meagre agricultural wage but was soon to be overtaken by the spinning mills.

The mechanisation of the spinning and weaving processes revolutionised these industries and gave the country an overwhelming advantage in productivity which could not be matched elsewhere in the world. In India, for example, a hand-spinner took 50,000 man-hours to process 100 pounds of cotton. In 1780 a Crompton 'mule' did the same job in 2000 hours. In 1790 a 'hundred-spindle mule' took 1000 hours and in 1795 a power-assisted mule took a mere 300 hours.

One of the most notorious of what the poet Blake later called 'those dark satanic mills' was set up by a Wormhill man in 1782. At the age of 22 and 10 years after the death of his father John at the age of 36, Ellis Needham took a lease from Lord Scarsdale of a site on the river Wye at Litton where he built a water spinning mill in partnership with Thomas Frith. This must have been a bold venture for one so young and suffering no doubt from straitened family circumstances after the premature death of his father. During the first 4 years the mill does not appear to have been a success and in 1784 a weir had to be made on the Taddington bank to increase the water pressure. In 1786 Ellis Needham made a determined effort to sell off the mill, advertising it in the Derby Mercury, the Manchester Mercury and the Nottingham Journal. However, with the help of William Newton of Cressbrook Mill, he managed to reorganise Litton and make it into a viable proposition, mainly through the introduction of parish apprentices.

Ellis Needham[181] married Sarah Beard at Duffield on 25 Jan 1787 and lived at Hargate Hall. In the land tax assessments he had 14 acres freehold. Ellis Needham was one of the most unscrupulous mill-owners at the outset of the Industrial Revolution, setting up his water-driven cotton mill at Litton (now restored and converted into flats) with extensive use of child labour at extortionate rates of pay (colour plate 20). Supplies of raw cotton came by canal to Chapel-en-le-Frith and thence by cart to Litton. Cotton mills required large quantities of relatively unskilled labour which could not be satisfied by the local communities. Workers were therefore drafted in from all over the country and particularly from the pauper parishes in London. They were contracted to the mill-owners by a form of indenture which committed the workers to a period of usually 7 years labour before they could be released again to their original communities. Most of them were children, called euphemistically 'apprentices', who started work from the age of 10. They were accommodated either at the workplace or in specially built local hostels. Ellis Needham wanted to establish an apprentices' hostel in the village of Taddington but faced a revolt from the villagers who were not prepared to shoulder the financial burden of supporting so many paupers. He was a dark and unscrupulous character whose ghost my grandmother claimed to have seen standing on the back stairs at Hargate. However my grandmother had a vivid imagination!

Cotton mills sprang up on every river valley in the county after Sir Richard Arkwright had demonstrated the value of water as a source of power at Cromford in 1770. By 1811 there were 120 mills in the county. Conditions in the mills using child labour were undoubtedly horrendous by modern employment standards but they did provide work and a trade of sorts for large numbers of people who would otherwise have endured lives of abject poverty. The fact that London parishes were prepared to export children to the North of England, often for up to 7 years at a

---

[181] Born 21 Sep 1760 at Perryfoot, the first son of John and Hannah Needham, and died Dec 1830.

time, is indicative of the fact that the alternative of leaving children unemployed in the large cities was seen as an even worse fate. Conditions in the mills were often exaggerated by those who were pressing for industrial reforms and their reports probably painted a blacker picture than was actually the case, certainly in the better run mills, of which Cressbrook under the management of Mr Newton was one example. Litton Mill under the regime of Ellis Needham however would appear to have been certainly one of the worst examples of exploitation and cruelty. There are well documented instances of epidemics at the Litton apprentice house and numerous deaths. A large number of Litton apprentices are buried on the north side of Tideswell churchyard, the burial fees at Tideswell being cheaper than at Taddington, the parish to which Litton belonged, though it is said that Ellis deliberately buried apprentices in both churchyards in an attempt to conceal the growing number of deaths.

Ellis occupied a number of influential local positions, being churchwarden for Wormhill from 1806-1812, a steward for the Tideswell Assemblies in 1802 and 1803 and a steward for the Buxton Assemblies in 1808 to 1809. Reports of lavish entertainment at Hargate Wall reached the apprentices who were always eager to pick up gossip about the management.

There were official inspections of Litton Mill by Dr Joshua Denman in 1807 and by Mr Middleton of Leam in 1811 which revealed illegal working conditions. Both visitors confirmed that the mill was clean, though there were suspicions that it had been scrubbed up before the inspections took place. Dr Denman found that the Mill Act of 1802 was largely ignored – there were night shifts which were forbidden by the Act, a working day, the length of which he could not determine, no attempt at instruction and excessive overcrowding in the apprentice house. During the 1811 inspection two apprentices complained of being worked too hard and not having sufficient support. Statements were taken on oath that the working day extended from 5.50 am to 9.10 pm with a dinner break of only half to three quarters of an hour. It was noted that the apprentices' food consisted of water porridge for breakfast and supper and oatcake with treacle or broth for the midday meal.

By 1811 Ellis Needham was in financial difficulties. He had advanced loans to a number of his friends and they had defaulted. He lost £1700 when Joseph Lingard[182] went bankrupt, £30-8-8d when John Baker did likewise, and Molly Baker of the Red Lion Inn at Litton failed to repay a £50 loan. Ellis and his sons took out loans themselves and were unable to repay them. A warrant was served on Ellis and John on 31st January 1815. From the bankruptcy accounts it emerged that Ellis had mortgaged Hargate Hall in 1812 for £10,000 to Mr Fogg. He could not redeem the property and in 1815 the family had to leave the house.

---

[182] Was he a relation of Anthony Lingard who was hanged for murder at Wardlow Mires in 1812?

After Ellis's bankruptcy 80 apprentices were left destitute and had to be supported on parish relief. Ten apprentices died between 1816 and 1818.

Robert Needham, Ellis's fourth son, tried to revive the business and ran the mill for 21 months but there were even more damaging financial failures and magistrates' inquiries. Robert died in December 1816, at which point Lord Scarsdale[183] cancelled the Needhams' lease of Litton Mill and creditors seized the apprentice house. Ellis tried to re-enter the cotton trade but he did not succeed and retired to Chapel-en-le-Frith where the Needham ladies ran a seminary for young women. He died in December 1830 and his estate was valued at a mere £100. Sarah, his wife, died on 3 Nov 1832 and is buried with her husband at Chapel.

A new mill was built at Litton in 1874 after a disastrous fire had razed the building to the ground. Little remains of the original design which was four storeys high, 20 windows long and 4 windows wide. The fire was started by sparks from over-heating of a cog joint which had been insufficiently lubricated with oil. Surplus oil had soaked into the floors of the mill, creating a huge fire hazard and local attempts to quench the flames came to nought. News of the fire was rushed to Buxton on the railway where the volunteer Fire Brigade assembled with their horse-drawn fire engine, reaching Litton only 90 minutes after the outbreak of the fire – a remarkably short response time given that the engine was not on standby, horses had to be gathered from across the town and harnessed, and the road from Buxton was hilly and in poor condition. They were able to save only the office and storeroom with some stock as the main body of the mill was beyond saving. About 300 people lost their jobs as a result, some moving to Cressbrook Mill and others to Stockport. The new mill was in use in 1895 for cotton doubling. This finally closed as a textile mill in 1965.

Water-driven Cotton Mill

[183] The Scarsdales were lords of the manor of Litton until Earl Curzon of Kedleston sold Litton in 1918. Some of the housing at Litton Mill reflects ownership by the family, eg Curzon Terrace.

Mr Middleton reported on conditions at Litton Mill, owned by Ellis Needham, with the story of a boy called John who was Apprentice number 253 there. At any one time there were about 400 children working in the mill as 'apprentices'. John was indentured around 1812 as an apprentice from the age of about 10 to 17, working 3 years at Litton Mill (until Ellis Needham went bankrupt) and four years at Cressbrook Mill before he was released to return to London. His story was first published in the Ashton Chronicle in 1849 and was reprinted in *Dark Satanic Mills* edited by E and R Frow in 1980.

"Ellis Needham, the master, had 5 sons: Frank, Charles, Samuel, Robert and John.[184] These young men, particularly Frank and Charles, used us very cruelly together with a man named Swann, an overlooker. They used to go up and down the mill with hazel sticks, out of the wood, and lay on us most unmercifully. Frank once beat me till he was frightened himself. He thought he had killed me. He had struck me on the temples and knocked me dateless. I was a long time before I came to myself again. Swann had a stick about two feet long with a pin or needle fixed at the end of it, and fastened in with a wax band. This he carried about with him and would come slyly behind us, and run it into the thigh or any other part of the body when we were not thinking about it. He once knocked me down and belaboured me with a thick stick over the head and face, cursing me in the most horrid way. To save my head I raised my arm, which he then bent with all his might. My elbow was broken. I bear the marks, and suffer the pain from it to this day, and always shall as long as I live. The bone was fractured, but never had any notice taken of it. It was very seldom we missed a day without being beaten in the most cruel and wanton manner. Old Needham was as bad as any of the rest; or worse if that was possible. He would sometimes come and begin to beat us as hard as he could, hitting us all over the body, until he seemed quite tired; he would then stop as if he had done, and move off as if he was going away; but he would come back again, and at it again, and move away and come again, time after time. I was determined to let the gentlemen of the Bethnal Green parish know the treatment we had, and I wrote a letter and put it in the Tydeswell post office. It was broken open and given to old Needham. He sent for me down to his house[185] one day at dinner time, together with another boy of the name of John Oats, who was concerned in it along with myself. He beat us with a knob-stick till we could scarcely crawl. Some time after this two or three gentlemen came down from London to make inquiries respecting us. But before we were examined we were washed and cleaned up, and ordered to tell them we liked very well, and were very well treated. Needham and his sons were in the room at the time. They asked us questions about our treatment,

---

[184] In fact he had 7 sons and 3 daughters, though it is possible that Ellis, the third son, and James, the fifth son, died in infancy.

[185] Hargate Hall.

which we answered as we had been told, not daring to do any other, as we knew what we should catch if we told them the truth. There was no school for us; but on a Sunday a man named Harrison used to come over from Tydeswell to teach us to read a bit. Every night when we got our suppers we sat round the table, and young Mr Frank read prayers to us out of the common prayer book. Sometimes Mrs Needham came to prayers along with us. We finished by singing a psalm. A man walked up and down between the tables with a stick to keep us from going to sleep. I have caught many a whack over my head. It was impossible to keep awake. This Frank and his brother, amongst other cruelties, used out of bravado, to take up the petticoats of big girls, and beat them most unmercifully. In this way I continued for about three years, until Mr Needham became a bankrupt."

Further evidence of the mistreatment condoned by Ellis Needham came to light in the examination of Robert Blincoe by Dr Hawkins in May 1833. Blincoe had been an apprentice at Litton Mill in 1808. Some doubts have been expressed about the truth of Blincoe's account but in one passage covering the cruelty endured by the apprentices at Litton there was the following exchange:

'What are the forms of cruelty that you spoke of just now as being practised upon children in factories?'

'I have seen the time when two hand vices of a pound weight each, more or less, have been screwed to my ears at Litton Mill in Derbyshire. Here are the scars still remaining behind my ears. Then three or four of us have been hung at once on a crossbeam above machinery, hanging by our hands, without shirts or stockings. Mind, we were apprentices, without father or mother to take care of us. I don't say they often do that now. Then we used to stand up in a skip without our shirts and be beat with straps or sticks. The skip was to prevent us from running away from the strap.'

'Did the masters know of these things or were they done only by the over-lookers?'

'The masters have often seen them and have been assistants in them.'

At the same time as the huge increase in industrial activity and mineral extraction, the spa town of Buxton was on the point of massive investment by its owner the Duke of Devonshire and equally large growth of its population.

Between 1780 and 1788 the fifth Duke of Devonshire, no doubt encouraged by the enormous profits from his copper mine at Ecton, built the Crescent, the Assembly Room and the St Ann's Hotel in Buxton (*colour plate 21*). The architect was John Carr of York who built in the style of Robert Adam. The Crescent cost the princely sum of £38,601. The octagonal Great Stables[186] with accommodation

---

[186] This subsequently became the Devonshire Hospital and has now been converted as an annex to Derby University

145

for 120 horses cost a further £16,470. The dome was added a century later in 1881 at a further cost of £25,832-3-1 when the building was converted and extended for hospital use. At the time the dome was the largest in the world, exceeding that of St Paul's in London and St Peter's in Rome.

When the foundations of the Crescent were dug in 1781, the shape and dimensions of the Roman baths were clearly discernible. The bath was in the shape of a parallelogram 30 feet east to west and 15 feet north to south. The wall of the Roman bath had been built with limestone, covered on the outside with a strong cement. The floor was made of plaster and strong oak beams had been laid on top of the walls to support the roof.

John Carr of York
By Sir William Beechey

In addition to the enormous expenditure at Buxton, William the 5th Duke borrowed no less than £170,000[187] between 1773 and 1790 to spend on land purchases. By 1883 the family owned 89,462 acres in Derbyshire alone in addition to their estates in Ireland, Yorkshire, Sussex and London's Mayfair (Chiswick House, Devonshire House and Burlington House) – 200,000 acres in all. Then there was the small matter of his wife Georgiana's gambling debts which were estimated to have reached £60,000[188] by 1789. The mountain of debt accumulated by the fifth Duke was a problem left to later generations to tackle.

One of the carpenters employed on building the Crescent at Buxton was the rustic poet William Newton (1750-1830), a native of the Peak District whose talents extended to engineering as well. He was employed by Richard Arkwright to build a mill at Cressbrook. Newton lost his job there when the mill burned down in 1785 but soon afterwards became a junior partner to Ellis Needham at the nearby Litton Mill in 1797. In 1810 he returned to manage the rebuilt Cressbrook Mill where he remained until his death 20 years later. He and his wife are buried at Tideswell, where he was a notable public benefactor. He is said, for example, to have piped the first public water supply to Tideswell and Litton largely at his own expense. He devoted all his leisure to the study of poetry, history and philosophy. An example of his verse, a sonnet dated 26th February 1797 is as follows:

---

187   £10.2 million at 2001 values.
188   £3.6 million at 2001 values.

I love to wander on the Mountain's brow,
Amid the terrors of the howling year,
When neither Moon nor twinkling stars appear,
But deepest darkness hides the scenes below,
When Winter's fierce conflicting Tempests blow,
And all the arrowy winds aloud career.

More grandly awful than the radiance clear
Of summer evening, when in richest glow
Far in the west the day's bright orb retires.
Congenial to my soul the Tempest's roar
Which lifts the mind above this earthly sod;
Humbles the proud, aspiring, vain desires,
Calls all my powers obedient to adore
The Cause of Nature, – for that Cause is God.

William Newton
Pencil sketch by Llewellyn Jewitt
After Sir Francis Chantrey RA

Once the new facilities were completed at the spa, there were plenty of the nobility who preferred to take the waters at Buxton than at Bath. Buxton had the additional merit of being cheaper but the expenses were nonetheless considerable. Lord and Lady Macartney enjoyed visits to the wells in July 1789 and June 1790. They travelled by public coach, accompanied by two servants from London to Derby. From there they continued via Ashbourne to Buxton. The total cost of the party's journey was £34-14-14, of which £2-1-1 was spent on turnpike tolls.

Once at Buxton her Ladyship accounted for the following expenses:

Four days' hire of Drawing Room	*£0-10-6*
Bedrooms	*£0-16-0*
Servant's Room	*£0-4-6*
Men's Room	*£0-7-0*
Our Dinner at the Great Room 19 July	*£1-7-0*
Our Breakfast	*£0-8-0*
Servants' Dinner	*£0-18-4*
Our Tea	*£0-5-4*
To be added for our wine	*£0-3-0*
Tallow Candles	*£0-1-4*
Washing	*£0-17-0*
Letters, parcels, etc	*£0-4-6*
Her Ladyship's use of the Bath	*£0-5-0*
His Lordship's use of the Bath	*£1-19-0*
Servants' outing to the Playhouse	*£0-10-6*
Outing to Lyme Hall, Cheshire	*£0-2-0*
Outing to Castleton	*£1-6-0*
Souvenirs	*£1-4-0*

Then there were tips to be dispensed:

The waiter	*£1-1-0*
The maid	*£1-11-6*
The shoe black	*£0-5-6*
The woman at the wells	*£0-16-6*
The helper at the stables	*£0-5-0*
An invalid bather	*£0-10-6*

All in all, their four day trip had cost around £88.

Once they had made their way to Buxton these wealthy visitors expected to be entertained and amused as well as cured. One of their favourite occupations was sight-seeing. They made a particular point of visiting the natural phenomena of the Peak District. In part the wars with France towards the end of the 18th century had restricted the practice of travelling to Europe, encouraging people to explore their own country instead, but there was also a genuine curiosity about large caverns and rocky outcrops, amongst the so-called 'Seven Wonders of the Peak'.

Peak Cavern at Castleton (also known as the Devil's Arse because its frightening entrance chamber looked as though it led directly to Hell), Eldon Hole near Peak Forest and Poole's Cavern at Buxton became prime tourist attractions.

The mysterious nature of the caves led to apocryphal stories like the goose (in some versions a duck) being released to fly down Eldon Hole and emerging from Peak Cavern two days later with its wings singed by the fires of Hell!

Chee Tor on the river Wye below Wormhill was also one of the Seven Wonders of the Peak and was such a favourite tourist site that it was frequently painted in exaggerated proportions and romanticised settings (*colour plate 22*). In the 19th century a guide could be obtained from the Red Lion Inn (subsequently the Bagshawe Arms) who would escort the visitor down to the Tor.

THE NINETEENTH CENTURY

Despite the booming industrial activity and associated prosperity which descended on the Peak District during the 18th century, clouds were once more gathering on the international front. The turn of the 19th century was a period of economic and national depression, made worse by the drawn out wars in America, on the Spanish peninsula and in France against Napoleon. The American colonies had been lost in 1781. The French monarchy and system of government had come crashing down in the Revolution of 1789, amid fears that the revolutionary movement would spread across the Channel. The subsequent rise of Napoleon Bonaparte and his early military successes caused a degree of panic in England and urgent measures were taken to prepare for a French invasion. English neurosis was only gradually calmed by the sinking of the French fleet at the Battle of the Nile in 1798, the defining naval victory at Trafalgar in 1805, the eventual successes of the Peninsular campaigns of 1808/09 under Moore and Wellesley and of 1810-13 under Wellington. Not until the spectacular and conclusive victory at Waterloo in 1815, followed by the capture of Napoleon himself and his exile to St Helena, was the threat finally removed and a huge sense of relief was felt throughout the country. Nine beech trees planted at Hargate Wall by Peter Parry Fogg in the winter of 1815 to celebrate Waterloo were still standing in 2005 which suggests that the relief was felt as keenly here as in the rest of the country.

During this uncertain period food prices rose sharply. In 1792 wheat (the staple ingredient for bread) was 43 shillings a quarter (of a hundredweight, ie 28 lbs) and by 1812 it was 126 shillings a quarter. There were sharp movements of economic inflation and deflation – in 1800 alone there was inflation of 36%, followed by 22% deflation in 1802. In 1800 an agricultural worker earned 10 shillings a week; rising to 12 shillings in 1812; falling to 7s 6d in 1817; and recovering to 11 shillings by 1850. There was however good money to be made from the onset of the Industrial Revolution and the Midlands and the North were the 'Silicon Valley' of the age. By 1815 a skilled Lancashire weaver collected £2-4-6 per week. Meanwhile a quarter pint of cheap gin cost 1d and beer was 2d a pint.

At the beginning of the 19th century a fundamental change occurred which was to have a major impact on the pattern of land ownership and the biggest impact on the appearance of the landscape since the arrival of human beings in the Peak District. This was the main period of Enclosures, when open common land was converted into fields, usually for the purpose of sheep-rearing (*colour plate 23*). Some enclosures would have been made in the Anglo-Saxon era and later in the 14th century but the majority of the stone walls would have been built at the end of the 18th and beginning of the 19th centuries, with the limestone being hacked out of the ground with pick and crowbar. The main Enclosure Acts for this part of the Peak District were passed by Parliament in the early 1800s, with the Act relating to Wormhill passing in 1822.[189]

The only common land remaining after 1822 was the village green by the well and the pinfold at Hill Green (the small three-cornered field on Tideswell Lane behind Mrs Wainwright's house) where straying farm animals used to be impounded until they were reclaimed by their owners. The guardian of the Pinfold was called the Pinner (*colour plate 24*). He had authority to impound straying stock and to impose a charge of one shilling a head when the owner claimed them back. In some villages there were stories of local boys letting out the stock of farmers they disliked and splitting the proceeds with the Pinner for their release from the fold!

The stocks which now sit on the Village Green in front of Knotlow Farm were originally sited on another piece of common land near Chapelsteads Farm and would have been used by the village policeman either to hold miscreants before they could be brought before a JP or as a humiliating form of punishment and deterrence for those who had been found guilty (*colour plate 25*).

In order to comply with the Enclosure Act people took whatever stone was readily available on the surface of the land, including from the Bronze Age tumuli, but most of the stone had to come out of the ground. The pits from which the stone was quarried can still be seen in some fields but others have been filled in and re-seeded. The cost in 1803 was quoted by Farey at 6-12 shillings per rood[190] for getting the stone, carting it and building the walls.

Other small quarries were used in the 18th and 19th century for the purpose of lime-burning in stone kilns – the only process known at the time for extracting lime from the stone. Fuel for lime-burning came initially from the coal-mines to the West of Buxton and then by rail with the opening of the railways in the 1860s. The land was divided into fields of about 3 or 4 acres, the optimum space for rotational grazing by small flocks of sheep. Wormhill's farmers of the 18th century would have managed 15-30 acres each – a size of farm which had not changed since the Norman Conquest. Enclosure was a contentious and unpopular development, depriving the poorer farmers of land and giving rise to rhymes such as :

> They hang the man and flog the woman
> That steals a goose from off the common
> But leave the greater criminal loose
> That steals the common from the goose

---

[189]   A copy of the original Act is in the Derbyshire Record Office at Matlock.
[190]   Seven yards.

But it was the salvation of English agriculture because common land had become over-grazed, weed-infested and barren. Once the land was transferred to private ownership, the incentive returned to look after it and maintain its fertility.

By 1794 20% of the limestone enclosures were cultivated, reaching a maximum in the early 1870s but by 1939 the arable acreage was half that of 1866. The enclosure movement was responsible for the gradual demise of sheep-rearing (in England in 1800 there were 360,000 short wool sheep; by 1866 only 258,000 and by 1948 only 98,000) and a corresponding increase in dairy cattle. Most of the walls remain at Wormhill, though some have been removed in order to make larger fields for the cultivation of barley and silage.

From the start of the 19th century the records and descriptions of the local area are considerably reinforced by the advent of guide books for the curious traveller and sightseer. One of these by A Jewitt was commissioned by the Duke of Devonshire to promote the tourist trade in Buxton. This guide does however cover much of the surrounding area as well. Hargate Wall, Jewitt noted in 1811, was the seat of E Needham Esq (in fact it was shortly to be mortgaged and would be re-possessed by Mr Fogg within 4 years) and the garden was already well developed –

From the leafy trees near it and the shrubberies with which it is ornamented it would be pleasing in any situation; here, from the nakedness of the adjacent country, it becomes doubly beautiful.

Wormhill, Jewitt observed, belonged principally to Sir W C Bagshawe and had been held by tenure of Wolve-hunt.[191] The family mansion, Wormhill Hall, was being used as a boarding school for young ladies by Mrs Hefford, late of Broom Hall near Sheffield. In the village was a public house known as the Chee Tor Coffee House, the proprietor of which claimed the privilege of guiding visitors to see that celebrated rock in Chee Dale.

Jewitt however was less impressed with Tideswell which he must have visited on a bad day

Tideswell is a town that bears more antiquity than beauty, indeed in its present state it may be considered the very reverse of beautiful; its buildings are mean, its streets crooked contracted and dirty, its shambles[192] disgusting, and its passages loathsome. The church is an elegant edifice and, though it has stood the severity of 455 Peak winters, is yet the handsomest building of the kind in this part of the Peak. The well, of which so much has been said by other authors, and which is

---

[191] There was a misperception, repeated elsewhere by other authors, that in mediaeval times rents in the village had been paid in wolf-heads rather than cash but there is no evidence to support this.

[192] A place where farm animals were brought for slaughter – the 19th century abattoir. In common with a lot of other roads in Tideswell, the Shambles was renamed to mark Queen Victoria's Diamond Jubilee in 1897. It is now Commercial Road.

supposed to have given name to the town, is now nearly choked up with weeds and rubbish.

In the 1820s some land at Hargate Wall was owned by the Duke of Norfolk. The 1822 Enclosure Act and plan show that the Duke owned the Second Milk Pasture and land on the dale side. Wheston Hall and the land that went with it passed to the 12th Duke of Norfolk by inheritance in the early nineteenth century. The Duke sold this property in 1828. Wheston Hall was then a much larger and grander building, part Elizabethan and part Georgian, first constructed by the Alleyns in the late 1500s and taxed on 8 hearths in 1670 (twice as many as Wormhill Hall in the same year, though this was before Wormhill Hall was rebuilt in its present form in 1697). The Alleyns were first recorded in the 1400s as one of the major families of the Tideswell parish (of which Wheston was and still is a part). A Thurston Allen was living at Wheston Hall in 1570 and the last of the family (by then spelled Alen) died out in about 1700.

In many respects Wheston was an unusual place for a settlement to be established. There is no running water or spring and water had to be carried from either Dale Head or the stream-fed trough on the Sitch road until a piped supply and electricity reached the hamlet in the 1960s. Many of the houses, including Wheston Hall, had a clay-puddled mere at the back which collected rainwater from the roofs, thus reducing the burden of carting water from some distance away.

Much of the history of Wheston remains unrecorded and a mystery. It is entirely fitting that there are several ghost stories associated with the Hall, un-dated and unrelated to any of the families known to have lived there. Speculation about one of them leads some to claim that it refers to the Maxwells who lived there during the 1700s. The story is that, long ago, an owner of Wheston Hall had fallen deeply in love with a girl whose father made her marry another man whom she detested. Her husband became a recluse and studied black magic and conjuring up the dead. The lady eventually found life with her husband insufferable and fled to her lover at Wheston Hall. One night her husband came to Wheston to claim her back but was fatally stabbed by the lover. The next morning there was a fresh grave in the orchard and the lover had fled, with neither the husband nor the lover ever being seen again. The lady herself died later at the Hall. Once a year the ghost of a lady is said to pass three times round the house. She is barefoot and clad in her nightdress. As she goes round the house, she shrieks and tears her golden hair.

A second and perhaps related ghost story was recalled by Clarence Daniel of Eyam, one of many writers about the mysteries of the Peak District. She introduced it with the spooky rhyme:

Long Years have passed, yet Wheston Hall
O'erlooks the Tor and Dale[193]
Where huge fantastic rocks upreared
Defy the Winter's Gale;
And rustics, clustering round the fire
Oft tell the ghostly tale.

Her ghost story was told her by 'Master John' who had moved into the Hall with his parents at the age of 19 in 1918. On each of the first three nights that he spent there, he was visited in his bedroom by the ghost of an old lady wearing a poke bonnet. The apparition disappeared when he shone his torch on her but he was sufficiently scared to move to another bedroom and never saw her again. The old lady in the poke bonnet did however reappear when some Wheston farmhands and neighbours were playing a Saturday night card game and failed to take notice, after the clock had struck midnight, that they were breaching the rules of the Sabbath by continuing to gamble on Sunday. The outer door burst open to reveal the ghost of the old lady. A blast of cold air blew the cards all over the place and scattered the chairs and tables before the spectre disappeared, bringing the game to an end and reminding the miscreants of their Christian duties.

A third ghost story about Wheston Hall relates to 'Soldier Dick' who was associated with a suit of mediaeval armour standing inside the main entrance. So afraid were the owners of offending the spirits by removing the armour when the house was rebuilt, that they buried it under rubble when they filled in the cellar, thereby appeasing the soldier's ghost and persuading him not to reappear thereafter.

A severe gale caused the collapse of the north-west front of the old Hall in 1952 and the house remained a semi-ruin until 1960. The east end was then demolished; the top storey was completely removed, leaving only the west stair tower and the front door to suggest its former glory.

Wheston Hall 1873

---

[193] Peter Dale.

Only in the middle of the 19th century is it possible to find the first full and official census records at specified points in time. The 1841 Census[194] is one of the earliest examples of a comprehensive account of everyone living in the village. It records, for example, 10 dwellings at Hargate Wall, though this appears to include the houses at Hill Top and Hill Green as well. The names of the houses are not recorded. The occupants were:

John Hayward (aged 50), farmer, with his wife, 3 sons, 3 daughters and a man servant – William Bray (13).
Henry Hayward (35), farmer, with his wife, one son and 3 servants – Jane Oven (20), Edward Vernon (11) and John Bestwick (18).
Edmund Dakin (40), farmer, with his wife, 3 sons and 2 servants – Mary Vernon and Edward Philips.
George Needham (25), farmer, with Martha Needham (65) and 2 servants – Charles Tymms (15) and Lyddia Gyle (14).
Thomas Phillips (75), farmer, with his wife and one son.
John Handley (66), farmer, with his wife and one servant – Mary Bagshawe.
Michael Tymms (61), agricultural labourer, with one son and a daughter.
Richard Taylor (22), agricultural labourer, with his wife and one son.
Joshua Plats (25), farmer, with his wife and one son.
William Redfern (60), farmer, with 3 sons and 5 daughters.

This makes a total of 50 people living at Hargate Wall, Hill Top and Hill Green and no less than 8 separate farmers. Five out of the 10 families had between one and 3 living in servants, though the census does not distinguish between domestic and agricultural workers. Most of these servants were in their teens and one was only 11. As in the previous century, families tended to be large to compensate for losses due to ill health and rudimentary medicine. Two of the houses contained 9 occupants.

Curiously the name of Peter Parry Fogg, who was the owner of Hargate Old Hall from 1815 to 1859, does not appear on the census. This suggests that he had let the Hall to one of the residents recorded in the census of 1841, possibly one of the Haywards.

On 22nd August 1859 Peter Parry Fogg sold the 'capital messuage' or mansion house at Hargate Wall plus 157 acres, including the site of the future Hargate Hall, to T (Thomas) Swann the Elder. Thomas owned Hargate until his death in 1878 when it was inherited by William Swann (his son). The 1891 census records Maria Swann, Thomas's widow aged 71, living at Hargate Hall along with her son William, a 31 year old farmer, two domestic servants and two agricultural workers.

---

[194] Details on microfilm in the Buxton Library.

The Swanns could evidently be generous hosts at Hargate Wall. The Tideswell Brass Band used to travel round the area in the lead up to Christmas, playing Christmas carols and receiving hospitality from their audiences. A history of Tideswell[195] recalls:

The Band returned from Mr Swann's at Hargate Wall where a rich table was always provided. On the way home they began to play before a haystack under the impression that it was a human habitation. One of the bandsmen called out 'Play up; they're getting up'. Over the top of the stack could be seen the light of the rising moon!

Population figures are much more readily available from the start of the 19th century when censuses were conducted regularly at 20 year and more usually 10 year intervals. In the previous century Buxton had been a quarter the size of Tideswell but the spa was to cause it to grow exponentially in the 1800s. In the 20 years from 1861 the size of the town more than trebled and in the 40 years after 1881 it nearly trebled again to become almost 8 times larger than Tideswell.

In 1800 :   760 Residents
In 1821 :   1036 Residents (and 184 houses)
In 1841 ;   1569 Residents
In 1861 :   1877 Residents
In 1881 :   6021 Residents
In 1921 :   15651 Residents

Bagshaw's, White's and Kelly's Directories and the Census records in the Derbyshire Record Office at Matlock show the statistics for the village and the names of the occupants for the period of 183 years from 1788 to 1971 :

Year	Houses in Wormhill	Village Population
1788	35	
1801	56	234
1811		295
1821		347
1831		313
1841		337
1846	70	337
1851	72	369
1861		418
1871		714

---

[195] *History of Tideswell* by W Walker 1951.

(Note rapid increase in population from this period onwards, as quarry workers at Tunstead, Great Rocks, Upper End and Peak Dale – than all part of the Wormhill parish – started to count in the figures)

1881	953
1891	1357
1901	1493
1911	1495
1921	1505
1931	1631
1951	1545
1961	973
1971	975

Crime continued unabated in the 19th century and, no doubt spurred on by the novels of Dickens and other contemporary authors whose books became accessible to a better educated and more literate public, there was a macabre fascination with murder and the gruesome punishment which accompanied conviction for this crime. Not far away at Wardlow Mires near Tideswell local lore claims that in 1812 the last man in England was hanged on a gibbet. This appears to be another example of erroneous folklore[196] since a murderer called James Cook was gibbeted on 1st August 1832 and gibbeting was not formally abolished before 1834. Nevertheless the local folklore says:

'I was interested in the man Anthony Lingard who murdered an old woman and was the last person in England to be gibbeted. His gibbet used to be in the old museum at Belle Vue, Manchester. My husband, Harry Bagshaw, often told me the story of his grandmother who went to visit the old lady at Wardlow Mires one Sunday evening for their usual gossip. She walked from Foolow. As they sat chatting round the fire a piece of cinder flew out. They waited until it cooled to see if the shape was a cradle, which meant a birth in the family; a purse, which meant money; or a coffin, which meant death. It was a coffin. Great consternation! Who was ill in their family? No one ...everybody in good health. Grannie went back to Foolow very worried. The first thing they heard next morning was that the old lady had been murdered. The Police found that the only thing missing was a pair of her boots, made by a shoemaker in Foolow. A short time afterwards a young servant girl was bragging about a pair of boots her sweetheart had given her. The police heard and got in touch with the shoemaker and asked if he could recognise them. He said he could as he had put a piece of brown paper in the sole of the left boot. The paper was found and the man tried and found guilty.'

---

[196] See *Peakland Pickings, Stories and Characters of the Peak District* by Neville T Sharpe 1999.

The fuller and better researched account by Neville T Sharpe shows that the victim was Mrs Hannah Oliver, the toll-keeper at Wardlow Mires. Lingard strangled her with a handkerchief in an attempt to make it look as though she had committed suicide. He stole not only the pair of red shoes but also a sum of money. He offered the shoes and money to a young woman who was pregnant by him if she would claim that the child was fathered by another man. The young woman suspected that the shoes were stolen property and refused to accept them. Lingard therefore hid them in a haystack and later recovered them before hiding them in his own house where they were found by the investigators of the crime. The shoes had been made for Mrs Oliver by Samuel Marsden, a shoe-maker of Stoney Middleton. Marsden recognised the shoes and remembered that he had inserted a piece of packing in one of the heels which ironically contained the words 'Commit No Crime'. It was the discovery of this piece of packing which sealed Lingard's fate when the heel was opened.

Anthony Lingard was hanged at Derby Gaol on 8th March 1815 and his body brought to Wardlow under military escort. When the escort reached Rowsley, they took a wrong turn and marched on through Beeley along the Duke of Devonshire's private road instead of turning left to Bakewell. At Chatsworth they were told by one of the Duke's servants that they could go no further. 'Duke he may be' replied the young officer, 'But I hold the King's commission. Quick March'. The outcome of this incident was that the road was no longer considered private under an ancient law which stipulated that the passage of a corpse along a road made it a public right of way.

The costs of this horrendous ritual were not insubstantial – £31-5-3 for the investigation leading up to the arrest; £53-18-8 for the gibbeting and £10-10-0 for the gaoler and escort from Derby to Wardlow. Such was the public fascination with the event however that the vicar of Tideswell found none of his congregation in church on the day of the gibbeting but all of them and more at Wardlow where he took the opportunity of delivering a sermon of fire and brimstone under the gallows.

Lingard's skeleton is alleged to have hung on the Wardlow Mires gibbet in chains until it was finally removed 11 years later on 20th April 1826 after complaints about the gruesome chattering of the bones in the wind. The site of this hanging would have been the so-called Gibbet Field at Wardlow Mires where other hangings are reputed to have taken place earlier, including one of a notorious highwayman called Black Harry who was finally apprehended in Stoney Middleton Dale in the 18th century. The nearby Peter's Stone[197] at the entrance to Cressbrook Dale has the alternative name of Gibbet Rock.

Other less stomach-churning entertainments appeared. A horse-racing track

---

[197] So-called because it was thought to resemble St Peter's Basilica in Rome. It has a reputation for disorientating visitors and climbers, several of whom have been injured there over the years.

was established on the Barms at Fairfield (the area of the commons given to the parish after the 1772 Enclosure Act) and the Duke of Devonshire awarded a 50 guineas plate for the first race. A stand was erected in 1831 and June Race Meetings flourished there for almost two decades before ending in 1840.

By the end of the 19th century hunting had become a well-established pastime throughout the country and the county. Edward Bradbury in his Derbyshire Guidebooks and Directories published in the 1880s reported that there were no less than three packs of Harriers hunting in the Peak District, though no packs of fox-hounds. The Buxton and Peak Forest Harriers met principally at Peak Forest and Dove Holes; The High Peak Harriers[198] mostly round Hartington and Monyash; and the Dove Dale Harriers in the Dove Valley (*colour plate 26*).

High Peak Hunt at Hargate Hall early 1900s

Many of the industries pioneered in the previous century continued, though not all remained as lucrative as they had been. Throughout the 19th century lead mines had to be driven deeper and deeper to find profitable seams of ore. When enormous deposits were found in Australia and America, the local trade became uneconomic. In 1830 there were 2280 lead miners in Derbyshire; in 1891 this had reduced to 803; and in 1901 to only 285.

Farming was certainly still an economic activity and there was a steady increase in rents and wages earned on the land. In 1850 the average farm rent was 26/- per acre; the average farm worker's wage was 11/- a week, rising in 1867 to 15/- a week; and rising in 1911 to 20s 7d. The 1881 version of Kelly's Directory records that the main crops grown in Wormhill at the time were oats, turnips and hay.

In 1875 Thomas Swann, who owned Hargate Old Hall and the farm contributed to a report to the Royal Agricultural Society. His evidence gives an insight into the

---

[198] The High Peak Harriers was the only pack to survive into the 20th and 21st centuries but this too faces an uncertain future as a result of the hunting ban of 2004.

agricultural regime conducted on a local farm in the wetter and colder climate of the second half of the 19th century

I farm 360 acres of my own property. The soil varies from a good rich loam to a poor thin red or, as we call it, 'fox-soil' on limestone rock, and in parts we have dun-stone and clay. Our average rainfall is 51 inches[199]. I commenced laying down land on my present farm in 1860. At that time my holding consisted of 80 acres arable, 70 acres meadow, 160 acres permanent pasture and 50 acres sheep walk. In 1874 it was 25 acres arable, 60 acres meadow, 225 acres permanent pasture and 50 acres sheep walk. It will therefore be seen that I have laid to permanent pasture 65 acres; and I have done this because I consider that in this district it pays better to grow cattle than corn, the climate being too cold and wet for the latter. And I find that my farm pays me better now than it did under the former system. I can breed more cattle, and what I breed are as good now at 2 years old as they used to be at 3 years

This farm was acquired and mortgaged in about 1890 by Joseph Wainwright who had previously also farmed at Tunstead and Great Rocks in addition to starting a quarry in Peak Dale. His quarry, along with numerous other small private lime burning enterprises, was bought up by Brunner Mond in 1891 and from then on the private lime burners could no longer compete with the big limited companies. The causes of Joseph Wainwright's bankruptcy 10 years later are lost in the mists of time but they could have stemmed either from his failure to sustain his lime business or his stud farm. In September 1899 *The High Peak Advertiser* reported that Joseph Wainwright had held a shire horse auction at Great Rocks stud farm which attracted large numbers of breeders from around the country. The stock was of the highest quality and the Prince of Wales was amongst the purchasers. The sale totalled 5228 guineas.[200] Nine hundred and fifty people sat down to a champagne lunch provided by Joseph Wainwright. Either his generosity was misplaced or his good fortune failed to last because within 2 years his mortgage with Robert Whitehead for the Hargate Wall estate was re-possessed. Contemporary maps show that Great Rocks Stud Farm was just to the east of the railway line in Great Rocks Dale and hence has been long since lost to quarrying operations.

There were further shire horse stud farms in the district including the major complex at Orient Lodge between Great Rocks Back Pastures and Green Fairfield. This too was demolished in the 1950s as quarrying operations extended to the west of the railway line but the following aerial photograph gives some idea of the size and scale of the enterprise.

[199] Closely matching the average recorded by my grand-mother for Buxton and 7 inches (15%) more than today.

[200] £5489-8-0 or, at 2001 values, about £300,000.

Orient Lodge and Stud Farm

Until the 19th century any education received by the children of the village came either from the vicar or from travelling teachers when charitable funds were available for teaching the poor. The first proper school-house (*colour plate 27*). was built at Wormhill in 1844 and the first resident schoolmaster was Edward Furniss. Daniel Dewick was the schoolmaster in 1857. In 1867 the school mistress, Miss Mary Hayes, received a salary of £19-0-5 per annum plus free accommodation in the school-house. In 1871 the school was re-built in its final form with the foundation stone being laid in Masonic tradition and full Masonic dress by the Phoenix Lodge of St Ann after a dedication service in the church led by the vicar, Augustus Adam Bagshawe. The inscription on the foundation stone read: Laid the 19th August 1871 by the Phoenix Lodge of St Ann No 1235 Bro. RR Duke, Worshipful Master, Bro. R Darwin Past Master, Bro. J Milward Past Master, Bro. AA Bagshawe MA PGC Vicar, Bro. R Griggs Architect. In 1888 there were 61 pupils on the register of the village school and it continued to be used as a primary school before it was finally shut down in the 1970s.

Former Schoolhouse and Pupils early 1900s

It is worth recalling that, in the 1800s, all of the fundamental public services like schooling, healthcare and welfare, which people nowadays take for granted as free at the point of use, had to be paid for by every member of the community. Social security, unemployment and other benefits, let alone state pensions, did not exist. The first old age pensions, 5 shillings a week for those aged 70 and above, were paid on 1st January 1909 and Sickness and Unemployment Benefit was not introduced before 1911. There was therefore a very real threat of absolute poverty, especially in isolated rural communities and amongst the old and infirm. The only prospect of relief from poverty came either from a generous employer or lord of the manor or from an established charity. Most parishes benefited from a number of such charities, most of them coming from endowments or legacies. There were 8 such charities at Wormhill in 1846 but half of them no longer produced an annual income either because the original endowment had become devalued or lost or because those entrusted to manage the sums had failed to do so:

- £3 per year for the services of a schoolmaster left by Robert Wilson in his will in 1714 (value in 1846 – nil).
- £40 left by Elizabeth Paltreeman in her will in 1782, the interest from which was intended to pay for the schooling of 4 poor children in the parish (value in 1846 – nil).
- £20 left by Richard Bagshaw in his will of 1749, the interest to be paid to the schoolmaster for the teaching of poor children in the parish (value in 1846 – nil).
- 6 pence per week left by Roger Wilkson for bread for the poor. This continued to be distributed in 3 penny loaves on the first Sunday of every month to the poor who attended the chapel.
- £30 left by Anthony Wright in his will in 1768, the interest to be given to the poor (value in 1846 – nil).
- Fifteen shillings per year left by Gervase Smith in his will in 1760 to be given to the poor at Christmas. This was paid out of the proceeds of a field called 'The Poor Piece' purchased about 1814 by Sir W C Bagshawe.
- Five shillings per year left by William Bagshawe (the Apostle) for the benefit of the poor.
- £5-10-0 per year from the Rev Francis Gisborne's charity, received by the vicar, converted into flannel and woollen cloth and distributed about Christmas time to the poor.

The progress made in medical knowledge and treatment during the 19th century brought with it a steady increase in life expectancy. Infant mortality reduced from 44% in the 18th century to 28% in 1840 and to 13% in 1921. Children started to be vaccinated against smallpox in 1867 and a serum was

Former Post Office early 1900s

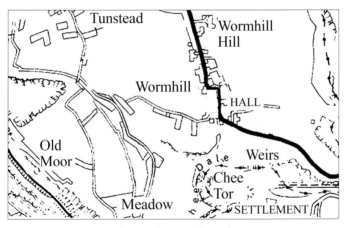

Line of original road

administered against diphtheria from 1894. Nevertheless 10,000 people per annum in England and Wales were killed by scarlet fever in 1850 and 75,000 people per annum were still dying of tuberculosis in 1900. In 1864 doctors estimated that 28% of children did not have an adequate diet to enjoy a healthy standard of living and the poorest families could not afford to eat meat more than once a week.

Improvements were made to the line of the main road running through the village in the course of the 19th century. The original road from Millers Dale ran along the back of Wormhill Hall, up behind the church, behind the vicarage, up the church lane before turning sharp right at the old Post Office (colour plate 28). This tortuous route was abandoned after a cutting was made from the Post Office down past Hassop Farm. A picture of the cutting in 2006 is shown in colour plate 29.

An impression of the local roads in the days before tarmac and extensive ownership of motor vehicles can be gauged from this next photograph of the cross-roads at Hill Green at the top of Wormhill. It was probably taken between 1900 and 1910, judging by the newness of the boundary wall around Hargate Hall. Note the narrowness of the carriageway, the 'pointing' sign-post, the boy posing on the wall at the corner, the compacted stone road surface and the absence, as yet, of the stone gateway into Hargate Hall Stables.

Hill Green Crossroads about 1905

At the outset of the 19th century transport and travel were still confined to an improving road network but one which was still of dubious quality and incapable of taking heavy industrial loads. James Brindley's canals were in full use but did not reach into hilly districts like the High Peak. The real revolution in transport came with the invention of steam power and the railways. In the middle of the century there was intense competition to build the new tracks.

Linking the London to Derby line through to Manchester provoked a huge debate as to whether the line should follow the Derwent Valley through Chatsworth, Baslow and Hope or the Wye Valley through Bakewell and Millers Dale. The 6th Duke of Devonshire offered to invest £50,000 if the line was constructed on the Derwent Valley route, though he stipulated that it would have to be tunnelled underneath the park at Chatsworth so that it could not be seen from the House. Furthermore, because he disliked travelling at speed through tunnels, he insisted that there would have to be a station at Rowsley where he could join the train to travel south and another station at Baslow where he could join the train to travel north! The Duke of Rutland initially refused to have a railway running up the Wye Valley through his estate at Haddon but changed his tune when the benefits to local towns, landowners and agriculture were explained. Eventually the Wye Valley route was chosen.

Millers Dale Station 1906

Millers Dale station was opened in 1863 and originally had three platforms – one for the up line, one for the down line and a branch line for Buxton. In 1905 a second viaduct was completed from the station and across the Wye valley to the south-east and parallel to the original viaduct, thus creating five platforms – two for the up line, two for the down line and the same branch line to Buxton. This permitted stationary trains to be overtaken by others on the double tracks. As the only main stop for express trains between Derby and Manchester, Millers Dale became a key junction and soon had its own post office and mail sorting office which serviced most of the Peak District. When it finally closed in 1967, the station is said to have been the last one in England to have had a post office on its platform.

The branch line enabled many local people to commute to work in Buxton for the first time, some walking daily to and from Millers Dale from Tideswell via the

Pinfold Lane to catch the train. When the station finally closed as part of the Beeching Cuts on 4th March 1967, the railway was providing 19 return journeys per day between Millers Dale and Buxton. Since its closure the railway line has been converted into a public cycle path and footpath.

Millers Dale Station 2006

The 1860s and 1870s saw a huge expansion of the railway network with the construction of the London Midland and the London North Western Railways from London to Manchester and three separate railway companies operating into Buxton. Two separate railway stations belonging to different companies were built side by side at Buxton reflecting the intense competition for the trade of the spa town. In these pre-mechanisation days this building programme was a highly labour-intensive enterprise with large gangs of 'navvies'[201] digging tunnels and embankments and building the many stone and steel viaducts required to carry a two-track line through the Peak District.

The railways provided the first real opportunities for people to travel widely and relatively cheaply. Up to this time many of the inhabitants would not have travelled further than the nearest market towns in their lives. It is said that, in England and Wales before 1880, most people did not move more than an average of 22 miles from their birthplace in their lifetimes. They were now able to go on excursions to the races or the seaside and visit London and other major cities, even if they had to endure the rigours of an open carriage on a third class ticket. Journey times were also dramatically reduced. A steam train on the London-Manchester route took 2½ hours from Millers Dale to the newly constructed St Pancras Station in London – as fast if not faster than in modern times. Thousands of people per annum were enabled to visit the Buxton Spa by rail, calling for a rapid increase in hotel accommodation. The Palace Hotel was built in 1868 to help satisfy the demand.

---

[201] Named after the original 'navigators' or travellers' guides.

Scarcely less revolutionary was the speed with which information and data could be transmitted via the 'telegraph' wires which advanced across the country alongside the railway lines. For the first time a speech delivered in the House of Commons in the afternoon could be transmitted verbatim to the local newspapers and read at the breakfast table the following morning. Family news, good and bad, could be communicated speedily by the 'telegram'. A telegram could be received at Millers Dale, transcribed and delivered to an address in Wormhill within an hour of being despatched from anywhere in the country. National newspapers became a feasible proposition because of the much improved rates of distribution and the Post Office could deliver mail nation-wide by the day after posting. The first national 'Penny Post' began in 1840 with the introduction of the world's first postage stamp, the Penny Black.

With the railways came an enormous increase in milk production. After 1870 milk was sent regularly to London and 8 million gallons was carried on the Derbyshire section of the London Midland Railway in 1888. The surge in demand for liquid milk was largely responsible for helping the High Peak to avoid the worst effects of the 1870s Agricultural Depression.[202] Milk from the village was delivered in churns to Millers Dale Station by horse and cart. In my childhood I remember seeing on the farm an old horse-drawn sleigh on steel-shod runners which had been used to transport milk to the station in snowy winters.

Despite the economic benefits, not everyone approved of the construction of the railways through pristine countryside. The writer John Ruskin (1819-1900) complained bitterly of the building of the railway viaduct across Monsal Dale:

There was a rocky valley between Buxton and Bakewell, once upon a time, divine as the Vale of Tempe; you might have seen the Gods there morning and evening – Apollo and all the sweet Muses of the light – walking in fair procession upon the lawns of it, and to and fro amongst the pinnacles of its crags. You cared neither for Gods nor grass, but cash (which you did not know the way to get); you thought you could get it by what the Times calls 'Railroad Enterprise'. You Enterprised a Railroad through the valley – you blasted its rocks away, heaped thousands of tons of shale into its lovely stream. The valley is gone, and the Gods with it; and now, every fool in Buxton can be at Bakewell in half an hour, and every fool in Bakewell at Buxton ...

Ironically the Monsal Dale Viaduct now carries listed building status! (*colour plate 30.*)

---

[202] This was caused by American prairie-grown grain flooding the UK Market. The construction of 53,000 miles of railway track in the USA brought grain to the coast more cheaply and the advent of ocean-going steamers reduced the cost and hazard of transatlantic transport. In 1873-4 the cost of sending one ton of grain from Chicago to Liverpool fell from £3-7-0 to £1-4-0.

There is some speculation, at the beginning of the 21st century, about whether the railway line could be restored to its former use by re-linking the track from Matlock to Great Rocks Dale. Recreating a central London to Manchester line would undoubtedly ease the pressures on the East and West Coast mainlines which are close to full capacity and the old viaducts and tunnels are apparently still in good condition. There are however places, eg at Rowsley, where the original line has been built over and some bridges have been removed. In 2006 the cost of re-instating the railway line was put at £100 million which would make it a very substantial infrastructure project, though not necessarily unaffordable in comparison to other major contemporary schemes. The Ramblers Association and the environmental lobby however might beg to differ!

Another development to appear in the latter stages of the century was a step change in the accuracy and availability of large scale maps. The whole country was surveyed; trig points were established on dominating pieces of high ground from which to take the measurements (one is on Bole Hill) and high quality maps were produced for the first time showing individual buildings, field boundaries and spinneys. The 1883 Ordnance Survey map of Hargate Wall shows the layout of the houses and buildings much as they are today. The main farm buildings are shown as a small square occupying only a fraction of the area which became the main cow yard and with an entrance in the north-east corner. The area now filled by the Big Shed and the Stud Yard is shown as an open field, though the line of Waterloo beech trees at the top of the field is clearly marked. There is a small building in what is now the back garden of the Farmhouse but there is an empty space where the Farmhouse and No 2 Cottage now stand. Hayward Farm, Dakins Farm and the Lambing Sheds are clearly recognisable as they are today. The Top Buildings were there but there were no trees in the First Paddock, no duck pond or mere between

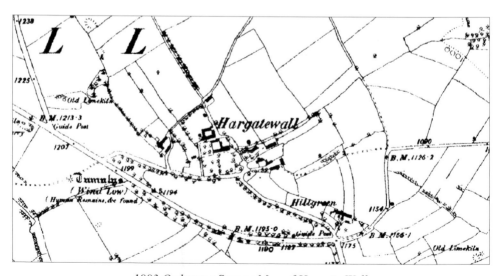

1883 Ordnance Survey Map of Hargate Wall

Dakins and the Bull Paddock. Nor was there a dividing wall between the Bull Paddock and the field containing Dakins Mere. The site of the future Hargate Hall is shown as an open field lined by a single row of trees.

On 17th May 1859 Wormhill achieved the status of an independent parish rather than being part of the parish of Tideswell. The new parish included the hamlets of Hargate Wall, Dale Head, Peak Dale, Upper End, Edge Foot, Dove Holes (also called Bibbington in some directories after the name of the lime burning company based there at the Victory Quarry), Great Rocks Dale, Tunstead, Blackwell Mill and the western part of Millers Dale. Perhaps partly in celebration of this new-found independence, St Margaret's Church at Wormhill was rebuilt in 1864 in Victorian Gothic style by the Bagshawes with seating for 225 people. T H Rushforth was the architect (*colour plate 31*). The renovation included some distinguished oak carvings in the chancel by 'Old' Advent Hunstone, the scion of the famous wood-carving family in Tideswell. The only remaining part of the Norman chapel is the base of the bell tower. A new organ was installed in 1895.

The hamlets of Peak Dale, Great Rocks, Upper End and Tunstead expanded rapidly to service the new limestone quarries and the growth in the population was sufficient to justify the construction of other chapels and churches in the parish – a Methodist chapel at Great Rocks in 1885, a new church in Peak Dale to seat 200 people in 1886 and costing £1500, and another Methodist chapel at Upper End in 1887.

St Margaret's Church

The 1883 Ordnance Survey map of Wormhill is less distinct than that for Hargate but nevertheless shows the school, the Bagshawe Arms public house, the Brindley Memorial completed 8 years previously, the vicarage, church and Wormhill Hall. The 'new' cutting taking the main road down from the Post office

1883 Ordnance Survey Map of Wormhill

past Hassop Farm is also clearly shown.

The vicar of Wormhill in 1871, Rev A A (Augustus Adam) Bagshawe, was a leading member of the local Freemasons and the Phoenix Lodge of St Ann. The Lodge met usually in Buxton but on various occasions between 1871 and 1876 an 'adjourned' meeting was held at Wormhill Vicarage. Foundation stones were laid by the masons for the new school in 1871 and the Brindley Memorial in 1875. A photograph of one such lodge meeting in 1873 on the vicarage lawn shows the vicar seated in the centre (fifth from left) and Robert Rippon Duke, the famous architect of Victorian Buxton, seated on the far right.

Phoenix Lodge of St Ann meeting at Wormhill Vicarage 1873

Augustus Adam was vicar of Wormhill for 40 years and, when he died in 1890, three stained glass windows and a font of Sicilian, Kynance and Derbyshire marbles were erected in the church as a memorial to him.

Around this time Ann Brightmore of Tideswell, who eventually died at the age of 103, was married at Wormhill church. Her father James Bell was gardener to squire Bagshawe. The bride proceeded direct to the church from her domestic service at the Hall, still carrying her long brush. The bridegroom, trowel in hand, came down from the church roof on which he was working.

Quite whether and, if so, when the custom of well dressing might have taken place in Wormhill in the 19th century cannot be proven with any certainty. There is however one reference by John Leyland, writing in 1891, who refers to well dressing having taken place at Wormhill within living memory, ie perhaps at the beginning of the 1800s, though the Brindley Well was constructed in 1875 and might have prompted the start of well dressing in the village. In more modern times, well dressing in the village has only taken place consistently since 1951 when it was revived for the Festival of Britain. John Leyland's reference reads:

Where the streamlet bursts from its earth-bound course at Wormhill Springs, the ancient custom of well dressing was kept up, as at Tissington, within living memory, and the peasantry of the neighbourhood used to awake the echoes of the ravine with the sounds of their rustic jollity.

Nowadays the remarkable thing is that this ancient custom is carried on by a

Blessing of the Well 1951 Festival of Britain
(the Author aged 4 at bottom left holding his grandmother's hand)

small group of enthusiasts within a village population which is less than 5% of its peak in the previous century. The fact that we can still find people with out-standing talents in graphic design and well dressing technique, not to mention the dedicated workers who give up their holidays to work round the clock to complete the picture against an unremitting deadline and others who man the kiosk by the well and refreshments at the village hall throughout the week reflects the strengths and dedication of a community which is as proud of its past as it is committed to its future (*colour plate 32*). Long may it continue!

THE TWENTIETH CENTURY

By the beginning of the 20th century the census records were becoming more consistent and from then on there is a full account of not just the numbers of the village inhabitants but also their names and addresses. My own research has focussed principally on my end of the village at Hargate Wall but a similar amount of detail is easily available for the rest of the parish. I must apologise therefore for the bias towards Hargate Wall in the records which follow but repetition of the same level of detail for the rest of the village would have consumed more space than could be justified and would have been of limited value to the more general reader. What follows is thus a mere taste of the sort of information which can be readily found for every house in the parish in the 20th century.

The 1901 Census for example records 5 dwellings at Hargate Wall and, although the houses are not named, it is easier than in the 1841 census to deduce which houses were occupied by which families :

At Hargate Old Hall: Joseph Wainwright (54), widower and limestone quarry owner, with his son, Gilbert E Wainwright (23), and 2 servants.
At Dakins Farmhouse: Joseph Dakin (68), farmer, with 2 sons and 2 daughters.
At Hayward Farmhouse: John Wilshawe (43), farmer, with his wife, one son and 2 daughters.
At the two Hargate Cottages: Charles Redfern (22), carter on the farm, with his wife and one daughter. Adam Mycock (45), cattleman on the farm, with his wife, 2 sons and 2 daughters.

This gives a total of 23 people living at Hargate Wall just before Robert Whitehead re-possessed the Hall and the main farm and just before he undertook to complete the construction of the new Hargate Hall and the rebuilding of the Old Hall and the farm buildings. In the 60 years since the 1841 census, families had reduced in size and only one house had living in servants.

In 1901, soon after the census was taken, Robert Whitehead acquired the free-hold of Hargate Wall and 496 acres on re-possession of the mortgage made with Joseph Wainwright of Buxton, Lime Burner, and Gilbert Edward Wainwright, Lime Burner (his son). Having advanced Joseph Wainwright 'certain sums of money from time to time' and having lent him the further sum of £20,000 (£1.1 million at 2001 values) which was owing to him, the land was handed over to Robert Whitehead, his heirs and assigns for ever. In the Abstract of Title there are two schedules referring to parcels of land on the 1883 Ordnance Survey Map. The schedules include:

29 acres and 3 perches bounded by lands of Mr Bradwell, Mr Webster, Mr Fogg, The Revd William Bagshawe, The Duke of Norfolk, The Earl of Newburgh and Mr William Sutton.

48 acres and 20 perches formerly in the tenure or occupation of Joseph Wainwright, afterwards of T Swann the Elder, then of William Swann.

67 acres and 35 perches formerly in the tenure or holding of George Needham and John Handley, afterwards of T Swann the Elder and then W Swann.

All the capital messuage or Mansion House known as Hargate Wall and all that other capital Messuage or Mansion House then in the course of erection and intended to be called Hargate Hall and land around them amounting to 157 acres, 1 rood[203] and 24 perches conveyed to T Swann the Elder on 22 August 1859 by Peter Parry Fogg and Isaac Nield.

23 acres formerly part of Wormhill Commons but since enclosed, previously owned by John Middleton, then T Swann the Elder and then W Swann.

3 roods and 39 perches in the same ownership.

29 acres 2 roods and 31 perches in the same ownership.

121 acres 2 roods and 5 perches at Dale Head formerly owned by Joseph Garlick, John Handley and Henry Wainwright, then William Henry Greaves Bagshawe who sold it on 2 May 1890 to W Swann and Thomas Swann the Younger.

17 acres and 18 perches formerly Wormhill Common in a place then called Castle Nidget Flat.[204]

The period 1900-1910 saw major investment in the Hargate Wall estate by Robert Whitehead. The new Hargate Hall was already under construction when Robert Whitehead re-possessed the estate in 1901 with the building programme having been initiated in 1898 by Joseph Wainwright before he went bust. Robert Whitehead completed the new Hall in exotic fashion by 1902 with a large centrally heated Orangery and a Stable Block decorated with marble and tiling (*colour plate 33*).

The main farm buildings were rebuilt and extended; the Big Shed and Shire

---

[203] Quarter of an acre.

[204] Note that Cameron's *Place Names of Derbyshire* pp 179-182 records a field at Wormhill called Castle Lidget which almost certainly derives from Lidgate, through the derivation of 'Castle' which could signify an early fortification remains an interesting mystery. Castle Lidget was the former name of the Commons area around Sitch Wood and Sitch Barn and extending up the Sitch Road as far as the lane going down to Haywards Meadows. In the 1822 Enclosure Plan Castle Lidget Flat belonged to Rev William Bagshawe (38 acres), John Bradwell (23 acres) and James Beech (17 acres).

Hargate Hall under Construction 1899

Horse Stud Yard were added with extensive new boxes and elaborate iron-work, a saddle and tack room and a clock tower over the entrance; and the Old Hall was rebuilt. The Farmhouse and Number 2 Cottage were added – the 1901 census clearly shows that there were only two cottages at the time Robert Whitehead re-possessed the estate. A yard of wooden boxes was constructed at the Top Buildings as kennels for hounds (still marked as Kennels in some plans). The Sitch Cottages were built in 1906 and the Sitch Wood was planted. Manure was carried to the field by horse and cart and a forkful placed under each tree as it was put in the ground. Before 1900 tree cover on the farm would have been sparse, although the 1883 ordnance survey map shows that the shelter belts on Horse Lane, round Top Town Meadow and the Long Copse were there at that time.

Stud Yard Hargate Wall about 1908

175

The land consisted of excellent pasture overlying a limestone base and was liberally fed by a moderately high rainfall which now averages 44½ inches per year. The oldest trees were an elm at the bottom of the lane at Dale Head (now dying of Dutch elm disease) and another elm which I felled at Coates Barn after it succumbed to disease in 1995. Both of them dated from about 1800.

In the first decade of the 20th century Hargate Wall Farm was run as a model farm with a shire horse stud (the top yard above the Big Shed is still referred to as the Stud Yard) and it is said that Robert Whitehead reckoned he was doing well if he only lost £2000[205] a year on the enterprise. The farm consisted of a mixture of dairy pasture and grazing; hayfields; some corn and arable; with miscellaneous crops of potatoes, cabbages and carrots (which Mr Dakin remembered were once grown in the field where the Sitch Wood now stands). The Dairy herd was made up of mostly Dairy Shorthorns. Itinerant Irish farm workers would come to the farm in the autumns to work in the potato fields and were accommodated in a wooden bungalow which used to stand in the front garden of the farmhouse, being called in from the fields by the bell in the clock-tower of the Stable Block at Hargate Hall. A purpose-built Wash-house was built in the front of Number 2 Cottage with its own copper boiler, where the occupants of the farm-house and cottages did their weekly wash on Mondays. Major profits were being made on the back of the ongoing Industrial Revolution and presumably Robert Whitehead made a significant profit from his various business ventures.

Robert Whitehead was the fifth and youngest son of John Whitehead (1815-1898) of Elton and Penwortham Priory in Lancashire and Eliza Ellen, daughter of Robert Allanson of Birtle Cheshire. Born in 1856, he was privately educated in Brussels, followed by University and the Royal Agricultural College Cirencester. He married Edith Harman, daughter of Henry Oram, in 1888 from a family of entrepreneurs from Bury and had three daughters. Robert Whitehead was a JP and

---

[205] About £111,000 at 2001 values.

High Sheriff of Derbyshire 1915-1916. He became deputy chairman of the Staveley Coal and Iron Company, a director of Cammell Laird shipbuilders and of various other companies. He was also prominent in the local Hunts and is said to have run a popular shoot at Hargate. One of the attractions which undoubtedly encouraged Robert Whitehead and other wealthy businessmen to live in the local area in the first half of the 20th century was the excellent telegraph communication and commuting facilities at Millers Dale which gave fast access to London, Manchester and Liverpool.

My father, George Drewry, was born in Buxton in 1889 where my grandfather was agent for the Duke of Devonshire. When he returned from the First World War in 1918 he married one of Robert Whitehead's daughters and settled at Hargate Old Hall, as it continued to be known for some years. From there he embarked on a career, also as an agent for the Duke of Devonshire, looking after the estates at Peak Forest, Highlow and Woodlands in the Hope Valley.

In the first two decades of the 20th century motor vehicles were still a rarity and the early models owned by the wealthiest members of the community were notoriously unreliable. Horses remained a standard means of transport for both farming and general travel. The horse and gig shown in the previous photograph in the farm yard at Hargate Wall was allegedly used by my family in the 1920s. Note the cheeky terrier hitching a ride on the foot-plate and the saplings over the wall on the right hand side which have since grown into mature horse chestnuts with a 3 to 4 foot diameter.

Buxton was at its peak as a Spa Town and had seen major investment by the Dukes of Devonshire. The largest construction projects like the Octagon in the Pavilion Gardens, the conversion and extension of the Devonshire Hospital with its new Dome and the Municipal Baths were funded by a combination of public subscription and the floatation of public companies through share issues.

Spring Gardens Buxton 1903
(Note the Tram)

177

Responsibility for their design and oversight of their construction rested invariably with the architect R R (Robert Rippon) Duke.[206] The Pavilion Gardens were built in 1871 to extend the spa 'season' into the winter and the Pump Room was built and presented to the town in 1894. The Empire Hotel was added in 1900; the Opera House, designed by Frank Matcham, was built in 1903 and King Edward VII visited the spa in January 1905.

While the Buxton spa was at the height of its popularity and fame, this was a Golden Age when private and municipal investment was readily available. At Hargate Wall Farm ornate field gate posts made of cast iron and bearing the initials RW were positioned at the top of the farm yard and are still there today. The water supply was laid from the perched aquifer on Withered Low and piped over 1½ miles in 3 inch cast iron mains. A 'perched' aquifer signifies a bowl of lava under the limestone which is impervious to water and therefore forces the water out in springs at the surface. The Spring chamber on Withered Low was marginally too low for water to be gravity fed up to the new Hargate Hall; so an iron windmill was constructed which pumped water up the hill to an underground chamber at the top of Bole Hill with return pipes to the spring chamber which gave the necessary headage. The remains of the windmill and underground chamber can still be seen. The windmill does not appear to have been in use for long and probably fell into disuse when the public reservoir was built at Bole Hill as the main water supply for the village, though a windmill is still marked on the site in the 1924 version of the Ordnance Survey map. The public reservoir, fed by the pumping station on the site of the Neolithic settlement of 3000 BC in the lee of Middle Hill, provided all of the village's water until a new pipe line from the Derwent Dams came through to Buxton at the end of the century.

Up until the 1950s sanitation conditions left much to be desired. Few houses had internal flush lavatories connected to a septic tank and most relied on the out-door 'Privy' and the uncomfortable dash to an unlit, cold and smelly latrine in the middle of a winter's night! The Privies were emptied once a week by the Council if you were lucky.

Before the arrival of electricity Hargate Old Hall originally had its own gas plant for lighting. This was fed from a methane plant in what is now the garage to the Flat. It became redundant when electricity came to the village in the 1930s. The Tideswell telephone exchange was established in 1925 with 34 subscribers in the local area. My father's first telephone number at Hargate Wall was Tideswell 7. A limited selection of radio programmes could sometimes be picked up on the temperamental 'wireless' crystal sets but television did not arrive before the 1950s. The first major event to be televised and broadcast across the country was the Coronation of Queen Elizabeth II in 1953.

---

[206] See *The Architect of Victorian Buxton* by Mike Langham and Colin Wells 1996.

Back of the new Hargate Old Hall 1909
Taken from the First Paddock

St Margaret's Church was enlarged in 1906 with a new organ transept being built on.

In 1909 Robert Whitehead, having completed the new Hargate Hall in 1902, rebuilt the main part of Hargate Old Hall. The Date Stone over the front door reads 19 RW 09. Most of the old Jacobean Hall which dated from the early 1600s was demolished.

Hargate Wall 1909

Note the flagpole on the eastern gable of the Big Shed roof in the farm yard. The brackets for holding the pole are still there.

The Village Street and Institute – early 20ᵗʰ Century

The present Village Hall or Village Institute, as it is sometimes called, was built in 1938 to replace the previous Men's Club and Institute which had originally been provided at the expense of Mrs J Deakin who was the tenant of Wormhill Hall. The original Institute, visible on the left of the next photograph, appears to have been a wooden frame building alongside the road and with doors facing south. There was a similar Men's Club and Institute at the Great Rocks quarry in 1936.

Village Hall 1938

The population of Wormhill peaked in 1931 at a total of 1631 before the hamlets of Upper End and Peak Dale were split off into a different parish. By comparing the data in Bagshaw's Directory of 1846, Kelly's Directory of 1881 and Kelly's Directory of 1936 it is possible to track the evolution of the parish over 90 years while it remained geographically the same size but grew enormously in population numbers.

View of Wormhill early 1900s

If we look first at the farmers listed in the three Directories, it is apparent that there were many more working farms than today, most of which were small-holdings and only two of which exceeded 150 acres even in 1936. The number of farmers reduced from 34 in 1846 to 27 by the end of the period. In some instances there is a remarkable degree of continuity of the same families farming in the parish and many of the residents of Wormhill in the 21st century can trace their forebears and relatives in the following tables. Likewise some of the farms still carry the names of their 19th century owners (eg Bateman Farm at Wormhill, Mosley's at Meadow, Taylor's at Tunstead, Dakin's and Hayward's at Hargate). The origins of other farm names are lost to history but it is possible to speculate, for example, that 'Hall Farm' (now Old Hall Farm) was the home farm which went with Wormhill Hall. 'Chapelsteads'[207] was the barns and stables (steads/steadings) which went with the Chapel (colour plate 34). Hassop Farm[208] may have been built originally in the 1600s by the Eyres whose principal estate was at Hassop. Glebe Farm at Wormhill and another Glebe Farm at Goosey Corner Millers Dale were clearly Church property and the latter may have had geese wandering across the road to make the 90 degree bend even more dangerous than it was already.

Smallholdings were typical of many English villages at the time and were a source of much curiosity to the first tourists from across the Atlantic. One of them asked a Peak District farmer how much land he had.

'Fifteen acres' came the reply.

'Gee, where I come from in Texas I can get on my horse, ride on my ranch for a whole day and still be only half way across my land at sundown'.

'Aye' said the Peak District farmer 'I 'ad an 'orse like that once'!

---

[207] The current farmhouse was built in the middle of the 18th century and is Grade II listed.
[208] Hassop Farm was built around 1800 on the site of an earlier farm and is Grade II listed.

Farmers	1846	1881	1936
Wormhill	Michael Bateman Joseph Catlin Martha Heapy Robert Hudson Thomas Longden Samuel Slack Joseph Wright Thomas Wright	Paul Austin Thomas Eley (Hall Farm) William & John Lees Richard Longden John Mosley Robert Mosley Jonathan Potter Joseph Wright	Joseph Bramwell Harold Mosley Edward Mycock (Chapelsteads) William Needham Joe Swindell John Taylor John Wainwright
The Hill	John Handley Joshua Platts William Redfern Isaac Wilshaw	George Cartledge Thomas Handley William Redfern	Thomas Kinsey Frank Redfern
Hargate Wall	Edmund Dakin Henry Hayward John Hayward George Needham	Joseph Dakin Martha Hayward William Swann	Samuel Dakin Norman Lomas Clifford Mosley
Tunstead	Thomas Taylor Joseph Wainwright James Wild	Ann Bramwell Samuel Howe Henry Wainwright	Joshua Allsop Wilfred Beresford Thomas Teeboon F&W Wainwright
Great Rocks	Hannah Bennett Edward Lees	Richard Boyd John Lees William Lees	John Bowler Matthew Longson John Wildes
Meadow	Henry Mosley Ralph Mosley Thomas Warhurst	Thomas Mosley Isaac Warhurst	Ann Dakin George Davidson Walter Wain
Upper End	Jonathan Garlick Thomas Mason Joseph Shirt	Isaac Warhurst	Abraham Cooper Ernest Howe James Longden Harvey Shipley
Edge Foot	Edward Potts	Joseph Garlick	
Dale Head	Thomas Handley William Wainwright		
Millers Dale	George Dakin Samuel Frost John Wilshaw		Roger Mosley
Totals	33	24	27

Taylor family, Old Hall Farm early 1900s

Amongst the other trades and occupations listed in the Directories there are further interesting revelations. Wormhill Hall, owned by the Bagshawes, was either let or unoccupied throughout the period. The village pub changed its name at some stage between 1846 and 1881. In the days of horse power 20-30 working farms were sufficient to justify a full time wheelwright in the village – the equivalent of today's garage. There was a Post Office in Wormhill by 1881 and two shops at that time but the vast increase in shops and other trades at Upper End and Peak Dale by 1936 reflects the enormous growth of those two hamlets resulting from expansion of the quarrying industries.

Millers Dale had two corn mills – one opposite the church on the Tideswell side of the viaducts known as the Meal Mill because it ground oats[209] and one on the western side which fell within the Wormhill parish[210] and was known as the 'Wormhill Mill'. Both of the mills were operated by the Dakin family in the 20th century before being sold to Staffordshire Farmers in 1949. Millers Dale provided even more employment with the arrival of the railway from 1863 when coal merchants, new inns and station shopkeepers established themselves there.

It is interesting that a community of 337 could sustain two working shoe and boot makers in the village in 1846. Note also that Lime Burners in the parish who were private owners in the 19th century had become limited companies by 1936.

---

[209] This was also known as 'Tideswell Mill' and was demolished in the 1970s to be replaced by a Water Board pumping station. Originally it had a substantial dam and mill pond to drive the water wheel. The water wheel has been preserved on the site.

[210] The dividing line is the railway viaducts running across the valley.

Wormhill Mill 1908

Other Trades	1846	1881	1936
Wormhill Hall	(Vacant)	William Brierley	(Vacant)
Schoolmaster	Edward Furniss		
The Pub[211]	Martha Heapy	Thomas Needham	John Wainwright
Shopkeeper/Post Office Post Office	Rebecca Tymms (Wormhill)	Martha Bradwell (Wormhill) Anthony Wyld (Wormhill)	John Wilde (Wormhill) Edna Booth (draper Upper End) Charles Brittain (grocer Peak Dale) George Davenport (Peak Dale) Doris Hadfield (Peak Dale) Annie Hallam (Peak Dale) Caroline Lomas (Upper End) Sarah Middleton (Upper End) Esther Noton (Upper End) Maggie Proudlove (Peak Dale) Lillian Wheeldon (Peak Dale)

[211]   The pub in Wormhill was known as the Red Lion in 1846 and the Bagshawe Arms by 1881.

Other Trades	1846	1881	1936
Wheelwright		Boaz Bagshaw	Frank Bagshaw
Miller (Millers Dale)	George Dakin Samuel Frost		Thomas Dakin
Shoemaker	Thomas Bradwell Thomas Wright	Peter Wright	
Stone Mason	John Mason		
Beer Retailer		Robert Lomas (Dove Holes)	
Coal Merchant (Millers Dale)			George Cooper Frank Lomas
Lime Burner	Thomas Brocklehurst James Swann	Samuel Bibbington (Upper End)	ICI Ltd (Great Rocks) S Bibbington Ltd (Dove Holes)
Other Inns and Refreshment Rooms (Millers Dale and Peak Dale)	Robert Holmes (Anglers Rest)		Sarah Byatte (Railway Inn) Thomas Hunt (Railway Station) Annie Turner (Midland Hotel Peak Dale)
Total Population	337	953	1631

An interesting and humorous account of life in Wormhill during and after the Second World War, along with many photographs of the village at the time, was published in 2003 by Claude Fearns,[212] whose family took the tenancy of the Bagshawe Arms and the farm in March 1939. They started with 10 heifers which cost them the princely sum of £240 and went on to become one of the first owners of an orange Fordson tractor in the village. Anyone looking for nostalgic reminiscences of the 1940s from the viewpoint of a Wormhill schoolboy and a host of references to villagers of the period will be fascinated by this little book.

The value of limestone as the chief ingredient for chemicals, cement, aggregate and fertiliser began to be fully exploited at the start of the 20th century. In the Tunstead, Chee Tor and Millers Dale limestone beds the calcium carbonate content is exceptionally high (97-99%), available in greater quantity than elsewhere in the country, and closer to the surface without the complication of over-lying shales. Close access to the railways made the transport of huge tonnages a feasible proposition and the Tunstead quarry (often referred to as 'Long Sidings') rapidly developed the longest quarry face in Europe at one and a half miles in length. Peak Dale and Upper End expanded rapidly to house the large workforce

---

[212] *White Peak Memories* published by Churnet Valley Books, Leek.

Peak Dale Quarry 1920

required. Many quarry workers however commuted to Tunstead from further afield, including a sizeable contingent from Tideswell who walked to and fro along Tideswell Lane in all weathers until a bus service was introduced in 1925. By the 1960s 40% of the total output was consumed by the chemical industry, 20% by agricultural fertiliser, 12% in the building trade and large quantities of limestone were used as a flux in iron and steel production as well as road foundations. Cement production was to follow and the quarries were to become a major source of local employment. Dolerite and basalt quarries (as at Waterswallows – now exhausted and closed) provided very durable stone of high crushing strength which was ideal for roads bearing heavy traffic.

At the end of the 19th century blasting of the rock was achieved by boring a short tunnel, pouring in gunpowder and installing a long straight straw also filled with powder to act as a fuse. After a stopping-plug had been driven into the hole, fire travelled down the straw and gave the operator just enough time to scramble away before the charge exploded. There were nevertheless a relatively high number of fatalities in the quarrying industry, and not just amongst the blasting operators.

As late as the 1920s the best paid quarry workers at Tunstead were earning a mere £3 per week. These were the 'fillers' whose job was to break up the stone into the required size by pick-axe and hammer, load it into the rail wagons for 10½d (4p) per ton and start all over again if the supervisor decided that the rocks were too large. One man could typically process up to 15 tons per day but he had to do so in the open air whatever the weather conditions and he received no pay at all if work was stopped even for reasons outside his control.

In many ways it is a curious fact that the quarry workers did not develop the same degree of militancy as their fellow workers in the coal mining, docks and transport industries which led to bitter disputes and the General Strikes of 1926. Quarrymen who had to operate in these primitive conditions, doing hard manual labour in breaking stone and loading rail wagons by hand, and exposed to constant risk of injury and death from falling rock, might have been expected to have more grievances than most. The fact that they didn't may have something to do with the more enlightened industrial relations which prevailed in this industry.

Sir Alfred Mond (1868-1930) joined his father's business of Brunner, Mond & Co after finishing university, went on to become the first Chairman of Imperial Chemical Industries (ICI), both of which ran the Tunstead quarry, and was finally elevated to the peerage as Lord Melchett. In 1927 he wrote in a periodical called Industry and Politics: 'In the industry in which I am mainly interested we have succeeded in avoiding for a period of over fifty years any serious industrial dispute. This has been largely due to a liberal, far-seeing policy, which did not consist in waiting for claims to be made and then yielding to them reluctantly, but in foreseeing reasonable demands and in granting them even before they were asked.'

The development of modern explosives in the First World War refined blasting techniques. In May 1933 King George VI, then Duke of York, pressed a plunger in a hut above Buxton Central Quarry and fired 3,700 lbs of ammonal,[213] bringing down 32,000 tons of limestone. This blast was fired from 600 yards away, a record distance at the time.

Lime is made by driving carbon dioxide out of the limestone by heat. In the old days stone was burned in open-topped kilns like very wide stone funnels and the burning process took 5 days. Nowadays burning is achieved much more rapidly and efficiently in high powered rotating kilns fuelled by gas ignition, followed by coal and coke reaching temperatures of 1400 degrees C. The lime burning process is now completed in about 6 hours. The total output of limestone from the county in 1999 amounted to 20 million tonnes. In 2004 the Tunstead quarry, owned by Tarmac and Anglo-American, was processing 2 million tonnes of limestone per annum, rising to 6 million tonnes per annum in 2005. Seven to nine train-loads of aggregate per day and one train-load of cement were taken from the sidings. Limestone was in use not only for road stone and the chemical industry but also as a flux for power stations and sugar beet. In October 2004 a new cement plant was commissioned at Tunstead and formally opened by the Princess Royal with an output of 800,000 tonnes per annum which effectively halved the United Kingdom's cement imports and enabled all but 1% of the quarry waste to be used on site. Atmospheric emissions were also drastically reduced. On the Old Moor site 250 million tonnes of stone remained available for quarrying from 2004 up to 2042 when the licence granted in 1988 expires. In the future fortunately the Old Moor quarry will be extended to the south and away from Wormhill and the quarry faces on the northern boundaries are already being landscaped.

---

[213] The high explosive used in First World War artillery shells and in the mines dug under the German lines on the Somme.

Tunstead Quarry 2006

A secondary mineral industry which began in 1946 was the production of fluorspar, used in the steel, chemical and ceramic industries, and of barytes, used for paint and paper. Both of these minerals had been discarded as worthless by the lead miners of the previous centuries and were readily available in huge quantities in the spoil-heaps outside the former lead mines and rakes.

During the Second World War my father, George Drewry, formed a platoon of the Home Guard from local volunteers. In the Home Guard records he is listed as a captain in the 2nd Derbyshire (Buxton) Battalion under the command of Lieutenant Colonel H C Lings DSO (late of the Manchester Regiment). The Home Guard was formed initially in May 1940 as a response to the threat of imminent invasion and was first known as the Local Defence Volunteers (LDV). Some

Wormhill Home Guard Platoon 1942

188

defaulters were keen to avoid these services which gave rise to the nickname for the LDV of 'Look, Duck and Vanish'! There was a severe shortage of weapons and, at the outset, they were armed only with shotguns. Eventually some ·303 rifles were procured and one Bren Gun. Training took place, amongst other places, in Peter Dale and the remains of some inert 3" mortar practice rounds can still be seen there.

Hargate Hall became a recuperation hospital for Allied casualties and my mother worked there as a nurse. When invasion fears were at their height in 1940, farmers were encouraged to place large metal objects in the bigger fields to deter landings by glider. One of these, a large cylinder, can still be seen at Hargate Wall Farm. A British liaison aircraft crashed in fog on Middle Hill, killing its 2 occupants who were found by Fred Mycock. A night raid by German bombers, aiming allegedly for the RAF bomb dump at Harpur Hill but more probably jettisoning their loads after an aborted raid on Manchester or Liverpool, saturated the local area with incendiaries. Most fizzled out in the snow and slush but one burned Earl Sterndale church to the ground. Another incendiary bounced off the roof of the Bagshawe Arms in Wormhill and landed in the muck midden. A couple due to get married at Earl Sterndale the following Saturday continued with the ceremony in the burnt out shell of the church.

Wainwright Quarry at Peak Dale was used as a Proof and Experimental Range under Army supervision for testing new weapons and munitions made by ICI at Birmingham and Glasgow. It was here that new weapons like the Blacker Bombard and the PIAT anti-tank system were tested by firing them at the quarry face.

Shortly before D Day in June 1944 Claude Fearns recalled watching his father dipping sheep in the river in Chee Dale, when a massive troop train emerged from the tunnel in the hillside opposite. In addition to troops in the carriages there were tanks, artillery and other vehicles on flatbeds, pulled by two steam engines at the front and pushed by a further two engines at the rear. As the train roared on south-wards towards Millers Dale, an excited Claude allegedly shouted out 'They are coming, Mr Hitler. And they are coming for YOU'!

A V1 flying bomb passed low over the village on its way to Manchester, landing short and detonating harmlessly on the Buxton moors (apart from killing one sheep!). Once the V1 launching sites in France were overrun by the advancing allies after D-Day, the Luftwaffe took to air-launching these first generation cruise missiles from aircraft off the North Sea coast. One such raid took place on 24th December 1944 when 50 V1s were air-launched against Manchester, the only occasion in the war when a V1 raid penetrated so far inland. Of these 30 are known to have crossed the coast but only one landed in Manchester itself. Our near miss is very likely to have been part of this raid which was largely ineffective, though the one bomb which did get through killed 100 civilians in Manchester that Christmas Eve.

After the Second World War in the 1950s there were about 10 people working on the farm at Hargate Wall but, with the introduction of mechanisation, the numbers gradually reduced. An experimental Drying Shed was built in the 'Dryer Paddock' for drying damp hay, which was fuelled by a large coke stove. It was not a notable success and always struck me as a horrendous fire risk but the building and the Dutch Barn beside it survived until 1996 when it was replaced by a new Stock-Yard. In the 1950s the main farm crop was hay with small quantities of potatoes and farm cabbages. Hay was harvested loose (baling did not begin until the 1960s) and stored in the big lofts above the cow sheds or in the 5 outlying barns on the farm, of which only one now remains. Pigs were kept in the Piggery and were slaughtered and hung in the Dairy. Mrs Mycock ran two flocks of chickens at Dakins and in the Lambing Sheds. The milking herd, now made up entirely of pedigree Friesians, was about 100 strong, with 88 in the main cow yard. There was a thriving Young Farmers Club and regular competitions were held in the village.

In 1951 the Peak District became Britain's first National Park. At 542 square miles, 24 miles wide and 39 miles long, it remains the largest National Park in Britain. Over 12% of the Park, mostly on the higher moorland, is now owned by the National Trust and the wilder parts of it are now fully accessible under the Right to Roam legislation passed in 2003. Half the population of England and Wales lives within 60 miles of the Park and there are about 5 million visitors per annum.

Monks Dale and the eastern end of Peter Dale were given the status of Sites of Special Scientific Interest and, in due course of a National and European Nature Reserve. In 2000 the reserve was extended to include the whole of Peter Dale, less the pastures in the dale bottom.

Monks Dale[214] Nature Reserve

---

[214] Confusingly this sign beisde the Hargate to Tideswell road actually overlooks not Monk's Dale but the lower end of Peter Dale.

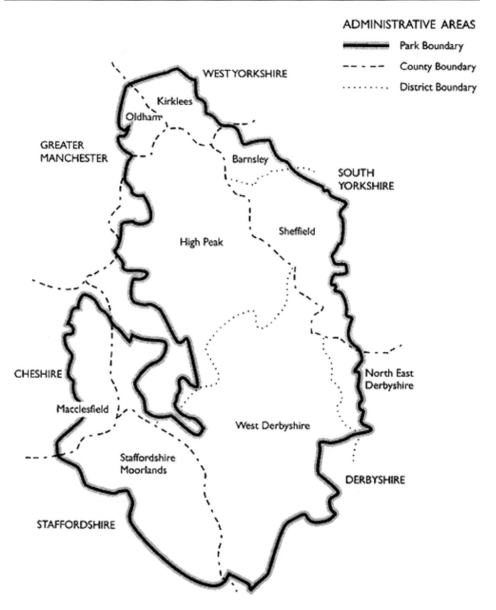

ADMINISTRATIVE AREAS

Park Boundary
County Boundary
District Boundary

WEST YORKSHIRE

Kirklees

Oldham

GREATER
MANCHESTER

Barnsley

SOUTH
YORKSHIRE

High Peak

Sheffield

CHESHIRE

North East
Derbyshire

Macclesfield

West Derbyshire

Staffordshire
Moorlands

DERBYSHIRE

STAFFORDSHIRE

Peak District National Park

CONCLUSION

Over the 5000 years during which the present day village of Wormhill has been inhabited by human beings it has of course evolved at an ever increasing pace with the progress of civilisation and technology. In more recent times each century and even each generation has looked back in awe at the 'primitive' nature of their predecessors' way of life and has remarked how different it must have all been then. Yet, in other respects, what is remarkable is how little has changed.

This village has always been a small self-contained community, based around a limited number of family groups. Only four families have owned the manor in the thousand years since the Norman Conquest and two of them have owned it for 300 years each. Some of the inhabitants like Sir Godfrey Foljambe became nationally important figures. Others, starting in the 12th century and continuing through to the present day, have sent their sons to fight the nation's wars and defend its freedom. Many other families of both distinguished and more humble origins have lived here, worked on the land and married within the district for centuries. Today's surnames are often the same as those appearing on legal documents in 1300.

Royal patronage which brought favours to the High Peak in mediaeval times and the economic high fortunes of the Industrial Revolution which brought prosperity to this part of England in the 18th and 19th centuries are of course a thing of the past. Yet that spirit of hardiness and self-reliance remarked upon by Chrichton Porteous as an enduring characteristic of the rugged landscape and its stoical inhabitants has always been here. It has spawned the likes of James Brindley who rose from the poorest of circumstances through sheer self-belief and determination to become one of the greatest engineers of his time.

The rich bounty of minerals which lies beneath our feet has provided work and livelihood to our community ever since the Romans arrived here in 78 AD. They worked the lead and the fluorspar; others later worked the lime, iron, copper, marble, coal and chert. Nowadays it is an American-owned company which works the lime and the cement. The mineral extractors of previous generations were constrained by arcane mining laws and the limitations of finance and technology. Today's extractors have finance and technology on their side but are rightly constrained by other limitations such as the overriding requirement to preserve the landscape of one of the country's finest National Parks.

One enduring activity which even a Neolithic settler would still recognise today is farming. Cattle and sheep have been reared here since 3000 BC. Crops have been grown according to the climate of the age – wheat in the Late Stone Age, barley, oats and rye more recently – and now in an age of renewed global warming maize is being grown not far away at Bakewell. The dry stone walls forming the boundaries of the fields have been a characteristic feature of the limestone plateau of the White Peak since Anglo-Saxon times, though more were built in the 14th century and more still in the 19th century when open common land gave way to privately owned enclosures by Act of Parliament. The fortunes of agriculture have ebbed and flowed throughout the history of the village. Depression brought about by external factors or Government indifference is nothing new and may yet be overtaken again by a cyclical upturn, however unlikely that may currently appear. Even our successors will presumably have to eat. And as the dwindling global reserves of oil run out, imported food may become more expensive as a result of the prohibitive costs of transport and hence less competitive with home-grown supplies. Equally, if the more dire forecasts of global warming prove correct, the growing world population may have to abandon tropical regions turned to deserts and rely on the more temperate regions like England for their food and homeland. So it may currently be fashionable to lament the prospects for British agriculture but it may be less than accurate as a prophecy for the future.

In the meantime our present inhabitants have turned their attention and energies, not for the first time, to diversification. Tourism and the holiday industry have been exploited here since the 17th century. The outstanding natural beauty of the High Peak landscape has been recognised and protected by its status as the country's first National Park, bringing much revenue from outside visitors even while its convoluted planning constraints bring some frustration to its residents, governed as they are by the demi-gods of the Park Authority. The thermal spa industry peaked at the start of the 20th century before a steady decline, only to be resurrected again at the start of the 21st with patronage, not this time from ducal landowners but from the National Lottery and other institutions. A new university campus and a thriving opera company add to the picture of alternative occupations which increasingly provide employment for local people.

Infrastructure and local utilities have certainly improved over the course of time. In one instance however things appear to have got worse rather than better but, in retrospect, this may not be seen as a bad thing after all. Communications with this part of the country have of course been revolutionised, as elsewhere, by the advent of terrestrial and satellite television, mobile telephones, the internet and wireless broadband bringing instant contact and information from throughout the world. Physical communications on the other hand have deteriorated. The road network is of better quality but no more extensive than it was in 1900 while car ownership and overall road use have increased beyond recognition. The ease with which virtually every family can travel to local towns for their shopping, schooling, entertainment and all other needs of modern life has led directly to the demise of the village Post Office, shop, school and pub. The canals have, for the most part, long since fallen into disrepair, even if some are being partially regenerated for recreational use. The railway line through the Wye valley, once one of the principal railway arteries of England, has been severed since the 1960s between Matlock and Buxton. How are we to fulfil the promise of the newly diversified occupations if the communications to transport people to and from the area in relative comfort and at reasonable speed are not in place? Are our visitors to be as unimpressed as the London gentleman arriving by broken down post chaise in the summer of 1755?

On the other hand; if we had a motorway running past the bottom of the village; if we had a high speed rail link to the four corners of the land; if we had a regional airport on our doorstep together with noise, light and air pollution of a high order; would we not be as overcrowded and dispirited as the outer suburbs of London and Manchester? Would we still find the peace and tranquillity which is expected of a National Park? If not, would people still want to live and visit here anyway? And who would be interested in the history of the place after that?

My final thought is that this little local history, along with most other histories of regions great and small, may be taking far too narrow a perspective of the much longer term evolution of the planet. This thought also brings us back to where we started. If the 'doom and gloom' school of modern scientists is to be believed, the Earth has undergone a succession of Ice Ages over the last half million years, separated by interglacial intervals of 10,000–100,000 years when warmer climates have allowed the evolution of various forms of life. According to this theory we are currently some 12,000 years into the latest interglacial interval, during which time human beings have evolved into modern man, and we should expect to be confronting the next Ice Age any time between now and 80,000 AD.

If the theory is right – and let us hope that it is not – much more fundamental questions would arise. Will the human race survive the next Ice Age? Will they migrate to the equatorial regions and seek to hold on until the ice next recedes? Will they migrate to other more temperate planets in different solar systems of the universe? When and if humans return here at the end of the next Ice Age in 100,000 AD, what will they find? Will the archaeologists of the day be excavating the remains of 21st century Wormhill – the footings of the houses, the faint traces of a church and some ancient bones in the churchyard which have not been obliterated and swept away by the glaciers? And what wild and wonderful interpretations will the historians put on the way of life of us 'primitive' people who live here today?!

Annex A

Owners of the Manor of Wormhill 1066-1700

Date	Owner	Monarch
1066	Siward Barn	Harold
1086	Henry de Ferrers	William I
1100	Sir Ralph Foljambe	William II
	Sir Geoffrey Foljambe	Henry I / Stephen
1184	Sir Henry Foljambe	Henry II Richard I
1208	Sir John Foljambe	John
1239	Sir John Foljambe	Henry III
1249	Sir Thomas Foljambe	Henry III
1283	Sir Thomas Foljambe (the second)	Edward I
1297	Sir Thomas Foljambe (the third)	Edward I
1314	Sir Thomas Foljambe (the fourth)	Edward II
1324	Sir Godfrey Foljambe	Edward II
1377	Sir Godfrey Foljambe (the third)	Edward III
1388	Lady (Isabel) Foljambe	Richard II
1392	Sir William Plumpton	Richard II

Date	Owner	Monarch
1405	Sir Robert Plumpton	Henry IV
1421	Sir William Plumpton (the second)	Henry V
1498	Catherine Eyre	Henry VI Edward IV Edward V Richard III Henry VII Henry VIII Edward VI Mary
1602	Rowland Eyre	Elizabeth I James I Charles I
1670	Adam Bagshawe	Commonwealth Charles II James II William & Mary

INDEX